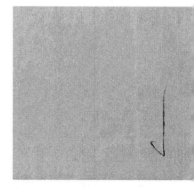

Gift:
Sydney . G .
  Eastwood Ward.
    Leicester Stake.
    SEPT. 1961.

THE FLETCHER HOUSE OF LACE
AND ITS WORK

THE FLETCHER HOUSE OF LACE
AND ITS WIDER
FAMILY ASSOCIATIONS

THE FLETCHER HOUSE
OF LACE
AND ITS WIDER
FAMILY ASSOCIATIONS

Compiled by

SAMUEL BILLYEALD FLETCHER
OF WEST BRIDGFORD, NOTTS.

Printed by
DERWENT PRESS LIMITED, DERBY
1957

PLATE 1

EDWARD FLETCHER

DEDICATION

*This Family Story is most solemnly
and affectionately dedicated to Edward
Fletcher and his wife, Phoebe, née Allen,
to whom any achievement or success
attained by their many descendants,
is due*

PREFACE

I MUST confess to being one of the original 'young instigators' who, as mentioned by our Compiler, persuaded him some four to five years ago, to attempt a publication in book form of Fletcher family history.

It was therefore with some trepidation that I learned from him last summer that his task was nearly completed, followed by his obvious query as to what happened next.

However, a few chapters read at random, and a glance or two at the new Family Tree connections, opened out for me such a vista of family lore extending the world over—that I was convinced it had to be published.

It is now my great pleasure to present the results in printed style of this task so willingly undertaken and so conscientiously compiled, with, for the enquiring mind, more dustcloths awaiting removal to give further lustre to the already many facets of this, our family history.

John W.S. Fletcher

Hieron's Wood,
Little Eaton,
Derby.   *January, 1957.*

Photograph by Harper Shaw, Wymeswold, Leicestershire

PLATE 2

78, 78A & 80 TAG HILL, HEANOR

Left to right: 80—The Eleys Residence.   78A—The Fletchers Residence.   78—The Allens Residence

CONTENTS

PART I
THE FAMILY STORY

xi

CONTENTS

PART II

INDEX TO DOCUMENTARY SUPPLEMENTALS

xii

LIST OF ILLUSTRATIONS

A SHORT INTRODUCTION TO THE STORY OF

THE FLETCHER HOUSE OF LACE

THE tabulating of a family record such as ours is not a common occurrence, so those who study it may wonder how this one came into being. The explanation is very simple and human. It is just this:

In the late spring of 1927, my father, Edward John Wood Fletcher, became ill beyond recovery, so we had to inform his brothers, Samuel and William Percy, of his serious condition—not an easy duty to perform, as their whereabouts were unknown. All we knew was that they and their families had left England.

It was then I remembered that grandfather's original nameplate, 'Samuel Fletcher & Co. Limited', still marked the entrance to his one-time warehouse in Stoney Street, Nottingham, so I called there and was advised by the proprietor [a son of the late L. P. Lymbery] to commence my search in Long Eaton, where I found that Samuel had emigrated to New Zealand and that William Percy was domiciled in Canada.

These first-fruits of research launched me on a long revealing voyage of discovery among the back-roots, side-shoots and currents of family history, the products of which have been of rewarding interest to myself and a source of good news to kindred in many lands.

During these excursions into strange waters, many unexpected obstacles have been encountered, surmounted, and as they passed astern, some of them became notable family landmarks.

The outstanding one of them all came into view in 1944 when forty-six direct descendants, members of the John, Joseph, Samuel, James, Catherine-Farnsworth, Robert, Mary-Houghton and George branches of the family, defrayed the cost of restoring the grave of Edward and Phoebe Fletcher, our common ancestors, whose resting-place graces St Paul's churchyard, Hyson Green, Nottingham.

There was a very happy ending to this act of family service. When all expenses were paid, a substantial surplus remained for disposal, so, after making a donation to church funds, the net balance, nearly twenty pounds, was handed to the Vicar, the Rev. J. C. Meers, requesting him 'to expend the same, at his discretion, on Christmas cheer and comforts for old and needy folk resident in St Paul's Parish'.

Three years later [1947] I drew my bow at a venture and made my first visit to Chaddesden Works, Derby, where John, Thomas and Edward, the sons of the late William Fletcher, gratified my long-cherished wish to see a lace machine in operation for the first time.

Before parting company we had a cup of tea and a friendly chat, during which the seed was sown that blossomed into the Fletcher Family Tree which permanently records the names of upwards of five hundred-and-fifty related twigs borne by its thirteen main branches. One hundred-and-forty-two photographic copies of it were supplied to members of the family living in this country or overseas.

These two major adventures were the spurs that goaded me into garnering a varied mass of lore from which we can trace the male line of our family back to the beginning of the eighteenth century, and probably much further.

Full appreciation of its historic value was indicated when, shortly after Christmas 1952, a group of our young Derbyshire clansmen requested me to collate all the family documents in my hands into one orderly record 'before the passage of years made it too late to do so'. I consented, but we mutually agreed to proceed on a much wider basis, hence the bulk of my own personal collection of family papers, reinforced by contributions from kinsmen belonging to all our main branches, is woven into the pattern of the compilation presented for your pleasurable regalement.

Of necessity, a small minority of those mentioned herein figure more prominently than the rest, but only because I badgered and coaxed until they allowed the limelight to shine upon them in furthering the overall plan.

We owe them all our sincere thanks, since without the unremitting patience they exercised in delving for and framing their particular branch contributions, there could not have been a really complete and worthwhile story to tell you.

SAMUEL BILLYEALD FLETCHER

The Compiler

OUR FAMILY ORIGIN

This is always a baffling problem when no reliable documentary records of proved accuracy exist to decide between conflicting differences of opinion and a variety of long-established beliefs rooted in our older generations.

Therefore, it is not surprising to hear that we are reputed to spring from Scandinavian or Scottish stock, or both.

Other believers are convinced that coal production on estates in and around Smalley, Derbyshire, was the business of our ancestors before those of later times took to lace-making.

A very large body, mainly older members, firmly believed that Pentrich contained the root of our family origin, and in bygone days it was a custom to drive there from Heanor 'to show the youngsters the place where Grandpa came from'.

This view cannot be lightly passed over, yet be all this as it may, Heanor seems the most likely district in which to trace the deep-down tips of our family beginnings.

Let us now measure the claims of each held-to-be place of origin by the unquestioned evidence available.

THE SCANDINAVIAN LEGEND

This makes intriguing reading because it has a background of fact—a contradictory statement on the face of things.

During the seventeenth century, two brothers named Fetchler or Fechtler, left their native land to seek their fortune in America. They had to cross England, but only one brother completed the full journey beyond the seas. He that remained behind married, settled down somewhere in Cheshire, adopted the style of Fletcher and fathered a tremendous family, nearly all sons. Succeeding generations were similarly fruitful. In course of time this strain of Fletchers spread through Lancashire and further northwards over the border into Scotland. Some made arrows for the Scottish clans they followed. Incidentally, the name Fletcher means 'arrow-maker' and is of French origin. Therefore, these craftsmen were found in

Argyllshire as followers of the Campbells and the Stewarts, and in Perthshire with the MacGregors. Fletchers are a sept of the last-named and entitled to wear the clan tartan.

When Bonnie Prince Charlie's army faded away near Derby in 1745, some of his Fletchers probably re-settled in South Derbyshire to earn an honest penny. Thereby, substance could be given to this legendary belief and also explain the numerical strength of our Fletchers in this quarter today.

Early in the present century, a direct descendant of the Scandinavian brother who completed the journey to America made search for kith and kin in various parts of this country. Long Eaton was included in this survey, but the measure of his success never came to light, so this romantic story must remain a legend. I have often wondered whether Admiral Fechtler, U.S.A. Naval Chief, springs from this particular source. His reactions, if questioned, might be most illuminating.

COAL AND COLLIERIES

The claims of coal now demands attention. For upwards of fifty years members of our senior branch have suggested that the archives of Stainsby House, once the home of Robert Fletcher of Kilbourne, Derbyshire, a colliery proprietor, who died in 1711, could throw light upon our family origin. This seemed feasible, but the evidence on the Fletcher Memorial in Horsley Church, reproduced here, appears to negative this delightful thought. The inscription reads:

"Near this place are deposited the earthly remains of a family of colliers, Robert Fletcher of Kilburne, buried November 24th, 1711; John Fletcher of Stainsby House, Esquire, son of Robert Fletcher, buried January 26th, 1734; Mary Fletcher of Kilburne, daughter of Robert Fletcher, buried January 26th, 1744; Sarah Fletcher, relict of John, buried March 1st, 1757, aged 90 years; Mary, daughter of John and Sarah Fletcher, buried May 22nd, 1729; Robert Fletcher of Oldgroves, eldest son of John Fletcher, buried February 20th, 1744; Mary, wife of John Fletcher of Stainsby House, youngest son of John, buried May 16th, 1761; John Fletcher of Stainsby House, buried January 19th, 1766; he, having no issue, left all estates and collieries to John, the eldest son of his only surviving sister Elizabeth, who married Francis Barber of Greasley in the County of Nottingham, a

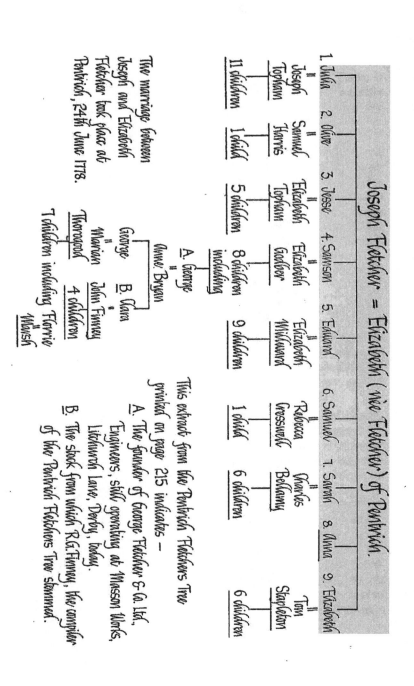

Joseph Fletcher = Elizabeth (née Fletcher) of Pentrich.

1. Julia = Joseph Topham — 11 children

2. Olive = Samuel Harris — 1 child

3. Jesse = Elizabeth Topham — 5 children

Elizabeth Godber — 8 children including

4. Samson

5. Edward = Elizabeth Mildward — 9 children

6. Samuel = Rebecca Cresswell — 1 child

7. Sarah = Charles Bellamy — 6 children

8. Anna = Tom Shapleton — 6 children

9. Elizabeth

A. George = Anne Bryan

George = Marian Thorogood — Thorogood

B. Clara = John Finney — 4 children

7 children including Harrie = Marish

The marriage between Joseph and Elizabeth Fletcher took place at Pentrich, 24th June 1778.

This extract from the Pentrich Fletchers Tree printed on page 215 indicates —

A. The founder of George Fletcher & Co. Ltd., Engineers, still operating at Masson Works, Litchurch Lane, Derby, today.

B. The stock from which R.G. Finney, the compiler of the Pentrich Fletchers Tree stemmed.

coal master. John Barber, in remembrance of the man who trained him up from a youth, and in regard to a family that had laboured for his emolument, erected this monument in 1767."

'The male line of this family died out in 1766, when possession was vested in the female side, the Barbers, which line is still in being today. On the other hand, our Fletcher male line is a proved unbroken one from the very early seventeen-hundreds, so at best we may only be laterally related to Robert Fletcher of Kilbourne. There is no evidence to support this available at present.

In the autumn quarterly issue, 1953, of *The Derbyshire Countryside* magazine, there is an article entitled 'A Legend of Horsley' by F. W. Munslow, which describes a horse race in 1751 between a Barber and a Bacon for the latter's family estates and a futile attempt by a descendant to recover them a hundred years later.

OUR PENTRICH ASSOCIATIONS

Pentrich is charmingly situated on a hilly ridge about five miles north of Heanor at the gateway to the Peakland of Derbyshire. Its character has changed very little and the days there are as unhurried today as they probably were a hundred, or even two hundred, years ago. Stone quarrying, farming, coal mining, cotton doubling and wire manufacture have been the staple sources of local employment.

Various places of note lie within easy reach of those who enjoy open country on foot. Wingfield Manor and Crich Stand are to the north; Matlock, north-west; Ambergate, south; Southwell, famous for its Minster, lies to the east; whilst Wirksworth is on the westward side of the village.

Many generations of Pentrich Fletchers found comfort, consolation and inspiration within the twelfth-century church of St Matthew and their last resting-place without its hallowed walls, but exhaustive and independent searchings by Dr Gerald F. Keating, John Piper, Jnr., and myself revealed no evidence of our common descent from this Fletcher stock.

All the data gathered, particularly from the church registers at Pentrich, failed to tie up with Heanor parish church records of the birth of Edward Fletcher at Heanor in 1797 and of his father, John Fletcher, at Heanor Wood in 1753.

The part Pentrich Fletchers Tree on facing page should convince you of the logical accuracy of our unanimity on this question.

3

'The late Mrs F. E. Marsh of Derby, a direct descendant of the Pentrich Fletchers through the male line, once believed we shared the same root. This belief was upheld by her attendance, many years ago, at the wedding of a Pentrich cousin, Alice Julia Topham, to Samuel, son of Samuel Fletcher of Nottingham, grandson and son respectively of Edward and Phoebe Fletcher, nee Allen, of Heanor. When Mrs Marsh realised, this constituted a branch connection only, she rightly reversed her views on our families' common origin.

Some day, maybe, we shall learn that the male line of the Pentrich Fletcher family stemmed from Heanor. 'Descent in reverse of an ancient conviction, but an intriguing possibility nevertheless!'

HEANOR—WHERE WE DO BELONG

Volume IV of the Stephen Glover MSS pre-1829 describes Heanor as a pleasant village eight miles north-east of Derby, and an extensive parish in the hundred of Morleston and Litchurch and deanery of Derby. The hamlets of Codnor, Heanor Wood, Loscoe, Langley, Milnhay and Shipley were among the dependencies of [formerly] Heynor, [later] Hainer, and [nowadays] Heanor.

Its inhabitants, then only a very few thousands, were mainly employed in agriculture, the manufacture of stockings, and working the collieries.

'Our Line of Descent', set out on the revised Family Tree, proves that our Fletcher male line had its roots in Heanor well over two hundred years ago. Furthermore, H.M. Commissioners responsible for the 1791 *Heanor Parish Awards* allotted John Fletcher of Taghill plot 43 of five perches and plot 47 of twenty-three perches when Derby Road and adjacent thoroughfares were widened and improved. Each plot was bounded to the eastward by a frontage to the said Derby Road. Additionally, *The Morleston and Litchurch Hundred Land Tax Duplicates* 1820-1831 record payment of 1s. 8d. annual tax levied upon John Fletcher, owner-occupier, house and garden, Taghill, Heanor. Upwards of ten years' later, 1842, *The Heanor Register of Electors* included Edward Fletcher, son of John, as lease-holder of a house and garden on Taghill, where from 1842 to 1848 *Pigot's Directories* list him as occupant of a shop, house and lace factory. Whether these premises were sited on the plots originally allotted to John Fletcher in 1791 is open to doubt. Modern and informed opinion suggests that before 1842 Edward had moved up Taghill nearer the Ripley Road, taken a shop with living accommodation, traded therein as a butcher and grocer and used a small factory in rear of these premises for his rapidly expanding lace manufacturing business in which several of his sons assisted and learned 'to make the hard way'.

Messrs I. & R. Morley, hosiery manufacturers, acquired this site and demolished the shop during reconstruction and alterations, but the old factory, so full of Fletcher memories, still continues to give good service to its new owners.

THE ALLEN AND FEMALE SIDE OF THE FAMILY

Research into this side of the family presented me with a setback that I could not leap-frog over, as my first discovery was that fourteen years' records (December 31st, 1798, to December 31st, 1812) of births, marriages and deaths were missing from Heanor parish church archives. Phoebe Allen, the wife of Edward Fletcher, was born in 1807, so inability to refer to this vital and essential entry among the lost of that period of registration prevented the uncovering of the Allen back-roots and the tracing of this side of our family pedigree. My subsequent enquiries reached as far as Salt Lake City, home of an immense Mormon library of genealogical reference works; but even that failed to remove the veil covering the roots of our Allens origin.

However, these further Heanor Parish Awards by H.M. Commissioners in 1791 of plot 11 to Thomas Gillott; plot 19 Edward Gillott; plot 32 Mary Wild; plot 42 Thomas Allen; plot 44 John Eley; plot 48 Edward Gillott; plots 53 and 54 Samuel Gillott, and plots 82 and 83 Richard Allen, all on Taghill, and allotted to 'possible connections on the distaff side', should strengthen Heanor's claim to be our Fletcher family cradle. Incidentally, plot 42 would be on one flank of plot 43 and plot 44 on the other, and I know that many Allens, Fletchers and Eleys were born and bred during three generations in the houses standing on these pieces of land. All three dwellings, two houses with a small shop between them, are on the right of Taghill as you proceed towards Parkfields and Fletcher's present-day lace factory. Can you blame me for venturing the claim that Thomas Allen, of plot 42, fathered Phoebe who became the wife of Edward, son of John Fletcher, occupier of 43? What do you think?

5

"The 1820-31 *Land Tax Duplicates and Register of Electors,* previously referred to, quote Richard and Thomas Allen; John Eley; and Edward, Samuel and Thomas Gillott liable for annual taxes on their Taghill allotments, and having the right as freeholders thereof, to vote.

I think it is reasonable to assert that the mass of facts and evidence we have garnered and examined, proves almost beyond doubt that the main root of our Fletcher family is deeply embedded in the soil of Heanor, and some day, perhaps, other 'twigs' will uncover a much older portion than that which has been laid bare here.

A Janus-like glance towards Pentrich and Heanor seems to be a fitting tailpiece to this question of very widely differing ancestral beliefs in our root of family origin.

In making search through the church registers at Pentrich, I failed to find any reference to the birth of Joseph Fletcher who married Elizabeth Fletcher of that village in 1778. Maybe, our Joseph, the son of Samwill and Mary Fletcher of Heanor Wood, adventured a little further afield to do his courting than was customary in those bygone days, married Elizabeth Fletcher of Pentrich, and thereby established a branch male line to the main Heanor root. Some of you may assert that our Joseph, then barely sixteen years old, *was* too young to be a bridegroom, but Phoebe Allen *was* only barely seventeen when Edward Fletcher led her from the altar a bride. She was also the mother of nine children before she reached the age of thirty. Lads and lasses of long ago matured rapidly and early, so on this human note our main branch contributors will continue the wider story which is written equally from both the male and female sides of the family. The first one to take up the pen will be John William Synyer Fletcher, the spearhead of the younger band of our stock that pressed me into service for this, our third family effort. John is the great-great-grandson of Edward and Phoebe Fletcher and he will now tell us something of interest concerning the senior branch of our clan, whose headman was John Fletcher of Parkfields, Heanor, in the County of Derbyshire.

Other representative contributors will add their stories in order of main branch seniority.

SAMUEL BILLYEALD FLETCHER
The Compiler

6

PLATE 3

JOHN FLETCHER

CHAPTER I

THE JOHN BRANCH

Compiled from contributions made by John William Synyer Fletcher and Jeanne Lander, née Fletcher, supported by notes from other members of this main branch.

JOHN, the eldest son of Edward and Phoebe Fletcher, was born at Heanor on July 27th, 1824, and died there on January 4th, 1893.

His father, obviously a man of enterprise and foresight, believed in having several irons in the fire and whilst successfully managing both a grocer's store and a butcher's shop, installed the first family lace machines in a little house on Tag Hill, Heanor, Derbyshire, prior to the 1840's. Unfortunately, the exact year of business foundation has not been discovered as yet.

One may wonder why Edward, a butcher and grocer, should venture his hand at lace making, but any history of this period will show that he was not alone in this. In those hard and troubled times many people, often from the artisan classes, invested what capital they had in one of the so recently invented lace machines, being quick to realise the possibilities of this new industry.

Circumstances were against these pioneers and many failed, but those who did succeed found themselves well rewarded for their enterprise. From these small beginnings, possibly only one machine in a house or outbuilding, the lace factories of today have developed.

It can be seen from this that the story of our family's industry from the beginning is in no way unique, but may find its counterpart in those of other lace manufacturing families living and working in this area.

Edward soon found it necessary to devote all his time to his lace machines and with the growth of his business and his family—the latter eventually numbering upwards of eighteen children—he moved to a small house in Forest Terrace, Forest Street, Hyson Green, then outside Nottingham, in about 1848, and housed his plant in Abbott's factory situated at the further end of this thoroughfare.

7

Increasing business expansion and regular family additions, soon made another move essential to larger premises at No. 6 Terrace Street nearby, and in this district he lived and worked as a lace manufacturer until his death in 1871.

Five of Edward's elder sons chose to join their father in the business and they, besides three younger ones—Robert, Henry and Richard—all eventually established businesses of their own in or around Nottingham lace market.

John, our great-grandfather, the eldest of the quintet, is our particular interest.

He married Mary, the daughter of Keyworth and Martha Earnshaw of Heanor, and they had ten children—five sons and five daughters.

Soon after 1848, John left his father to go into business for himself as a framework knitter in Gedling Street, Nottingham, but very soon moved into a workshop in High Street, Old Basford, where his wife also had a millinery business.

Eventually, John and Mary retraced Edward's steps back to Heanor and the lace factory on Tag Hill to settle there permanently, but where they first lived after their return is not quite clear.

There are, however, good reasons to believe that they made their home for awhile at 78a Tag Hill, where John and most of his generation were born, or next door at 78 [see illustration, Plate 2] before Parkfields became their residence where, some years earlier, John's younger brother Joseph and his family are reputed to have lived for a short time.

John's son, John Keyworth, lived at Park Grange, which can be seen from the windows of Parkfields. Joseph Edward, a younger brother of 'J.K.' lived with his family at The Fall House, which you almost pass as you journey towards Ripley.

This dwelling is over three hundred years old and is mentioned in William Howitt's *Boy's Country Book*. After the death of John Fletcher Senior, John Keyworth moved to Parkfields, and his brother, George Henry, occupied Park Grange.

Comparatively recently, it was our privilege to meet Mr and Mrs Marshall, once proprietors of Heanor Laundry and the then owners of Parkfields, who invited us to look round their home. It is a beautiful old house in a quiet, secluded garden, and it seems surprisingly remote from the world in spite of the fact that the Derby

8

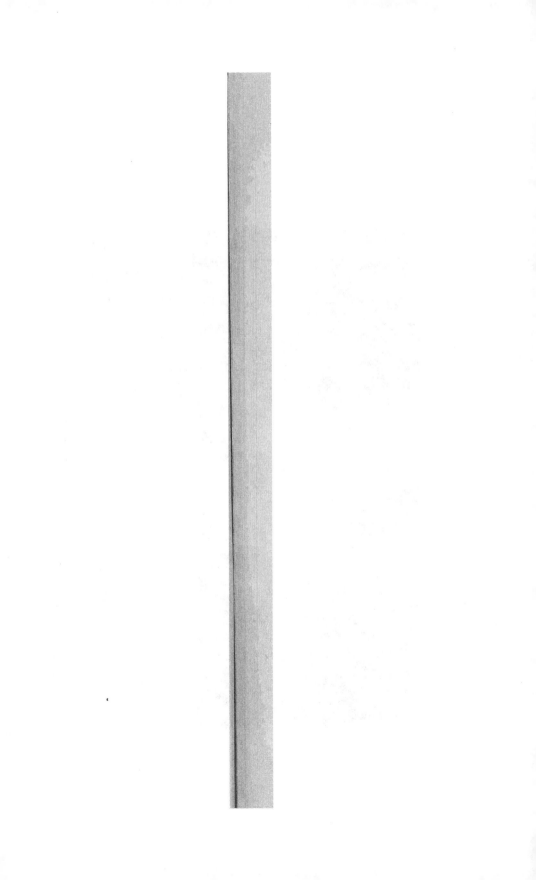

PLATE 4

60TH BIRTHDAY CELEBRATIONS, 1905, AT DERWENT BANK

Road, with its heavy traffic and industry, is only a hundred yards away.

The house, of course, has been modernised to suit present-day requirements, but Mrs. Marshall knows all its history, which room was used by each member of the family of 'Old John' or 'J.K.', and here and there she was able to point out alterations or improvements which had been made during their period of ownership.

There is a story that, as a sideline, 'Old John' worked a small private coal mine in the Heanor district, possibly only a surface affair; but my father [*Jeanne's*] can remember my grandfather saying that when he, grandfather, was a young man, he hardly ever saw the daylight in winter as it was still dark when he went down the mine in the morning and dark when he came up again at night.

I have very rarely heard any mention of this from any other member of the family, so maybe these coal-getting operations took place on John's own land, and were considered worthwhile to provide fuel for use in his factory.

We have now reached the point in our story where a considerable something much more intimate and progressively interesting could be said about individual members of 'Old John's' family circle.

William Fletcher. William, the first child of John of Parkfields and his wife, Mary [née Earnshaw] was born at Heanor, July 29th, 1845, and, as he grew up, took a more than lively interest in his father's business, there learning the mechanical art of lace making in company [later] with his younger brother Thomas.

On June 2nd, 1870—Whit-Tuesday to be exact—William married Leath Ann Thorpe of Nottingham and took up residence next door to his father in Heanor. He was then twenty-five years old.

As their younger brothers—John Keyworth, Joseph Edward and George Henry—in their turn entered the family business, William and Thomas decided to set up a separate concern of their own for the manufacture of lace, and this they did in 1871 as W. & T. Fletcher at New Street, Long Eaton. From the later reading of their father's Will it would appear that he [John] made considerable assistance available to them in launching this venture during his lifetime.

Nottingham had by this time become accepted as the centre of the lace trade and it was in the city that the buying and selling of the commodity was carried on. It was quite natural, therefore, that when John finally became established with his factory at Heanor, he

9

should open an office and warehouse in Nottingham in Pilcher Gate [pre-1876]; later on Weekday Cross; then Halifax Place, and finally in Stoney Street. William and Thomas did likewise in 1883 on High Pavement, and later on in St Mary's Gate.

With his business interests now centred in Long Eaton, William decided to move nearer to them, so he, his wife and their firstborn Clara Jane [born 1871] made their home there, first in South Street and then in Main Street.

As the business prospered, the family increase kept pace with it, since four more daughters—Lavinia [1872], Eleanor [1874], Mary Winifred [1877] and Gertrude [1878] were born before John Thorpe [1879], William's first son and heir, and Thomas [1881] to complete the additions made during the family's domicile in Long Eaton.

Some ten years after entering into partnership together [1881], William and Thomas decided, for reasons at present unknown, to enlarge their business, so they moved into factory premises near the railway bridge on Osmaston Road, Derby, to meet the hoped-for increased demand for their lace products.

William successfully dealt with the problem of re-housing his family in Derby, firstly in Leopold Street, and then by moving into St. Peter's Vicarage where his third son, Joseph Edward [1883] was born.

Trade continued to flourish, so William and Thomas decided to start lace manufacture in Russia and, in 1887, built and equipped a factory in Moscow for this purpose.

This great venture received additional sponsoring from outside interested parties. William went to Moscow to supervise the setting up of the concern, which was completely self-contained, having the manufacture, dyeing, dressing and finishing of all lace under the one roof, with the result that the finished product could be merchanted direct from the factory.

In addition, houses for the employees were erected within the precincts of the works, complete with the [then] most modern and up-to-date ideas incorporated.

On his journeys to and from Moscow, William brought back gifts of sealskin hats for his sons and beautifully embroidered aprons for his daughters, some of which gifts are still treasured family possessions.

'Brisk' was the word for the state of trade both at Derby and in

Moscow for the next decade but, in 1897, some insoluble problems arose, and finally, after a quarter-of-a-century in business together, the partnership between the brothers was dissolved.

William, now fifty-two years old, and with an eye to the future welfare of his three growing sons, the eldest of whom—John Thorpe —was even then ready to take part in the family calling, decided to look around for suitable premises in which to restart business on his own account.

These were found in the Victoria Mills, Draycott, owned by Ernest Terah Hooley, a noted financier and speculator of his day who, in proposing to extend and enlarge the Mill, offered William the lease of the new portion.

Unfortunately, so many varied hold-ups and delays arose that William decided to look elsewhere for more suitable premises and eventually found what he wanted—a small uneconomic foundry on Nottingham Road, Derby. This he bought [1899] and on the site laid the foundations of the company known as *William Fletcher and Sons* [*Derby*] *Limited* today.

The organisation that preceded and followed from leaving the Victoria Mills made living accommodation nearer to business a necessity, so William left St. Peter's Vicarage and moved the family into The Poplars, Spondon.

An accident befell his wife here for which the Derby Canal Company had to pay heavy compensation and, with this unexpected windfall, William branched out into a fresh line of activity. He built a dairy near the entrance gates of his house on the Derby-Nottingham Road and traded there with some success.

However, having moved the centre of his lace business interests back to Derby and made Melbourne House, Osmaston Road, the next family home, the dairy was sold to the Derby Co-operative Society who still use it as such today.

Assisted by his sons, grandfather William set about the creation of a lace manufacturing concern second to none and, as time went by, additions and improvements were progressively made, including three lace shops containing 47 Jardine 222-inch go-through machines; a plain net plant of 46 units [1906]; designing and draughting departments; a yarn doubling and processing shop, along with full repair and maintenance facilities.

Profiting by his experiences in Moscow, he built houses for his employees and a works institute [1904] which latter recently celebrated its golden jubilee.

The recreation of his own family business began the close association of grandfather with Sir Ernest Jardine, whose wife was a cousin to William. Various travels abroad ensued, generally business and pleasure combined, such as the visit in 1905 to the Great St. Louis Exhibition where, and in other centres, including Philadelphia and Salt Lake City, they saw lace machines and met Dr. Alexander Dowie, the Mormon chief and first prophet of Zion, who himself was a lace manufacturer.

They also went to the Milan Exhibition [approximately 1906-7] with their sons, both named John, and included Venice in their itinerary, where they had their photographs taken by Sir John Jardine, Bart., our mutual kinsman, as the party sat in a gondola on the Grand Canal.

In 1912, the business became a limited liability company with grandfather and his three sons as directors.

All the products of the factory were sent to Nottingham where an office and warehouse for the merchanting and distribution of the lace and net were established. These premises have varied over the years from Pilcher Gate, St. Mary's Place, Halifax Place, and Stoney Street to Fletcher Gate. Today, our Nottingham accommodation is confined to an office at 20 Fletcher Gate.

Shortly before the end of the 1914-18 World War, William died at the age of seventy-three and was laid to rest in the churchyard of St. Matthew's, Darley Abbey, Derby, to where, a few years later [1921] his wife, Leath Ann, re-joined him, aged seventy-five years.

During the middle twenties, trade as a whole was not in a particularly prosperous state, but nevertheless, when the next generation made its appearance in the business with *John William Synyer, eldest son of John Thorpe Fletcher* and *Charles Edward*, eldest son of *Thomas Fletcher*, to be followed later by *Peter*, second son of *Joseph Edward Fletcher*, a change for the better gradually took place and the tempo of this upward trend has increased since the second World War [1939-45]. After hostilities ceased, *Cyril Henry, the younger son of John Thorpe Fletcher*, with many years of banking experience behind him, joined his relatives in the Nottingham Road, Derby, factory, and added his share of effort towards this progressive revival of trade.

12

PLATE 5

ON THE GRAND CANAL, VENICE, FIFTY YEARS AGO

Left to right: JOHN THORPE FLETCHER; SIR ERNEST JARDINE; WILLIAM FLETCHER; a son of a business friend who happened to be there

Photographer: the present SIR JOHN JARDINE, BART.

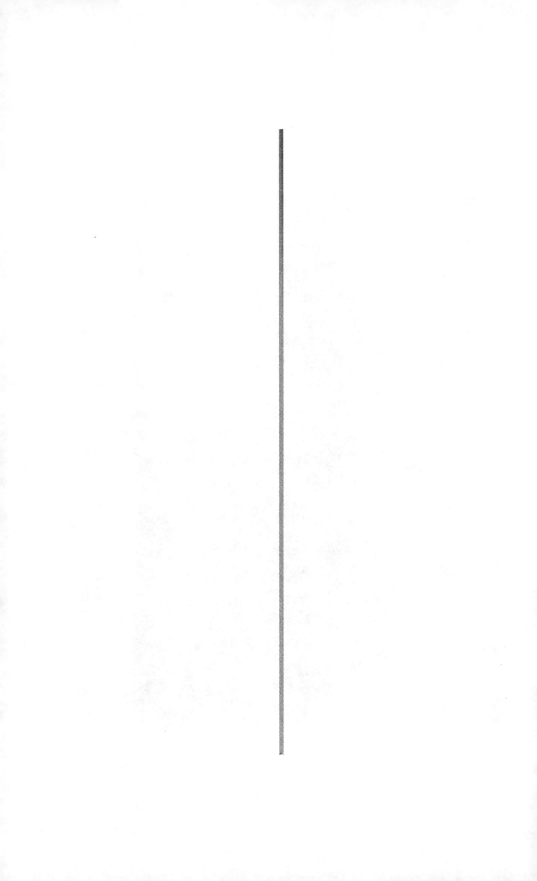

The post-war years have, without doubt, been a time of prosperity and activity within the factory, particularly for renewing and re-equipping the plant. In the midst of this period, in July 1950, *John Thorpe Fletcher* passed on at the age of seventy years, having held his position as head of the business since his father, *William*, died in 1918. His son, *John William Synyer*, was then made a director to fill the vacancy.

A few years later [1954], *Thomas Fletcher*, who followed his brother as Chairman of the Company, died at the age of seventy-three years, before having a full opportunity to appreciate to the full, the value of the additions and other improvements made during the period we here review.

During this period, improvements and extensions were made which include new offices and cloakrooms, and a board room in which are hung the family portraits of Edward, John and William Fletcher—father, son and grandson respectively.

The portrait of Edward came to light in 1947, having been in the possession of Sir Ernest and Lady Jardine for many years. It was recognised as the portrait of the grandfather of Lady Jardine during the sale of the late Sir Ernest's effects and, on being informed, the present Sir John withdrew it from the sale and presented it to the family.

Later on, this portrait was photographed and a framed copy was presented to Samuel Billyeald Fletcher to mark the appearance of our first family tree, which he compiled in 1946.

About three years after the start of our Nottingham Road factory, *William Fletcher* left Melbourne House and bought Derwent Bank on Duffield Road, Derby, a fine old house standing in about seven acres of lawns and gardens overlooking the River Derwent.

I, Jeanne Lander, can just remember it, as this lovely dwelling was my home for a year when I was four years old. The garden at the back of the house descended in terraces, with rose gardens, shrubberies and herbaceous borders to give variety and added beauty to the scene. The tennis courts, the secluded summer arbours and other pleasant amenities made Derwent Bank the perfect setting for the garden party Grandfather gave there on his sixtieth birthday. Over a hundred relatives and close friends were invited. A marquee was erected on the lawn. Caterers from Derby provided all the refreshments and nothing was spared to make this gathering of the

13

clan a memorable one and, to judge from the photographs of the happy throng, even the sun was shining that day.

It will not be out of place to say here that the family firm of William Fletcher and Sons [Derby] Limited has over 250 employees working under conditions that compare favourably with those of any other lace factory in the trade. There are no canteen facilities for mid-day meals as, with few exceptions, the employees live within walking distance of the factory. A canteen trolley is taken round with tea and light refreshments in the morning and the afternoon.

STORIES AND PRIVATE LIFE OF WILLIAM FLETCHER
[continued]

Many are the further stories told of Grandfather during the time he was building up his own business in Derby at the start of the century.

One of the most human of these relates to the personal engagement of an experienced twisthand who had worked previously for him at Osmaston Road. After his interview, he was told to return on the morrow to sign his contract.

On the following day, to his consternation, Grandfather greeted him with the words 'There's a new boss today', on which, the would-be employee enquired 'Had the business changed hands overnight?'

'No, m'lad', said William—who invariably addressed his male employees in this way—'our Jack's wife has got a son'.

The twisthand—Walter Gelthorpe—signed on, rose to be foreman of the lace shop, and stayed with the firm for the remainder of his life, passing away within recent years at the age of eighty-six.

On another occasion, a rather pompous and self-important representative wished to see Mr William—all employees addressed him so—having not previously met him. The traveller, looking round, saw a short, rotund elderly man in a cloth and white apron and enquired for the proprietor. 'I don't know where he is, my man' said Mr William, not wishing to interview this particular visitor, with 'Keep on looking' thrown over his shoulder as he proceeded on his way.

His employees held him in high regard, both as a man and as an employer, so much so, that when he started his own business, many of W. and T. Fletcher's employees joined him in his new venture.

14

. All of these, with one exception, have now passed on. The exception is *William Henson*, now in his eighty-sixth year, who still works a good and full shift five days a week. He is the life and soul of the shop and has served the family for close on sixty-eight years; and he it was who made the first rack on the first machine at Draycott and likewise when the factory started at Nottingham Road, Derby.

Only recently, there passed away *George Cope Brown*, designer, after well over sixty years' service. Many of our older employees have served since the beginning at Nottingham Road, Derby, each for over fifty years, while those with forty years to their credit are quite numerous.

It is noteworthy that when the machine-made lace industry was founded in the U.S.A. in the early part of this century, a number of twist hands from Derby, attracted by the prospect in the New World, and the added factor that the lace machines there were built by Jardines of England, emigrated to form a nucleus of trained men to nurse the growth of this new industry.

Names of these, such as *Charlie Cresswell*, still living in retirement at seventy-seven years of age, *Alec Benlow*, *Charles Eaton*, *George Adsetts*, *Harry Shaw* and others, come to mind, a few of whom still correspond with the Old Country.

In the early days of this century there were many inventions and innovations, and Grandfather William was quick to take advantage of any of them, for either business or personal benefit.

For instance, the telephone was a definite business man's need and, although he enjoyed driving down from Derwent Bank to his factory with his sons in his carriage and pair, it was not long after the 'horseless carriage' had finally proved itself that he changed his mode of travel to Daimler car.

This 'early bird' of the road was superseded by a Humber [R318] and, later still, by a 30 h.p. Sunbeam landaulette [R402], the last word in 1913-14 comfort and reliability. This last-named unit of transport was in constant use by the firm until the late thirties when, very regretfully, it was scrapped, mainly, it is suggested, because it consumed a gallon of petrol every five miles.

We now move forward a generation into the field of Grandfather's family, so here is what I, John W. S. Fletcher, have to retail concerning my father and his offspring.

15

John Thorpe Fletcher, his eldest son, born 1879, at Main Street, Long Eaton, was educated at the Moravian School [now entirely attended by girls] at Ockbrook, near Derby, and entered the family business when his father was actually founding it on Nottingham Road, Derby.

He was made responsible for the sales side of the firm and from then on became widely known and well respected in Nottingham Lace Market. Despite the hard work entailed, he found time for recreation—cricket and amateur soccer were his favourite out-of-door sports.

He captained, for many years, the firm's cricket eleven, which consistently won many trophies in and outside the Derby and District League.

In Association football, he played for Hills' Ivanhoe, a well-known Derby amateur club of its day and, in company with his brother Tom, took part in the sensational F.A. Amateur Cup victory over Crook Town in season 1901-02. Father also frequently appeared as an amateur for Leicester Fosse, the forerunner of the present Leicester City, members, at the moment, of the Second Division of the English League.

He married *Florence Synyer* [1903], daughter of Henry Synyer, an official of the old Midland Railway at Derby. They made their home at 7 Kedleston Road, Derby, where I, 'J.W.S.'—his elder son—was born on June 19th, 1907.

A few months after this event, the family moved to Highbury, Chadfield Road, Duffield, a village five miles north of Derby, where my brother, *Cyril Henry*, arrived in July 1912.

Our removal to Maxey House, Castle Hill, Duffield, just preceded the birth [1914] of our sister, *Phyllis Mary*, who completed their trio of children. The needs of these olive-branches compelled father to confine his outside interests to Freemasonry as member of the Ecclesiastical Lodge, and to golf at the local Chevin course.

For physical reasons, 'J.T.' was rejected for service with the Forces during the 1914-18 World War but played his part in the local Home Guard. It is said 'that he always managed to be in charge of the arms and ammunition wagon—a taxi—when the troops were on the move to the local rifle range, a march of some three or four miles distant from headquarters.

In 1918 he succeeded his father William as head of the firm and, with all his children away at school during the 1920's, found time to make an appreciation of the position and to formulate plans for future management of the family business.

Owing to severe trade depression, 'J.T.' had much to think on at this time, but thanks to the guidance he gave, and the forethought displayed then, the firm is in a strong position today.

Thirty-one years ago—January 1st, 1926, to be exact—his elder son, *John William Synyer*, joined the firm to learn the trade from the floor upwards. A few years later, Cyril Henry, the younger one, adopted banking as a profession, which he did not pursue permanently.

Then, with the calendar at 1939, the claims of marriage and service with the Forces, removed the younger members to other spheres and within the space of six months, 'J.T.F.' and his wife were left to keep the home fires burning whilst he shouldered the business problems which war prevented his sons being beside him to share, as he also grappled with the duties that the Yarn Allocation Committee for the Lace Trade membership thrust upon him.

Life during the war became a little grim, as his wife's health began to fail and although she lived to see the end of hostilities, she died in 1946.

These worries, along with this major loss, completed the undermining of 'J.T.'s' own health until finally, a back injury he sustained while adjusting blackout curtains, hurried his death, which took place in July 1950, aged seventy years. He was laid to rest near his father, William, and others of the family, in St Matthew's Churchyard, Darley Abbey, Derby.

John William Synyer, the eldest child of John Thorpe and Florence Fletcher, saw first light of day on June 19th, 1907. He followed his cousins Richard Cullis Fletcher and Thomas Frederick Fletcher to Bromsgrove, Worcestershire, where he attained a fair measure of success in both work and play until he joined the 'business that father built' in 1926.

From that date onwards his chief concern has been 'learning the trade' to merit being appointed a director in 1951 after his father's death.

In lighter vein, his sporting talent had its outlet as member, and later captain, of the works cricket eleven, whilst in the winter months rugby football, in which he eventually reached County Championship standard, was his first love.

A further interest was the Territorial Army. In 1929 he enrolled in The Sherwood Foresters [T.A.] and, in 1939, was embodied for early service with the British Expeditionary Force in France, later to return to Europe with the B.L.A. into France, Belgium, Holland and Germany, before release from service in 1945.

In 1939, 'J.W.S.' married Phyllis Elaine Stancliffe of Kilmacolm, Scotland, a niece of the late Alderman A. R. Flint, solicitor, of Derby. She was one of the first women to be sworn in as police officers in the country by the Derby Borough Force at the outbreak of war in 1939.

With the arrival of *Michael John* in 1943 and *Judith Anne* in 1947, the interests of this great-great-grandson of *Edward Fletcher* pass to less energatic relaxations such as gardening, stamp collecting and, occasionally, vintage motoring.

Cyril Henry, the second son of John Thorpe and Florence Fletcher, was born in 1912 and followed his brother to Bromsgrove, whence he started on a banking career in Nottingham, before coming to the Derby district just before the 1939-45 World War.

His sporting interests were shared between rugger with Derby Tigers and golf at the Chevin course, of which clubs he was a keen member for a number of years.

In 1938 he joined the 68th A.A. [Anti-Aircraft] Regiment, Royal Artillery, which was embodied at the outbreak of the second World War. Later on, further service with the L.A.A. [Light Anti-Aircraft] Regiment at Brigade H.Q. and in Operations Room. *Cyril Henry* was attending Infantry Battle School at Battle Abbey when Germany surrendered, from where he joined the East Lancashire Regiment at Oberhausen and district for police duties, etc. until discharged towards the end of 1945.

After his release from the Services he resumed his career with the Westminster Bank Ltd. in the Belper and Derby district, but severed the connection there to enter the family lace business which he serves in an administrative capacity.

In June 1939, *Cyril Henry* married *Eileen Benn*. They have two sons—*Alan Henry*, born 1941, and *David John*, born in 1943.

Phyllis Mary, John Thorpe, and *Florence Fletcher's* only daughter, was born in 1914 and, at an early age, was despatched to Harrogate

18

for educational purposes, after which, with plenty of tennis for recreation, she had a session or two at the Derby School of Art.

In 1939 she married T. A. Walton, accountant, the son of Thomas Walton, well known in Derby banking circles and diocesan affairs.

Her husband being posted abroad, *Phyllis Mary* also joined the family business in an administrative capacity, only giving up this work on the arrival of her daughter, *Susan Jane*, in 1943.

This joy was almost immediately shattered by the news of her husband's death in an air disaster in India.

Peace then came and, in 1948, she married *P. P. Ayre*, the eldest son of *Ernest Ayre, Esq.*, of Mickleover, Derby, Chairman of Joseph Mason and Co. Ltd., paint manufacturers, of Derby.

This marriage was blessed by the arrival of a second daughter—*Sally*—a happiness that was short-lived through the death of her first daughter, *Susan*, from sickness, shortly afterwards at the age of six years.

Their home remains in Duffield, not far from where her father, *John Thorpe Fletcher*, lived for so long in the village.

Thomas, second son of William Fletcher, born in 1881 at Long Eaton, also attended the Moravian School at Ockbrook, near Derby, where he showed his prowess on the sports field.

After starting work in father's Nottingham Road factory, he still had the time and inclination to take part in several branches of seasonal sport, including cricket with the works eleven, and association football, in which he enjoyed many personal triumphs in local circles and much further afield.

As an amateur, many honours came his way in connection with the winter game, including the never-to-be-forgotten defeat of Crook Town by Hills Ivanhoe in the F.A. Amateur Cup, in which he and his brother 'J.T.' figured in the early part of this century [1901-2].

About the same time, he toured America with the Pilgrims XI and on the Continent. He also played for Derby County many times in the seasons 1903-4-5 in first-class football.

He learned his trade from the mechanical side and became works manager, a position which has now been taken over by his elder son, *Charles Edward*.

Thomas succeeded his brother John Thorpe as chairman of the firm in 1950, a position he held until his death in 1954, when he was interred in Darley Abbey Churchyard. His second wife, Norah [née Stuart] survives him.

In the later years of his life he became a Freemason and a member of the Hartington Lodge, Derby.

Charles Edward, the elder son of Thomas, was born in 1909 and left Bromsgrove School in 1926 to join the staff of the Nottingham Road family factory where, in the course of time, he understudied his father and, at his death, became works manager of the business.

His sporting achievements rendered considerable service both to the works eleven and to the local Derby rugby club.

As a member of the Royal Air Force Volunteer Reserve, he was early embodied, and served in North Africa where he was wounded and invalided out in 1943 with the loss of the sight of one eye.

Now that he occupies his late father's position, he can lead a little more leisurely life with his wife at Allestree, near Derby.

In 1936, he married *Elsie Mary Phillips*, daughter of Bert Phillips, a well-known local angler, who no doubt can rival, or even surpass, the tales that arise from *Charles Edward's* personal achievements in his country garden.

Derek Stuart, the younger son of Thomas, was born to Norah, his second wife, in 1922. He was educated at Derby School and, on leaving, became an apprentice at Rolls-Royce Ltd., Derby. His greatest interest was flying, and during the 1939-45 World War, he joined the Fleet Air Arm as soon as he was eligible. Much to his family's distress, this promising young life was cut short by his death in a training plane which crashed into the sea off the coast of Scotland in 1944.

Joseph Edward, the youngest son of William Fletcher, an old boy of the Moravian School, Ockbrook, was born at St Peter's Vicarage, Derby, in 1883 and, like his two elder brothers, joined the family business to represent the firm in the plain net section of the trade to which, the chairmanship of the company and the responsibility for other important matters have been progressively added.

In 1916, he joined the army and saw service in France and Belgium, and with the occupation forces in Germany until he was demobilised in 1919.

Gertrude Russell [who died in 1932] of Derby, became his wife and bore him five children, the eldest of whom, *Eileen Joan*, passed on in infancy.

William Russell, their elder son, born 1912, on leaving Bromsgrove School, was trained as an electrical engineer, and finally obtained a post with the British Broadcasting Company.

In turn, he was stationed at various locations—Lisburn, Northern Ireland; Burghead, Scotland; Stoke-on-Trent; Bridport; Colombo, Ceylon [1948-51], and Malaya, where he made a similar round of service.

Since 1955, he has been in residence near London, and has two sons, *Gordon Munro Russell* and *William Russell Edward*, both at school.

Peter, the younger son of Joseph Edward, completed his education at Bromsgrove, entered the family business in 1932, and became understudy to his father in the plain net side of the concern.

In 1940 he enlisted and was commissioned with the North Staffs. Regiment in Northern Ireland. Two years later, he transferred to the Indian Army and served with the 4/3 Gurkha Rifles [North West Frontier Force] in the Waziristan area until he was released in 1945 to resume his business activities where he left off five years earlier.

Peter remains a bachelor member of his father's household and finds his main relaxation from the routine of commerce in the delights of photography.

Jeanne, elder surviving daughter of this quintet of children, born in 1920, left Derby High School in the late thirties to take up a course in beauty culture. This was cut short by World War II in which she served as a radio operator for three years in the Women's Auxiliary Air Force.

It was during this service that she met her future husband, Peter Lander, whom she married in 1944. They now live in Littleover, Derby, with their adopted daughter, *Julia*.

Rhona Mary, the youngest of Joseph Edward and Gertrude Fletcher's olive-branches, came into this world in 1924 and was still at school at the beginning of the second World War. Towards the end of hostilities she met Murray Halford, a Canadian Service man and later, in 1947, she went to Canada to marry him. They and their children now live in Toronto.

21

We must retrace our steps a little to record something concerning these five ladies who were all born before his eldest son entered this vale of tears.

Clara Jane, the senior member of them all, was born at Heanor in 1871 just prior to the family's move to Long Eaton. In the nineties she married C. G. Eggleston of Derby, who survived the arrival of their son, *George William Cantrell* by only a few years. *Aunt 'Clarrie'* has lived on quietly in Derby ever since and is now in her eighty-sixth year.

George William Cantrell left school during World War I, enlisted, and forthwith drafted to the 3rd Battalion Lancashire Fusiliers, attached to the Royal Flying Corps. Eventually, he gained his commission and was demobilised in 1919. A position was then offered him in the family business, which he accepted, and he has been in charge of the Yarn Processing Department for many years.

Tennis was his main recreation in his younger days, he being a team member of the local club known as the 'Erratics'. Nowadays, still a bachelor, he lives with his mother, and finds relaxation in gardening and other similar soil pursuits, when tempted to indulge in them.

Lavinia Ann, the second of this bevy of five girls, was married during the 1890's to W. J. Piper, a member of a family who had a large controlling interest in the *Derby Daily Telegraph*, later merged, along with 'W.J.P.' into the present *Derby Evening Telegraph*.

'*Walter*' and '*Vinnie*' lived for many years at No. 7 Kedleston Road, Derby, the former home of *John Thorpe Fletcher*.

They were blessed with a son and a daughter, both of whom, despite the calls of war, have survived their father, who died in 1940, aged sixty-eight. 'Vinnie', now in her eighty-fifth year, lives at Idridgehay, Derbyshire, with her daughter and son-in-law.

Walter John Fletcher Piper, their only son, was educated at Derby School and, in the first World War, obtained a commission from Sandhurst into the Indian Army in which he served 1917-21. By profession, he qualified as an accountant and then married his cousin, *Gwendoline Maude*, daughter of *Sidney Edward Fletcher*. Their home is in Upminster, near London. They have no family.

Evelyn Margaret, the only daughter of 'Walter' and 'Vinnie', did much to alleviate suffering in the first World War by nursing, and also through membership of the British Red Cross, Women's Voluntary Service and ambulance driving in the second one.

She married Dr Gerald F. Keatinge who became, and still is, medical adviser to the Butterley Colliery Company Limited of Ripley, Derbyshire.

John Charles Fitzgerald Keatinge, their son, on reaching National Service age during the second World War [1939-45] was commissioned from Sandhurst into the Guards Armoured Division in 1943. As in the case of so many promising young people 'he fell in action' near Caen, Normandy, during August 1944, and now lies at rest in French soil.

Moira Margaret Keatinge, their daughter, completed her general hospital training in 1944, joined the Q.A.I.M. Nursing Service and was sent to Normandy and later to India. She has since married a doctor, *John Watson*, and lives in London with him and their two children, the elder of whom is a son, *William*.

Eleanor, the third daughter of *William Fletcher*, met and married *Charles Edward Wood*, of Edward Wood and Sons, contractors. They lived at The Croft, Littleover, Derby, and had two sons.

Uncle 'Charles' was a great man for the outdoor life and worked a small farm, but his one paramount passion was riding to hounds. This he did with the *Meynell Hunt* for very many years, accompanied by his two sons, *Charles Edward* junior and *James William*.

Such enthusiasm, however, led to a fatal fall in the field for father in 1933, but mother outlived him till 1956, when she was laid to rest at the age of eighty-two years.

Charles Edward, their elder son, became a solicitor after leaving Bromsgrove School. The second World War then claimed him, and he served in the Royal Corps of Signals in North Africa and the Sudan before returning to his original calling, with time off occasionally for a ride to hounds. He is married, with one daughter, *Georgina Caroline*, and lives in London, although his practice is in Derby.

James William Wood, the younger son, also a Bromsgrovian scholar, was trained as an engineer, with spare time activities in the Staffordshire Yeomanry [T.A.]. On the outbreak of the second World War, his unit went to Palestine, where 'J.W.' saw service, and in Africa. On returning to civil life, he continued engineering for awhile, then gave it up, took to himself a wife, and now has a large farm down in Sussex—and a family.

Mary Winifred, the fourth daughter of William Fletcher, remained a spinster all her life, becoming her mother's companion, especially so after the death of her father.

On the passing of her mother, she went to live at Llandudno, a place which never failed to interest her, where she resided until her death in 1941 at the age of sixty-four years. She was laid to rest with her parents in St Matthew's Churchyard, Darley Abbey.

Gertrude, the youngest of these five daughters, continued unmarried and took a great interest in the domestic affairs of Derwent Bank.

During the 1914-18 War, she became a member of the V.A.D. and spent many long hours nursing the wounded. This had a fatal, adverse effect on her health, and so she passed to her rest and reward for good service rendered in 1916 at the age of thirty-seven years.

Thomas Fletcher, the second son of John of Parkfields, was born in Heanor and his early life and interests were very similar to those of his elder brother *William*. Both learned the art of mechanical manufacture of lace in their father's factory and when the younger sons of John began to take an active interest in the business, he and William set up their own concern in Long Eaton in 1871.

The year 1881 brought about the move to Osmaston Road, Derby, and six years later [1887] Thomas and William were engaged in laying the foundations of their Russian factory in Moscow. A decade of great activity ensued until 1897 when the partnership between the brothers was dissolved and Thomas took over the whole business, complete with the Moscow subsidiary concern, and also retained the original title.

Little is known regarding the private life of Thomas up to this time [1897]. We do know that he was then trading as W. & T. Fletcher, lace manufacturers, and that his two elder sons, Frederick William Cope and Sidney Edward, were established in similar businesses of their own at Sandiacre.

These two sons were soon brought into father's business. Then, in company with his third son, Thomas William, they took managerial charge of the factory and office in Nottingham, situated in St. Mary's Gate and later in Stoney Street, until the youngest of the trio went to Moscow to look after the firm's interests in Russia where he remained more or less permamently.

A period of some twenty years passed during which, judged by other concerns in the same trade, business in both factories thrived.

Then came the 1918 Revolution in Russia. The Moscow factory was seized and Thomas William was thrown into gaol.

The firm was absolutely stripped of its entire resources in capital, buildings and equipment to the tune of nearly £500,000. Insult to injury was added a few years later when these robbers wrote to, and asked Frederick William Cope Fletcher to send mechanics to Moscow to recondition the machinery they had so ruthlessly stolen [see local newspaper files].

Eventually, with the help of some of his former employees, he escaped in nothing but the clothes he wore, and after travelling in an open truck of a goods train to the Finnish border, finally arrived in Aberdeen late in the same year. Owing to the great privations he suffered in the Russian prison, Thomas William returned home a very sick man and passed away a few years later.

This disastrous end to the Moscow factory venture, with the great financial loss involved [see earlier note] for which, as far as is known, no compensation has ever been made, was a very great blow to the mother firm, W. and T. Fletcher.

It was indeed so crippling to its original owner that, in 1922, his business complete was taken over by John Jardine Ltd., who re-named it The Melbourne Lace Company and appointed *Frederick William Cope Fletcher* to manage the new concern.

Unfortunately, our detailed knowledge of the family affairs of *Thomas Fletcher* during the middle and later part of his life continues to be scanty. We *are* able, however, to definitely assert, that he had and most certainly cultivated an interest in local government to such an extent that he was elected an Alderman and, at the close of the last century, was honoured as the Mayor of the Borough of Derby.

The period commencing from the middle twenties was not a happy one for the lace trade generally so, as part of a reorganisation plan launched in 1928, The Melbourne Lace Company, in its entirety, moved into the Victoria Mills, Draycott, now also become the property of John Jardine Ltd., and the factory of W. and T. Fletcher, with nearly half-a-century of lace manufacture behind it, was put up for disposal.

'F.W.C.' continued as manager with The Melbourne Lace Company until 1930, when he set up on his own account in lace and net merchanting in St. Mary's Gate, Nottingham.

During the second Great War [1939-45], he was responsible under government authority, for all yarn allocations to the plain net trade, later reverting to the role of a private merchant of these materials. In this he continued, a highly respected member of the trade, until his death in 1949 at the age of seventy-four years. His business then became a limited company with his elder son, Richard Cullis, as a director, but late in 1956 it was finally wound up.

Frederick William Cope Fletcher had two sons—*Richard Cullis* and *Thomas Frederick*—both of whom were educated at Bromsgrove School in Worcestershire, where they were the forerunners of a line of other young male Fletcher relatives who followed them there.

Richard Cullis, the elder boy, joined the staff of British Celanese Ltd. From this he retired some considerable time ago and now lives, a bachelor, at the Lizard in Cornwall.

Thomas Frederick, the younger son of 'F.W.C.', left school in 1922. He then joined the L.M.S. Railway at Derby as an apprentice and, during this period, was a stalwart of the Derby Rugby Club until he obtained an appointment on the railways in the Argentine, South America. A number of years later he entered one of that country's main industries—meat packing—and then married. He and his wife and two children—a son, *John Alan*, and a daughter, *Diana Beatrice*—are still residents in that faraway part of the world.

Sidney Edward Fletcher, the second son of Thomas, enjoyed a somewhat chequered career after the demise of W. and T. Fletcher, but although now in his early eighties, is still interested in a timber concern.

Gwendoline Maud, his eldest daughter, is the wife of Walter John Fletcher Piper, a grandson of William Fletcher. They reside at Upminster, near London.

Bertha Marjorie, the youngest one, became Mrs Greasley, and the mother of a daughter, Sally, now Mrs. P. Greenhill, a resident in Wimbledon Park, S.W.19.

Edna, the second of these three girls, married J. H. Grimes, and lives at Huddersfield.

John, of whom little is known, is Sidney Edward's younger son.

26

Laura Martha Marshall Fletcher, one of Sidney Edward's sisters, married a well-known Belper solicitor, Percy Pym, whose son, *Joseph Peter Radford*, has now followed in his father's footsteps.

Little is known of the rest of this section of our family, except that the two youngest daughters of Thomas Fletcher, *Jane Louisa* and *Hilda Mary*, both unmarried, live away in the country at Allestree, near Derby.

JOHN KEYWORTH, JOSEPH EDWARD AND GEORGE HENRY FLETCHER

Their part in the John Branch story, compiled from notes.
supplied by members of their families

JOHN FLETCHER substantially advanced the interests of William and Thomas, his two elder sons, during his lifetime, so, to balance matters, the three younger ones were made jointly responsible for continuing the family business after his death for the benefit of their sisters and themselves.

This they did and maintained the policy of doing the finishing in Nottingham [Halifax Place] and the manufacturing in the original Fletcher factory at Heanor.

This soundly built three-storied building, containing 13,872 square feet of floor space [still in use today by I. & R. Morley Ltd.] was erected by Edward Fletcher on a plot of ground [877 square yards] situated behind his butcher's shop [last occupied by Mr Bosworth] and two adjoining dwellinghouses, when he purchased the land and properties [a copy of the indenture of sale is reproduced elsewhere] from John Gronow of Charlton Kings, near Cheltenham, Gloucester, on December 26th, 1838.

The resources of these premises adequately met rising trade demands for the next ten years, but by then, the great changes in construction, particularly in size of plant units, during the last quarter of the nineteenth century, had created a production problem for the three partners so, in 1904, they built a much larger and more modern factory near Heanor Gate station.

This venturesome changeover from the old to the new ran into troubled waters immediately. A sustained slump in the trade blew up and this, together with later setbacks and complications, some mutual in character, brought about a dissolution of the partnership [about 1910], an agreed division of the business, and their individual establishment as master men in the lace industry.

'J.K.' took over the finishing end in Nottingham as his portion, but 'J.E.' and 'G.H.' remained in Heanor and began independent manufacture there by sharing the factory and its thirty-odd lace machines and other equipment on a fifty-fifty basis.

JOHN KEYWORTH FLETCHER, an outstanding character among the family's older members, was born at 18 Derby Road, Heanor, April 13th, 1861, and died at 100 Tavistock Drive, Nottingham, November 29th, 1933, in his seventy-third year.

He married Mary Ellen Cash [who died November 7th, 1952], daughter of Harrison and Maria Cash of Mansfield, who presented him with two sons and two daughters, and the family, in turn, resided at Park Grange [1885-1895], Parkfields [also Heanor, 1895-1914], Radnor House, Nottingham [1914-1921], Abbey Wood, Newark [1921-1922], Charnwood, Gregory Boulevard, Nottingham [1922-1931] and 100 Tavistock Drive [1931-1933].

John Keyworth [and other brothers] received his education at the hands of Edward Richard Leafe, a Derbyshire schoolmaster. Directories of the eighteen-seventies list him as Principal of the Academy, Heanor, but two well-informed members of the family describe the site of his school as being near the 'Rose and Crown', Smalley, or as 'held in an outlying building of Parkfields which became the coach-house in later years'—a distinction with a difference, perhaps, though no reflection on the quality of tuition given is intended.

Schooldays over, 'J.K.' started work in his father's factory to learn the trade from rock bottom. It was soon evident, however, that the young newcomer's bent was not mechanical and that his main interest centred around the finishing and merchanting of lace which, in future phases of his business life, took him as far afield as Paris and other parts of Europe.

Briefly, the phases and centres of these activities were: working for father in Heanor and Nottingham [1875-1893]; his partnership with brothers Joseph and George [1893-1910], and on own account as plain net finisher and merchant at 47 Stoney Street, Nottingham [1912-1929].

The quiet joys and privacy of retirement then beckoned him so, in February 1929, 'J.K.' sold his business to Mr A. S. Chappell who, as John Fletcher & Co., is still active in the trade at the foregoing old-established address, and, so we are told, resides in West Bridgford.

Despite the inroads that are made into the time of a prominent business man, John Keyworth had a sense of service that compelled him to use most of his leisure for the public good.

He was a Justice of the Peace for Derbyshire; a County Councillor; Chairman of the Heanor Urban District Council; and a keen supporter of the District Nursing Association in its successful efforts to secure the services of Queen's Nurses for the town.

The great value set upon these human endeavours by fellow-residents can best be shown here by reproducing the phrasing of *an Illuminated Address*, prepared by Frank Ealey of Langley Mill, which was publicly presented to John K. Fletcher, Esq., J.P., C.C., when, at the age of fifty-three, he left his native Heanor in 1914 to settle in Nottingham:

"On behalf of the inhabitants of Heanor Urban District we desire to assure you of our gratitude for the many acts of kindness you have extended to us by your interest in and support of every object which has conduced to the general good. Especially we thank you for the tact and devotion you displayed when Chairman of the Heanor Urban District Council in procuring for us a pure water supply, first by securing the necessary support at a statutory meeting so as to endow us with legal power to apply to Parliament; your subsequent services on the Parliamentary Committee of the joint Authorities were instrumental in the passing into law of the Ilkeston and Heanor Water Board Act of 1901 the provisions of which are a clear indication of how thoughtfully you discharged your responsibilities and thus gave us an unfettered partnership in a municipal enterprise which has been a priceless boon to dwellers in your native town. Our memory of these events impells us the more deeply to deplore your decision to leave Heanor, but we trust you may be blessed with long life and that the assurance of our sincere personal esteem will conduce to your future happiness."

John Andrews	W. Stainsby
E. V. Eames	John Holbrook
W. Hardy	B. Stoddard
James Walker	R. Wright
Hy. R. Watson	H. J. Windle, *Treasurer*
E. Wheldon	P. Hanbury, *Secretary*

March 25th, 1914

29

When this treasure in art writing, embellished with pictorial miniatures of Heanor Church, Parkfield House, the Derbyshire Coat of Arms, parts of the Meersbrook Water Undertaking, framed in ornamented Old English gilt, was presented, an inscribed silver salver, a pair of solid silver vases and a fruit dish were companion gifts as marks of intimate respect for 'J.K.', his wife and their family. [This prized family souvenir now hangs in The Heanor Urban District Council Chamber].

Edith Evelyn, like many ladies of her generation, was an unflagging member of the rota shifts on service in Cammell Laird's Nottingham munitions canteen during the 1914-18 war. She married Charles Hingley [son of Albert Hingley of Kingswinford, Staffordshire] who, in addition to being an executive and representative of Lovatt and Lovatt, earthenware potters and merchants of Langley Mill, from 1903 to 1940, was also managing director of Amblecote Glassworks, Staffordshire [1933-51] until he died.

Harwood, the elder son of John Keyworth Fletcher, was educated at Retford Grammar School and married Alice Fisher. He worked in the lace trade for a short time, first for his father, and then for a year [1910] on his own account at 22 High Pavement, Nottingham, before he accepted a post at Lawn Mills, Mansfield, which his uncle Harwood Cash offered him [1911-14].

Some of us will never forget Gommecourt where, on July 1st, 1916, the Robin Hood Rifles were almost wiped out to a man. Jack Bishop, the Nottinghamshire cricketer, was one of the very few who lived to answer the roll, but 2/Lieutenant Harwood Fletcher was among the many who fell.

His son, *Harwood Silas*, an old Lichfield Grammar School boy, like his father did, prepared before danger threatened and had already learned to fly when the last war broke out. He enlisted straightaway and served as Pilot Officer R.A.F. from 1939 to 1942 when he was invalided out after doing ferry piloting during the latter part of his service.

Today, his interests are centred in motor engineering. These have taken him to Spain, Canada, America and South Africa, where, as the representative of General Motors Limited, he lived for two years and enjoyed social contacts with Arthur Fletcher of Blue Sky, North Boksburg, and his family in leisure moments.

He took Moyra, the daughter of Dr O'Mullane of Nottingham, to wife, but no children have blessed the marriage.

Eileen, the only sister of Harwood Silas, lived with her mother in West Bridgford until the latter's death a year or two ago. She married Richard Taylor, engineer, of Taylor Brothers, Sandiacre, but no additions to the Family Tree stemmed from this union.

The Nottingham Corporation Water Department, Castle Boulevard, have, at the moment, the benefit of Eileen's [now Mrs. Barnes] services as secretary, and those who wish can contact her at 39 Trevor Road, West Bridgford, Nottingham.

Nora, the younger of 'J.K.'s two daughters, worked in the making-up department of his business throughout 1914-18 and in the same day-and-night canteen as her sister Edith during these war years.

She married Philip, son of H. J. Windle, banker, of Heanor, in which town Nora and her husband live in quiet retirement.

George, the younger brother of Nora, had a distinguished record in both world wars. He began working for father on leaving Retford Grammar School but, in August 1914, took leave of lace, joined up with Kitchener's Army and went overseas to the Salonica front as a gunner in the R.H.A.

In war, aptness for leadership is valued, so George was soon commissioned and proceeded to France to conclude his 1914-18 active service. During 1939-45 much of his military service took place in the Bristol area where, as a salvage party leader, with the rank of captain, he was responsible for re-organising and restoring services and amenities in that part of England after heavy enemy bombing visitations. George married Eve Tyzack of Sheffield.

Anne, their daughter, was a driver in the W.R.A.C. during the last war, but left the service when she married Trevor Tomlinson. They have one son, Peter, eight years old.

John Harwood Harrison, brother of Anne, served in the Royal Navy throughout 1939-45. There are, I am sorry to say, no recorded details of this Jack Tar's signal service available, but in civil life he has a truly comfortable post with Baldwins, manufacturers of electric blankets. He and his wife [a Manchester lady] have made their home in The Park, Nottingham.

Joseph Edward Fletcher, the fourth son of John and Mary of Parkfields, born at Taghill, Heanor, 1863, in the little house which fronted the factory Edward Fletcher built in 1838, went straight from Edward Richard Leafe's school into his father's works to learn the lace trade from the bottom.

It was soon borne in upon the older hands that a budding mechanical genius, destined to acquire an outstanding technical knowledge of a lace machine and the ability to produce many novelties from it beyond the skill of most, had arrived in their midst.

On reaching twenty-four years of age, this talented young man married Fanny, the daughter of John Limb who farmed Church Farm at Brackenfield, near Alfreton. She was born in 1867 and became a great worker for the Heanor Nursing Association. Forty-four years together followed, during which they had three family homes, of which their first two were rich, both in notable associations and local history.

In 1887, they went to live at The Falls, Heanor, previously the home of the Tantum family and William Redfern, uncle of William Howitt, and they remained there for eight years. It was there that the housemaid committed suicide in the gardener's cottage across the yard, which was empty at the time. She had not been in service with them very long, and it was through some private trouble that she hung herself.

In 1895 they moved to The Dene, Heanor, which had been the home of William and Mary Howitt. The Dene was a very old house, part of it having been built in 1700.

This portion overlooked the large, walled-in garden, below which there was an extensive orchard containing a wide variety of fruit trees, and the house was supposed to have a ghost also.

Mrs Howitt [William's mother] was in residence at the time when her brother Tantum, of The Falls, was returning home late at night on horseback from dining with Squire Mundy at Shipley Hall. He knocked up the landlord of the Crown Inn [near Heanor church] and demanded a drink. The landlord, resentful at being fetched out of bed, took his time opening up, so Tantum flicked him with his riding crop, whereupon mine host brought out a carving knife and stabbed him. At the crucial moment of death, Mrs Howitt said the form of her brother appeared in her room, but whether his wraith has walked elsewhere since is not recorded.

The Falls still stands, but The Dene was pulled down some years ago to permit road widening, just after the family went to live at The

Croft, Eastwood, in 1926 where, five years later, Joseph Edward died.

When this work was completed, some remnants of oak and stone, taken from the old home, were fashioned into a lych-gate at Heanor cemetery as a memorial to William Howitt, the author, who was born at The Dene in 1792.

In this writer's lifetime, woodlands still covered the slope between those two historic dwellings, but all that remains of that sylvan retreat today is Woodend. Additionally, the buildings just below Heanor parish church towards Nottingham, erected on what was once Dene enclosed ground, are a further memorial left to mark the changes brought about by the ruthless march of time.

Joseph Edward avoided notoriety, preferring service not seen by the public eye. He was a lover of cricket and golf, but open-air instrumental music, particularly that rendered by Heanor Brass Band, to whom he presented a complete set of instruments, had a warm spot in his heart also.

After the agreed division of 1910, the ball did not run kindly for him in the lace trade so, in 1927 or thereabouts, he left the industry and, for the next year or two, produced artificial silk and wool dress fabrics from a small hosiery knitting plant he established at Eastwood

John Leslie, the eldest of five children, was born on December 31st, 1891, at The Falls and, during his education at Retford, he was not only in the Grammar School Rifle Club team that won the Frankfort Shield at Bisley, but was also runner-up for the Chelsmore Cup, which he lost after a shoot-off.

Day-by-day school lessons put aside, John Leslie worked in father's factory [1910-14] until enlistment in Kitchener's Army soon found him on active service with the 9th Battalion King's Royal Rifles overseas where, in September 1915, he was wounded at Yypres.

Duties at home that followed with the 7th Reserve Battalion Sherwood Foresters [Robin Hoods] stemmed from a commission, the rank of Musketry Officer, and the post of Range Commandant. This triumvirate of power and responsibility for teaching the uninitiated how better to shoot and control themselves under small arms fire lasted until September 1918, when 'J.L.' went back to France again to complete his First World War service.

Four more years of peace work [1919-22] ensued in father's factory at Heanor. Then, very wisely, he went over to Harwood Cash [nowadays Harwood Cash & Co. Ltd.] of Farnsfield, cotton doubler, Lawn Mills, Mansfield, and made good there. Today, he is a director of the firm and the weight of office is made easier to bear by indulging in his only hobby—game shooting, which takes him to Scotland and Shoots in Yorkshire.

Looking back over the years, it can truly be said that John Leslie 'made better than good' when he married Etta, the daughter of Harwood Cash. They have two children, and reside at Woodlands, a nice country house, near which father was Head Observer at K/2 Observation Post, Farnsfield, during the years of darkness [1939-45] before and after Dunkirk.

Etta Kate Cash Fletcher, their elder girl, married Reginald Lisle Rockley Jones, a wines and spirits and soft drinks merchant, and the son of Rex Louis and Janet Jones [nee Rockley] of Mansfield, Notts. Reginald and Etta have a little daughter, Patricia, who through her grandmother on the male side, springs from the famous bill-poster family whose huge pictorial advertisement hoardings once caught one's roving eye in town and countryside.

Josephine Ann Cash Fletcher, their other daughter, is a very keen horsewoman and has a great knowledge of horseflesh. She rides to hounds with the Grove and Rufford Hunt, a colourful, adventurous sport, to which an occasional stirrup cup, the good company and picturesque settings of the meets give an added zest. As Chairman of the Newark Division Young Conservatives Association she gives much thought to improving the state of affairs and safeguarding the affairs of State.

Charles Heathcote, the second of Joseph Edward's two sons born at The Falls was, in his day, *Victor Ludorum* at Retford Grammar School and, after completing his education there, worked [apart from one short interval] in the family factory at Heanor until his father retired from the lace trade. This break occurred when he joined the army and, in 1915, was discharged on medical grounds. Today, after eighteen years' service, he is Northern Area Supervisor for Messrs Stenor Ltd., Richmond, Surrey, a nationally-known concern. During twenty-five years' captaincy of Shipley Colliery Cricket Club, Charles was twelfth man for Derbyshire on several occasions and official scorer at times. He married Janet, daughter of Edward [who had charge of the pumps at Basford Gas Works] and Elvia Collingham [née Hooton] of Swinderby, Lincolnshire.

Joan Kathleen, their only child, was educated at St Joseph's Convent, Lincoln, and married Leslie Richard Heathcote [no relation to the famous inventor of that name or father-in-law, either] of West Hallam who, besides being a builder by trade, is Chief Inspector of the Ilkeston Special Constabulary and also Honorary Secretary of the South Derbyshire Conservative Association.

Brenda Jean, the only grandchild, as yet, in this section of the clan, has the love of music in her blood—she excels on the piano, I am told.

Joseph Edward, Junior, entered this vale of tears at The Dene, Heanor, and had his education at Retford Grammar School. He never had anything to do with the lace trade but was studying medicine at Edinburgh University when, in 1914, he was called up, commissioned in the R.A.M.C. [Royal Army Medical Corps] and sailed with that unit to Salonica.

Some twelve months later he was recalled from that theatre to continue his medical studies. These were completed under Dr Hogarth at Nottingham General Hospital where, from approximately 1922 to 1924 he was a member of the residential staff prior to going into partnership with Dr Gillespie at Eastwood, Nottinghamshire, a connection that endured for some years.

Naturally, in course of time, this young physician took unto himself a wife and was presented with two sons and a daughter—Joseph Edward, Susan Elizabeth and James Harwood. They all reside at Donnington, Boston, Lincolnshire, where Dr Joseph Edward Fletcher is still in practice.

Mabel, the elder daughter of Joseph Edward and Fanny Fletcher, has a liking for local history [Heanor] and tells us that William and Mary Howitt [1792-1879] attained material literary distinction in that direction. The children's poems of Mary were very popular and she is reputed to have written 'Won't you come into my parlour said the spider to the fly'. They were buried in the little churchyard at the back of the Quaker meeting house that stood opposite to The Dene.

Apart from being a normal housewife and mother, Mabel makes no other claim to personal accomplishment or outstanding achievement. She married the Rev. Jonathan Henry Bodgener, M.A., at Heanor Methodist Church [October 2nd, 1912]. He travelled as Methodist minister in the Heanor-Ripley circuit and was also called to serve in Liverpool; Southport; Seacombe, Lancashire; Lytham

St Annes; Oxford; Wallasey; Harrogate; Wallington and Worthing, Sussex, where he and his wife are now living in well-earned retirement. Their three sons are all enjoying the advantages and grasping the opportunities that follow in the wake of a good education.

John Fletcher Bodgener, A.A.L.P.A. [Associate Auctioneer Landed Property Agents] attended Kingswood School, Bath, and married Doreen Mary Horne. He served in R.A.F. Bomber Command during the last World War and at present is with Warmington and Son, Surveyors, Land Agents and Valuers, London.

Peter Henry Bodgener, A.M.I.C.E. [Associate Member Institute Civil Engineers] was also educated at Kingswood School,Bath, before proceeding to King's College, London University, to advance his studies. He was awarded a commission [First Lieutenant] and served with the Royal Engineers in Burma and Japan. On returning to civil life, Peter became Assistant Bridge Engineer to Chelmsford County Council, married Esmèe Mabel Struan Cosin and, with their three small daughters, Susan Alice, Catherine Mabel and Mary Hester, six, four and two years old respectively, have made their home at Ladywell House, Great Baddow.

Geoffrey Cruse Bodgener, A.R.I.B.A. [Associate Royal Institute British Architects] received most of his education at Ashville College, Polytechnic School of Architecture, before completing his service in the R.A.F., first as Wireless Mechanic [Sergeant] in Aden, and then as Instructor in Architecture at Cairo. On returning home, he taught in the Polytechnic School of Architecture until he obtained the post of Chief Assistant to Mr Edward Mills, a well-known London architect.

Geoffrey reached a more settled state when he married Margaret Lester. They have two young sons—four-year-old Peter Henry and James Lester who is two. Their home is at 11 Elios Place, Blackheath, London.

Doris Fletcher, the youngest of Joseph Edward's five children, never married and, like her youngest brother and sister Mabel, was born at The Dene. After her father's death she went into private service as lady-companion and friend until she passed away at Heanor on February 14th, 1955.

One of the most lasting tributes to the memory of Doris and her charm will be all the interesting notes relating to The Falls and the home of her birth which she compiled and made available to me during her long illness.

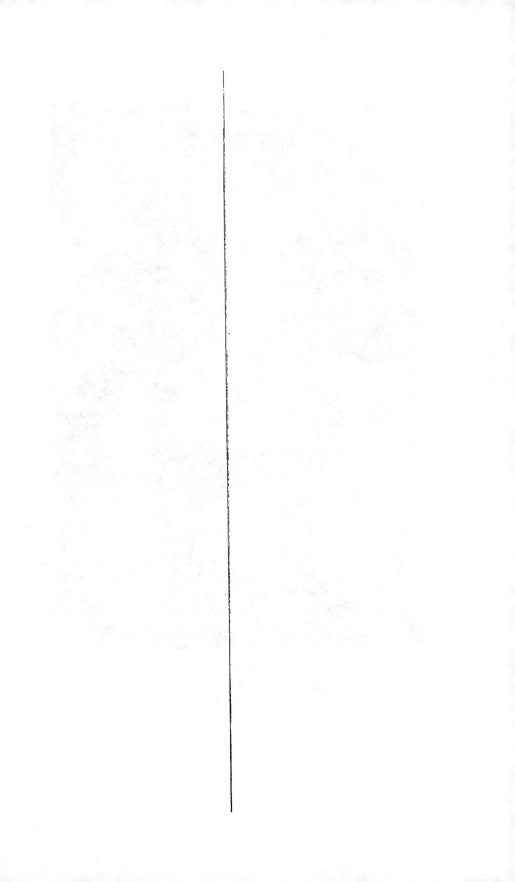

PLATE 6
Above: LACE MENDING ROOM
Below: GO-THROUGH MACHINE

George Henry Fletcher. By an unpredictable turn in fortune's wheel, this fifth son and youngest child of John of Parkfields became head of the family lace business founded in Heanor by Edward Fletcher one hundred-and-seventeen years ago [1838]. He was born at Heanor on November 9th, 1870 and, twenty years later [1890] started work in the old Taghill factory which, as Ilkeston No. 1, was the first building of any kind to have the telephone installed in the area. The present factory built at Heanor Gate in 1904 was, in 1906, the first establishment in Heanor to generate its own electric light on the premises. Danks Ltd. of Nottingham installed the essential plant and when Mrs John Keyworth Fletcher operated the ceremonial switch, onlookers came from as far away as Birmingham to witness a wonder happening which converted gas-light into all-electric service.

Today [1955] this one-shed factory of three shops' and 26,105 square feet floor space, which George Henry ceased to control in 1924, now houses fifty up-to-date machines producing a variety of exports for all the markets of the world except those behind the Iron Curtain. This plant varies considerably in gauge width to meet particular needs. Normal kinds of lace are made on types ranging from 174 to 360 inches; plain net is run off on 204 inch units, and knitted patterned lace suitable for ladies' wear is produced on machines ranging from 72 to 120 inches. The last-named material— an American innovation—has been greatly improved both in quality and design by the application of special Fletcher manufacturing techniques.

We must now retrace our steps some sixty years or more to record the marriage of George Henry to Jessie Roper of Newstead. Her father, ——— Roper, was entirely responsible for the general layout of the gardens and grounds at the Abbey where his wife also had full charge of the dairy. These, and similar domestic associations, may substantially explain why their three grandsons are so happy in their large, well-kept Smalley Hill gardens and why they also maintain traditionally good tables in their homes.

In his married and private life, most of which was spent at Park Grange, which is close to Parkfields, George Henry, a man of medium build, fresh in complexion with clear blue eyes, was retiring in disposition and avoided the limelight. His principal hobbies were tennis, cricket and hockey which he played for Heanor clubs in early

37

life, whilst his wife, a very keen gardener, did a great deal of social work in the town and for the church. In later years, however, particularly after he retired from active business, the garden at Park Grange became George Henry's sole out-of-doors interest until he died in 1939. His wife pre-deceased him in 1934.

Fifteen years before his passing [1924] the management of *George Henry Fletcher & Sons Ltd.* was turned over to George Colin, Frederick Leslie and Stuart Kirkland Fletcher and, throughout the thirty-one years' interval that has ensued, they have fully justified the confidence their father placed in them. The original lace concern at Heanor and Pilcher Gate continues to prosper in their care and, under the name of A. W. Hayes & Co., the manufacture of hosiery has been added to their activities at 56-60 Houndsgate, Nottingham.

All three brothers are co-directors of both firms and take the chairmanship of each board for a year, in turn.

George Colin Fletcher, the eldest of the trio, lives a full and busy life. He was born in 1894 at Park Grange and educated by the Rev. Harry Grassby at the Wesleyan Minister's Private Academy, Heanor, and at King Edward VI Grammar School, Retford. In 1910, he started working for father, but fourteen years later, as previously mentioned, was made a joint owner-partner with his two brothers in the firm.

They went their several ways during the 1914-18 war. Colin's choice was the Royal Flying Corps [re-named the Royal Air Force] in which he served as first class air mechanic until peace was restored.

No matter whether his interests are in business or the great out-of-doors, 'G.C.' will not allow the grass to grow under his feet. In addition to his lace and hosiery commitments, he is the Chairman of the Paris Net Co. Ltd., the Aura Net Co., both of Long Eaton; Draycott Dyers, Victoria Mills; and Heanor Gardeners Society.

At home, his main relaxation is ornamental gardening and the liberal use of glass to grow grapes, figs, peaches, apricots, nectarins, tomatoes and other choice hothouse fruits. When the quiet of the countryside calls, Colin tends his farm [between Buxton and Ashbourne], fishes in the stream [Dove] that flows at its foot, or has a little sport with gun, ferrets and dog. If he really wants to let off steam he turns to tennis and politics.

Incidentally, I, the Compiler, also enjoy a country ramble so one day, perhaps, this cousin may show me the shafts of the mines called

Heanor Fan and Hard Meadow from which his grandfather John Fletcher raised coal for personal use in home and factory.

By far the most important pursuit of all—the seeking of a wife—has been left to the last to record in this section.

George Colin married *Doris Marguerite*, daughter of *Charles Joshua Wilshire*, a talented Cornishman of Penzance, chartered accountant, secretary and director of Lovatt's Potteries Ltd., Langley Mill. Their present home is Twyford, Smalley Hill, Heanor, a little nearer to Derby than the factory. They have one son and three daughters, whose turn it is to figure in the story.

Nora Eileen Fletcher, their eldest child, studied interior decorating at Nottingham College of Art and was holding a lucrative post at Long Eaton when war broke out in 1939. She then enlisted in the Forces, had the distinction of being one of the first women in the country to be radar-trained and rose to the rank of Captain, H.A.A., A.T.S., with service 1940-45. Her unit of heavy anti-aircraft artillery was sited on the Isle of Hooe in the Thames Estuary and formed part of the protective screen that defended London. She is now the wife of Geoffrey Woodward, Major, T.A., and the mother of a one-year-old son, Adrian. Their home is in Dobholes Lane, Smalley.

Geoffrey Lawrence Fletcher, the only boy in this quartette of olive-branches, had his early education at Heanor Secondary School and then proceeded to Loughborough College where he gained a diploma in aero-engineering.

During the Second World War, Geoffrey served as a Civil Servant for five years [1940-45] at the Royal Aircraft Establishment, Farnborough, making research into surface tension of water and its effects on seaplane floats. This scientific work brought a thesis into being from his pen which the Government printed as a permanent record for ministerial archives.

Nine years ago [1946] Geoffrey joined his father in the Paris Net Co. and today is also specialising in Levers lace production at the Heanor factory.

Another important step in the right direction was to marry Shiela Grainger, who has already presented her spouse with a son and heir—two-year-old Robert. This event augurs well for the Fletcher House of Lace, the endurance of which seems assured for generations to come if our products can compete successfully in world markets.

Doreen Wilshire Fletcher, A.R.I.B.A. [*Hons. Arch.*], measured by her scholastic attainments is, undoubtedly, a talented lady. She had her preliminary education at Heanor Secondary School before going to Manchester University where she studied architecture and ultimately qualified as an Associate Royal Institute British Architects. She was employed by Manchester City Council as architect in charge, responsible for building Wythenshawe Grammar School, but resigned this appointment to marry. Doreen has made her home in Ceylon, where her husband is Assistant Town Planner for this beautiful island. They have one young child—a son.

Pamela Mary Fletcher, L.D.S. [*Edin.*], *R.C.S.* [*Edin.*], the third daughter and youngest child, had her preliminary education at Heanor Secondary School. She then proceeded to Edinburgh University to study dental surgery and was successful to the degree of becoming a Licentiate Dental Surgeon and a member Royal College Surgeons. She was at one time in practice professionally at Newcastle, Staffordshire, but is now doing school dental work in Stoke.

Pamela married John Tindall, B.Sc. [London], who is interested in pottery and employed by the Institute of Ceramic Research. His father, John Tindall, Snr., of Skipton, is Manager of Martins Bank. John and Pamela have no family and reside at Newcastle, Staffs.

Frederick Leslie, the second son of George Henry and Jessie Fletcher, was born at Park Grange in 1896. He, too, attended Mr Grassby's preparatory establishment in Ray Street and was a scholar at King Edward VI Grammar School, Retford, until 1912 when, at sixteen, he started work in the family lace factory, that well-known landmark on Derby Road, Heanor. Three years later [1915] Leslie was a Tommy in Kitchener's Volunteer Army in which he served till 1919 as a corporal, Fifth Army, R.E. despatch rider in France and Belgium. He also served in the Home Guard during the last war.

Kaiser Wilhelm dealt with, Leslie resumed his place in the family firm of which, in 1924, he was made a co-owner-partner-director, and in that capacity, his business activities and interests have been confined to lace and hosiery ever since.

In disposition and tastes 'F.L.F.' is very similar to his father. His relaxations and recreations include swimming, billiards and tennis, of which the last-named holds pride of place as favourite. Gardening as such does not appeal, but as you walk round the grounds of Memtah, the home of Leslie and his wife, you will soon be aware of his liking for the landscape side of the art.

Prominence in public affairs has not been sought either, though he has given valuable service to the British Legion and been honorary treasurer of the Heanor branch for ten years.

In 1925 the marriage between Frederick Leslie Fletcher and Ada Wheeler, of Liverpool, was solemnized. They have one child, a daughter.

She, *Vivienne Jessica Fletcher*, married George Harry Whiteman of Heanor, who served as L.A.C. with the R.A.F. in Egypt, Syria and Greece from 1941 to 1945. Since returning to civil life this young man has learned the lessons of hosiery management at I. & R. Morley's factory. He is now in G. H. Fletcher & Co.'s hosiery department and is likely to be his father-in-law's successor in the firm, since 'F.L.F.' has no sons of his own.

George and Vivienne [born 1928] have one child—three-year-old Richard Fletcher Whiteman, born in 1952.

Stuart Kirkland, George Henry Fletcher's youngest son, has little to say about himself. He enlisted in August 1915 and served with the R.A.M.C. as a private in Mesopotamia and on other fronts until November 1919 when he was discharged and awarded a medal and bar. His business commitments must be substantial, as apart from the joint holdings in lace and hosiery with his two elder brothers, he has been managing director and principal share owner of Berrey and Underwood Ltd., Nottingham, since January 1937.

Stuart and his wife [née Adelaide Truzzell] have four children— three daughters and a son—and their home is at Overdale on Smalley Hill.

John Stuart Fletcher, the last arrival, was educated at Stamford School, plays tennis for Derbyshire and is one of the younger members of the Fletcher family lace firm.

Helen Margaret Fletcher, the youngest daughter and tennis star of international repute, has travelled to the courts of Belgium, Brazil, Denmark, France, Holland, Mexico, the United States of America, the West Indies, and met many notable people, including the Queen of Denmark, the Duchess of Kent and Sir Anthony Eden since she was first accepted to play as a senior at Wimbledon in 1950.

Helen began her career by playing tennis for Heanor Grammar School in 1945, but took to horse-riding the following year, fell off

41

and broke her right arm. This incident may explain why she became one of the very few top flight left-handed exponents to grace the game. Whilst still at school she entered her first tournament—the 1947 Derbyshire Junior Championships, and won the Singles title, and in the same year reached the last sixteen at the Junior Wimbledon. Shortly after leaving school in 1948, she became the winner of the Nottinghamshire Junior Open Tournament, the Derbyshire Junior Championship, and reached the Junior semi-finals at Wimbledon where Susan Partridge beat her 2—6, 4—6.

At this point, it can safely be said Helen would readily agree that much of the credit for her early progress and later greater achievements belongs to Major Applewhaite of Manchester, and Grenville Morris, the Welsh International and Nottingham Forest footballer, who coached her in the arts and skills of court craft which enabled their pupil to become a member of Great Britain's Whiteman Cup team for the years 1951-52-53-54. She was also ranked Number 9 and Number 10 in World Singles and Number 2 in Great Britain during 1953 and 1954.

Moments of joy deferred were many, but it was a great day for Helen when she beat Shirley Fry, World Number 3, in the Singles 10—8, 6—2 on June 5th, 1953, at Manchester, and an even greater one dawned when she and Jean Quartier conquered 'Little Mo' Connelly and Louisa Brough in the Doubles at Surbiton where the battle went to three sets.

Her last appearance of note before tennis lovers was made in the French Championships at Paris in 1954. There, instead of gaining further laurels of victory, she caught a bad dose of mumps and had to leave the courts to spend a fortnight in a French hospital. A few months later Helen became the wife of Michael Barker, a civil engineer in practice with the City of Nottingham Corporation. Her marriage, a fashionable occasion of more than local interest, attended by two hundred-and-fifty guests, took place on November 13th, 1954, and gave Helen the added distinction of being the last of many Fletchers to be wedded at Heanor Parish Church—a record held by a male member of the line from the previous September.

The ties and happy events of family life are the centre of her interests today, they have two young sons. Lack of information concerning *June Mary* and *Elizabeth May Fletcher*, the elder sisters of Helen, prevents more than the mere mention of them in these records.

42

Jessie Mary, the only daughter of George Henry and Jessie Fletcher, was very fond of instrumental music, particularly the pianoforte, and devoted much of her time to the care of her father and Park Grange after her mother died in 1934. She married Richard Lahiff, a South of Ireland gentleman, who qualified in medicine at Cork University and practised in London until he and his wife removed to Sandiacre where they lived in quiet retirement until Jessie died last January [1956].

ELIZABETH, PHEBE, MARY, MARTHA AND JANE FLETCHER
OF PARKFIELDS

In this, the concluding portion of the senior branch, we must tell you what happened to the five daughters of John and Mary—the last words to the ladies, the cynic may say. For a variety of causes these final words are very few, but it is better to include them rather than spoil the completeness of this part of the family story.

Elizabeth, by marrying John Hanford of Derby, brought yet another grocer into, and also added two sons to the wider family circle.

John Robert Hanford, an encyclopedia concerning and possessor of a photographic gallery of Fletcher 'twigs', spent much of his life in the lace trade at Derby. He married Nellie, the daughter of Josiah Manning, a Midland Railway carriage and wagon foreman, of Shrewsbury, who presented him with two daughters.

Joan Eleanora, the elder girl, who ventured into matrimony with Thomas Faulkner of Derby, an instrument repairer in the Royal Air Force, has four children—Mavis Mary, Sheila Ann, Joan and John.

Ida Dorothy Mary, her younger sister, became the wife of Norman Edward Goodhead of Littleover, a Midland Railway cartage assistant in the Derby area. They have a daughter, Patricia, and a son, Roger.

Reginald Hanford, the younger son of John and Elizabeth, never married and, so it is said, left what money he possessed to his faithful charlady.

Phebe, who made Henry Mellers of Nottingham her life partner, became the mother of four daughters.

43

Mary Mabel Mellers, the senior of this quartette, became the spouse of Percy Newbound, the hotelier, who had public interests in Bridlington and other seaside resorts. Their offspring was confined to the fair sex—three daughters.

Esmé Millicent, the eldest girl, married Edward Derreck Hamilton Brewster [Newbound] Mumford: the Newbound was added by Deed Poll after marriage.

Zoë became the wife of Squadron-Leader Roger Maurice Saunders [Liaison Officer attached to the French Forces], who made the Supreme Sacrifice at Calais in 1940.

Sylvia, the youngest of the trio, wedded Bernard George Potts. Exactly nine years ago, Mother told the Compiler 'None of her daughters had any children'; that Esme and Sylvia were with her in Bayswater, London, and Zoë was living in Devonshire. No further news has come to hand since.

Jane Alice Mellers married Sanford Barnsdale, a perfumier and nephew of Sir John and Lady Robinson. After their marriage, they lived and manufactured scents in France for some years before re-settling in England at Barrowby, near Grantham, where Jane Alice died, leaving no issue.

Eleanora Martha Mellers, who passed away during the winter of 1954-55, married Morton Rallinshaw, a Nottingham engineer, who had big business interests throughout the United Kingdom.

They had one daughter, *Eleanora Marjorie Morton,* now the wife of a gentleman named *Cornford,* intersted in transport, whom she met when they were both in H.M. Forces [1939-45], and a son, *Henry Oswald Morton,* who died of sunstroke before reaching his 'teens.

The Rallinshaws were the perfect host and hostess in their Lenton home, the large garden of which fronted and overlooked Derby Road nearly opposite the church. They made one feel their welcome there.

Nell and Morton arranged a huge Fletcher family garden party when, in the summer of 1914, King George V and Queen Mary visited Nottingham and opened University College [now Nottingham University] at Highfields. Some that were there may still have a photograph of all the many guests seated on the platform erected in the grounds from which an unrestricted view of the Royal cavalcade was enjoyed. Those were indeed the days of grace.

44

Phebe Agnes Marjorie Mellers was not strong and did not marry. She was, however, an outstandingly brilliant professional interior decorator and had a flat in London, where she died during the Second World War.

Mary, the third of 'Old John's' five daughters, and a lovable character, had a fund of gripping family stories with which she charmed members of the younger generations.

One of her stories, which related to the small kitchen window that looked on to the stable-yard at Parkfields, had a more than mysterious flavour. Aunt Mary said that the pane of glass therein was the herald of misfortune as it made the same peculiar noise whenever bad luck, accident, death or other mishap was about to hurt the family circle. This warning sound chilled the blood of any member who heard it and came to be regarded as the ghost of Parkfields.

A more practical story, passed on by Cicely Wilshire, tells how hard her mother and aunt Elizabeth worked for father in those days of yore. Before a piece in the brown could leave the factory it had to be mended. Therefore, those two young ladies had to go down the dark, unlighted lane beside Parkfields, late at night, to work on it in the factory so that each perfected consignment could be on the seven o'clock train from Langley Mill to Nottingham the next morning. Since Mary's span of life was 'three score and eighteen' [August 10th, 1855—February 17th, 1934], the women of her day were far from being of the weaker sex.

Mary married Edward Eley of Marlpool, a member of a well-known family long established in the Heanor district, whom the directories of his day described as grocer, farmer, agent and gentleman. They had two children—a daughter, Cicely Fletcher, and a son, John Edward who died in early life.

Cicely Fletcher Eley was born at Marlpool and married Laurence Stanley Wilshire of Heanor, a potter at Lovatt and Lovatt, Langley Mill, Derbyshire. They had one child, Joyce Mary.

Like many millions more courageous British mothers, Cicely helped to keep the home fires burning in two world wars, but was denied the joy of welcoming the return of her husband from the first one. Laurence enlisted in Kitchener's Army in September 1914, was granted a commission [second-lieutenant] and served successively in the Dardanelles, France, Italy and France again, where he fell in action on April 14th, 1918. He was a very fine singer and

45

when stationed at Plymouth, Lady Astor frequently made use of his services at concerts which she sponsored in the district.

Joyce Mary was born on December 20th, 1915, so very likely does not remember her father. She married Harold Arthur Brown and presented him with two children—one of each gender.

Ian Laurence Brown, the elder of Cicely's two grandchildren, is a keen philatelist, so if you would like to encourage him, send a few of your spares to grandma to add to his collection.

Glynis Brown, the younger one is—well, 'just Ian's very young small sister'—and that means a great deal to the immediate family circle.

Before leaving this section of the story, the writer would like to point out that the father of Edward Eley was twice married and that a daughter of this other union, Maud Minnie Eley [half-sister of Edward] became the wife of William Hamilton of Mansfield, Notts. Strange to relate, one of their children, William Gething Hamilton of Codnor, Derbyshire, is the assistant manager of I. & R. Morley Ltd., Heanor, and thereby largely responsible for what happens in these extensive modern works of which, what was once known as Edward Fletcher's original Taghill lace factory is today an integral part.

Martha, John's fourth daughter, became the wife of Frederick Wasteneys of Dronfield, a draughtsman employed by Cammell Laird, the well-known engineers. She left no issue and lies at rest in the family grave in Heanor cemetery, but what subsequently happened to her husband is not recorded in the Fletcher archives.

Jane, the youngest of these five girls, was an expert in many forms of needlework and fond of painting in oils and water-colour on opal, wood and canvas. She married Charles Alfred Millington of Langley Mill, a traveller who worked for her father, and became the mother of a son, Tom Fletcher, and a daughter, Dorothy.

When her mother died, Jane [accompanied by her young family] returned home where, for several years, she organised the domestic staff, safeguarded the comfort of her father, and acted as hostess to the many guests who visited Parkfields.

Jane passed away on August 4th, 1902, aged 37, whereupon Aunt Mary Eley welcomed the two children, by then in their 'teens,' into her home and there Dorothy [known to us as Mrs Flint] lived till she married.

Tom Fletcher Millington was a man of character. This can be deduced from the hard fact that he served the Heanor factory for fifty-two years, first as a draughtsman and then as man-in-charge of the entire lace plant. Service with the Royal Air Force at Farnborough [1914-18] was the only major break in this unique half-century-plus record at the close of which he died in harness some three years ago [1952].

You already know that Tom lived with his Grandfather Fletcher for a considerable time, and nothing pleased him more than to yarn to his three children about 'the twigs on the Family Tree' and his life at Parkfields.

He married Elsie Mary Blanche, daughter of Steven Bircumshaw, a traveller for Field's Brewery, and grand-daughter of Thomas Williamson, a man of property in his day in the Brinsley area of Nottinghamshire.

Though Heanor born, Tom made Moorgreen his permanent abiding place and there, he not only developed a thriving poultry farm, but also turned his home into the Home Guard headquarters [1940-45] where, as officer-in-command, he organised all the necessary indoor parades and meetings.

It was in this self-same village that his wife established a private school for morning sessions only where she taught her own offspring and the children of local colliery officials, bank managers, farmers and similar families. This venture met with opposition from the Nottinghamshire education authority but on appeal, Whitehall, London, said it could function provided the pupils were up to the required standard. A visit by an Inspection Board revealed this essential condition, so the school was permitted to continue and prospered.

Thomas Herbert, the eldest of Tom and Elsie Millington's three children, trained for teaching at Chester College and then went to Sweden to take a course of training in Swedish drill. The Royal Tank Corps claimed his services as wireless operator throughout 1939-45, chiefly in the Middle East. He married Mary Lilian Evans, one of the secretaries attached to Lord Bath's Warminster Estate, and a daughter of Ernest Evans, a sculptor of repute. Some of Mr

47

Evans' work can be seen in Worcester Cathedral and Madison Court, the ancestral home of Lord Beauchamp.

Today, Thomas Herbert is Art Master and Physical Training Instructor at the Modern Secondary School, Cotmanhay, Derbyshire, and the father of two children, Brenda Mary and Peter Thomas.

Frances Mary, S.R.N., Q.A.I.M.N.S., the elder daughter, entered the nursing profession and had her training at Charing Cross Hospital, London, where she became a qualified State Registered Nurse and a member of Queen Alexandra's Imperial Military Nursing Service. During the last war [1940-46] she was also Theatre Sister-in-Charge of the Ophthalmic Ward, Gibraltar, and today [1955] is still actively interested as lecturer and examiner on behalf of the Northamptonshire British Red Cross.

Frances married Captain John Harry Ward, R.A.O.C., an industrial engineer [Esso Petroleum Company] who served on the Staff of the Madagascar Military Mission [1941-46] and for services rendered there he was awarded the E.R.D. [Emergency Reserve Decoration].

Their home at present is in Northamptonshire, where John Harry travels extensively as lecturer in the interests of the Anglo-American Oil Company.

Betty, B.A. [London], First Class Eng. Hons., the junior member of the Millington section of our family, had the special distinction of being the first child in Nottinghamshire to gain a scholarship from a private school—her mother's in Moorgreen. This scholarship, tenable at Heanor Secondary School, was a stepping-stone which led to Nottingham University and her B.A. [London], with first class honours in English.

She married Roy Cecil Abbott Bradshaw, B.Sc., Staff Captain in England and India [1944-47] and Research Chemist, British Baking Industries [1947-51] until appointed to the Ministry of Food and sent to Washington, U.S.A., to serve with the British Joint Services Mission. There, with the rank of lieutenant-colonel, he travelled all over America seeking and exchanging information on food preservation, distribution and storage in their relation to atomic warfare. Since 1953 he has been Food Technologist, Quaker Oats, Chicago, where he has a private laboratory. Betty and Roy and their three young daughters are now settled in the States, so perhaps some of the sixty or more of our kindred out there may like to contact them at West Lake Street, Liberty Ville, Illinois, U.S.A.

48

Dorothy, the only daughter and younger child of Charles Alfred and Jane Millington, spared no pains to make me feel quite at home when I called upon her to collect news of the Flint sept of our clan for inclusion in the Family story. Not only did she satisfy my literary need, but also regaled me with a flow of anecdotes from her box of memories, mostly about Grandfather Fletcher and some of his descendants, as we enjoyed afternoon tea together.

It seems that 'Old John' ran his own dental service for the locals and extracted the teeth of allcomers free with a 'fearsome-looking corkscrew-and-hook instrument of torture' always kept handy for use. Occasionally, a sufferer became very nervy on sighting this weird tool, but was reassured—or fled for his life—when the operator said 'it won't take a minute if thee hed'll stop on'.

He was very liberal with the carving knife and liked to tease his young lady guests [whom Laura Turner was frequently among] about their self-confessed inability to eat all the helpings served to them at his table. On occasion, he would pretend to see one of them looking longingly for more, and said 'tack up thee cart my wench for another load if thee's still hungry'.

So that this flashback into the realm of old-time happenings may be plain, I must let you know that Laura was my grandfather Samuel Fletcher's step-daughter and that those fair owners of bird-like appetites invariably left their platters clean.

'Old John' always remembered the house servants at Yuletide, so one year he asked Neddy Prince, a rather simple chap, whether he'd like 'bacca' or money for his Christmas gift. Ned thought hard for a few moments and then said, 'I'll have a bit o' both, Mester'. I must not forget that one when some generous soul gives me an alternative choice.

One day, a very young, self-important traveller entered the Nottingham Road works of William Fletcher [Derby] Ltd. to see the boss. Not liking being kept waiting awhile, he patronisingly asked a nearby industrious man in overalls [William of Derwent Bank in working kit] 'if he knew who owned this factory'. 'They tell me I reckon I do' came the quiet reply—as completely devastating as it was totally unexpected by that inexperienced commercial.

Many more shafts of wit could be quoted, but we must now move a little nearer to the present day to tell you that *Dorothy Millington* was a reader-off at the family lace factory for nine years [1905-13] before she married George Flint, son of William Flint.of Heanor who, in turn, was a pattern-maker for Lovegroves of Nottingham, a tallow-chandler, and farmer at the back of the parish church. One son and a daughter were born to them.

George Flint soldiered with the Royal Garrison Artillery [1914-18] and served the Fletcher Heanor factory as draughtsman and designer for some thirty years when failing health compelled retirement into private life where he has found enjoyment tending his garden and a measure of physical activity prosecuting his other main hobby— joinery and general woodwork.

Dorothy makes no claim to any personal achievement or distinction but confesses that she finds pleasure and relaxation in fancy needlework, knitting, all kinds of embroidery, and a wide range of home-made cookery and preserves. You will therefore need only one guess to decide what *is* her only main hobby—the comfort of the Flint family circle.

George Morton Flint spent most of his school days in Heanor, and of him, at the age of forty-one, I feel it can truly be said 'that the progressive development of the flying-machine, whether for civil or military purposes, or for possible adventurous space travel, has been, is, and always will be his one great ruling passion and practical interest'. At work, during leisure, or in the service of his country, his thoughts and endeavours have been steadfastly pointed in this direction, and apart from organising and conducting his own small dance band at Heanor and nearby district 'hops', no deviation of a major character, except his marriage to Sylvia Kathleen Hopkinson, has been permitted.

He served for five-and-a-half years [1939-45] in the Royal Air Force, Bomber Command, as aero technician; rose to the status of aero engine inspector with the Avro Engineering Company at Langar; flies and constructs model aeroplanes; and has been a member of the Air League of the British Empire since 1933.

The scope of active association with airborne traffic epitomised in the foregoing impressive record clearly explains why the technical advancement in construction and improvement in performance of 'transport in the sky' retains George Morton Flint's interest today. May Dame Fortune smile upon his efforts in this sphere!

Dorothy Mary Flint left Heanor Secondary School fitted for the post of clerk with Heanor Urban District Council and thereby became a national local government officer. Her place of duty was in the Sanitary Inspector's office, and during her leisure hours she indulged in tennis, cycling and hacking, a form of horse-riding that has always been popular with young ladies of her age and sporting temperament—for a time. Dorothy Mary now has a home, a hubby and a nine-year-old daughter [Jane Ann] to look after, so maybe the saddle has given way to the easy chair in which she fashions those delightful pieces of fancy work that charm the eye of the admiring beholder.

She became the wife of Denis Alan Lloyd, a schoolmaster by profession, and the son of George Lloyd of Heanor and previously of Leicester. He was taken prisoner-of-war in Europe, August 25th-26th, 1941, whilst serving as a wireless operator in a Stirling bomber and was in captivity for four-and-a-half years.

Brighter days dawned for him as Denis is now Science and Maths. Master at Scargill Secondary School, and his wife, himself and family are all quite at home at West Looe, West Hallam, Derbyshire.

THE EARNSHAW SIDE OF THE JOHN OF PARKFIELDS BRANCH

Written by Jeanne Lander from notes supplied by
Miss Millicent Monk of 12 Upper Street, Rusthall,
Tunbridge Wells, Kent

Mary Earnshaw, wife of John Fletcher of Parkfields, Heanor, was born on December 31st, 1824, and was one of a family of thirteen children of Keyworth and Martha Earnshaw.

Keyworth—pronounced, it is believed, 'Keworth'—was the name of the Earnshaw family estate believed to have been in Cumberland and now, alas, no more.

The family were builders in and around Heanor, but individually, with the exception of *Keyworth, John* and *Thomas,* little is known about Mary's brothers and sisters. Miss Monk, who kindly supplied the notes for this résumé of the Earnshaw family, is the grand-daughter of *Keyworth,* Mary's brother, and has been able to help with information concerning him.

He married a *Miss Martha Chandler* at Ilkeston about one hundred years ago and they and their family lived for some years at Glaston Hall, Rutlandshire, whilst Keyworth, in the capacity of either fore-man or manager, helped to lay the Kettering and Manton railway.

51

He was for some years a member of the Metropolitan Water Board and also built several houses in Brighton. One of his sons, William, emigrated to Detroit and became established there as a builder. Five of his sons joined him in the building trade there.

John had a considerable reputation as a faith healer and sick and ailing people were often taken to him with every confidence that he would cure them.

Thomas became landlord of the Plough Inn at Dorking, where he died.

Their brothers *Joseph* and *Benjamin* were in the building trade in Heanor and their two sisters *Martha* and *Phoebe* were dressmakers in the district.

It was as a result of the friendship existing between the sons of the Fletcher and Earnshaw families that John Fletcher met and eventually married Mary Earnshaw.

Sometime or somewhere in the future this thumbnail sketch of the past may catch the eye of a curious Earnshaw searcher, so, to further his or her investigations, an old branch of the Earnshaw family tree is appended.

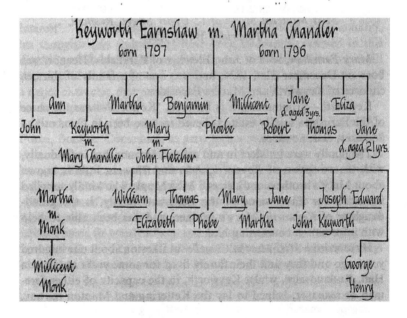

PLATE 7
MRS. JOHN FLETCHER
née MARY EARNSHAW

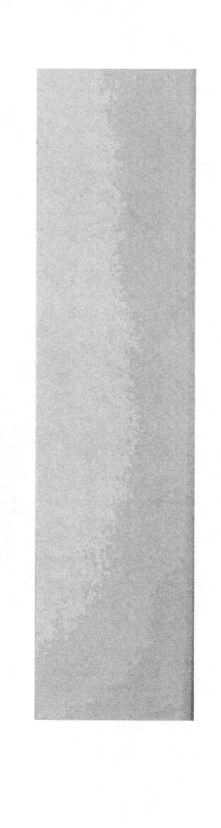

Most experimenters with future possibilities or delvers into the uncovered factual lore of the past, automatically become more interested in an, as yet, unsolved problem once they have established the actualities of the most recent one.

Your Compiler is in this position concerning the deeper origins and wider connections of the Hearnshaw families of Nottingham and Bulcote, and the Fletchers who farmed in the Mansfield area, in their relation to our own.

My interest has been heightened considerably since Mr John William Hearnshaw, Managing Director of John Jardine Ltd., sent me the following intriguing information on the subject.

'William Hearnshaw, his paternal grandfather, was Manager of Wright's Bank, and occupied that position until a few years after, by purchase, it became Lloyds Bank, Carlton Street, Nottingham.

He married Anne, the daughter of William Fletcher, a farmer who also dealt in cattle in the Mansfield area, a member of a large Fletcher family, tillers of the soil who, before removing to Bulcote, Nottinghamshire, lived at Wingfield Manor, near Pentrich, which seems to tie them up with the lace Fletchers.

This family [Bulcote] consisted of the following: James Fletcher, Mary Hannah Fletcher, Helen Fletcher, Anne Fletcher [my grand-mother], plus one other sister who married another man named Fletcher and became the mother of two bachelor brothers who farmed in the Mansfield district. They had a spinster sister, Lizzie, who I believe is still living. The two brothers were named John and Fred.

William Hearnshaw and Anne Fletcher had one issue who was my father, Roger Fletcher Hearnshaw. He, in his turn, had two issues, myself and my sister Marion who is Mrs T. H. Sheldon of Cotham Manor, near Newark.

Apart from my mother and myself, who have lived in Burton Joyce since my father's death in 1935, there are no Fletchers or Hearnshaws of these families left in Burton Joyce or Bulcote.'

Some doubters will, by virtue of the *h* prefixing Earnshaw, be quite ready to use this small difference in spelling to discount the likelihood of any relationship existing between these two families or we Fletchers, but experience has proved this to be an unreliable guide to use.

53

On other pages herein we have quoted two instances where, by Deed Poll, two Fletcher families became known to future generations as Fletcher-Bullivant and Astle-Fletcher respectively.

When you realise there has been, by gradual use, the transposition, deduction and addition of the letters 'A', 'C', 'E' and 'T', in re-forming and ultimately forming the present style of the Fletcher surname, you must support my belief that a link to bind the Hearn-shaw, Earnshaw and Fletcher families together, is reasonable and well-founded.

I venture to predict that the missing part of this chain of relation-ship will, as so often before, be found in circumstances both amazing and totally unexpected.

[*Compiler's Note.*—It was at South Wingfield Farm, occupied by Samuel Fletcher, that a band of Luddite machine wreckers [1811-16] first called to demand a weapon and a man to use it, to strengthen their unit that marched towards Nottingham to join the main body of rioters. Samuel and his sons refused to accede and were left in peace. Maybe, it was from descendants of this particular Fletcher stock that the Hearnshaws chose their spouses.—S.B.F.]

ELIZABETH FLETCHER NUMBER ONE

This second child and eldest daughter of Edward and Phoebe Fletcher was born at Heanor on March 3rd, 1826, and died there on May 7th of the same year. She was buried at Heanor.

PLATE 8

JOSEPH AND LAVINIA FLETCHER

CHAPTER II

THE JOSEPH BRANCH

*Compiled from notes supplied by Marjorie Henton and
Zillah Marshall, and extracts from family letters*

JOSEPH, second of the five elder sons of Edward, who learned how
to make lace in the old original Fletcher factory on Tag Hill, was
born at Heanor on April 1st, 1827.

He may, at one time, have thought All Fools' Day an unlucky
star to be born under, but for him the reverse was the case as, later
in life, he became not only a noted pioneer, but also the active family
leader in the trade.

Shortly after attaining his majority, he married Lavinia Ann,
daughter of Joseph Robinson, the landlord of the White Hart Inn,
Bulwell, who by trade was a carpenter, of Quaker stock, and a kinsman of Sir John Robinson of Bestwood Hall.

Long ago, when Nottingham was all open fields from where the
Theatre Royal now stands down to Hyson Green, this Robinson
family had farming interests on land at the top of Sheep Lane
[Market Street], but whether they were owners or tenants is not
recorded, though one authority is sure that the first-named was the
position.

Joseph Fletcher had a flair for being first in the field throughout
his business career. Where he adventured, others followed. After
marriage, he became one of the first of our Fletcher tenants at
6 Terrace Street and the first of Edward's sons to set up as a lace
manufacturer when he installed his first holding of machines in
Abbott's Factory, Hyson Green, in 1852.

Joseph was also the first and only son ever to partner his father as
Edward Fletcher & Son, lace manufacturers, when in 1860 their
warehouse address was High Pavement, Nottingham.

Until quite recently, we younger members of the clan have always
believed that John, the eldest, was the first of Edward's sons to
become a lace manufacturer in Heanor and live at Parkfields. We
now know that Joseph was, without any doubt whatsoever, first in

the field there too, as from 1865 to 1868 he made and traded in lace between Heanor and Nottingham, or Heanor and Derby, or both, and lived at Parkfields, until the family left the district under rather tragic circumstances.

The outlook had become set fair in every direction when, without warning, an epidemic of typhoid fever gripped almost the whole household in turn, except mother. She nursed them all devotedly, but despite every care, Elizabeth, their eldest child, a lovely lass in her middle 'teens, died.

This blow upset and embittered her father so much, he broke off all connections with Heanor immediately, moved into Terrace Royal, which stood on Clarendon Street corner near Nottingham Arboretum, and there his family resided intil The Hall, Long Eaton, was purchased in 1874 or 1875.

This Georgian type of house, once the residence of Canon Atkinson, the first vicar of Long Eaton, was built in 1777 on land owned by William Howitt, and the year of its erection is affixed to one of the spoutings.

You passed through delightful grounds to reach the steps that led to the entrance hall of that very happy Fletcher home. Drawing, dining and breakfast rooms and the library surrounded the entrance hall, from which the main staircase gave access to the front bedrooms whilst a backstairs flight led to the servants' quarters which overlooked the paddocks and stables that housed the carriage-horses and hunters used by members of the family who indulged in driving and riding to hounds. There was also a well-filled wine cellar, a maids' pantry and a spacious oak-beamed, white stone-floored kitchen, equipped with ovens, turnspits [meat jacks] and those many other devices beloved by good cooks in the bad old days. Shining brass and copper ware adorned the substantial kitchen dresser tops, and long-handled warming-pans hung from the beams, whilst the dairy was always well stocked with pies, hams, sides of bacon and bowls of cream from which butter was made. These were indeed heartening sights for those who liked to eat well and sleep cosily on wintry nights!

There was an inside lobby near the back entrance in which local residents sat when they came on Sunday mornings to fetch hot dinners for old and needy Long Eaton folk. These meals were not mere crumbs from the rich man's table. They were always of the

56

same fare as was served in the Hall dining room and were taken away in white cloth-covered backets. Granny made small individual pies, custards and puddings to meet each person's tastes and needs.

All such creature comforts were earned the hard way from very humble beginnings. Throughout their early married life, Joseph and his wife worked from five o'clock in the morning till after midnight making and mending their own lace.

Granny has often told us she was once working very late on a 'piece' of silk lace worth many pounds and that she and Grandfather slept with this precious bundle under their bed for the rest of the night. It is fair to suppose that they had no need of an old game cock or other form of alarum to wake them up early next morning.

In 1862 a long stride towards enjoying this much higher standard of life was made when the Joseph and Thomas partnership began combined operations in Long Eaton by installing their machine plant in Austin's Factory. This was the first partnership between brothers in the Fletcher family and the impact it made on the industrial and corporate activities of the district was both revolutionary and beneficial.

They initiated and introduced many reforms into the art of manufacturing lace and finishing the product. Under their joint influence the town became a hive of industry and a land of promise, which may explain why their brothers and many other Fletcher kinsmen followed them to Long Eaton in search of good fortune, which some of them found there in the trade.

To centralise and facilitate local merchanting, overseas marketing and lace production, Joseph and Thomas occupied a warehouse in Nottingham at 42 High Pavement; appointed Mons. Coulon continental agent in France; and built themselves a new factory somewhere in Long Eaton which came to be known as Fletcher's Factory and was the last word of its kind in the immediate area. It was six stories high, and the topmost one, in which all the mending was done, had a glass roof, which made conditions ideal for this exacting work.

Today, it is still said that this palatial building provided one of the biggest local fires in living memory when it was totally destroyed some years after the joint partners were laid to rest.

To locate where the exact site of this particular 'somewhere' was is not easy, as widely differing authorities compel the belief that there were several Fletcher factories in Long Eaton [such as in Peel Street] of which more than one went up in smoke....

. The 1883 volume of Wright's *Nottingham Directory* lists the Joseph and Thomas Fletcher Factory [note the fullness of title] as being in Tiger Street. This site must be a near possible, as could the one in New Street listed in other issues. The most likely spot, however, is that now occupied by Wallis and Longden, lace machine builders, whose Trent Works are supposed to stand on a section of two pieces of land 21,570 yards, purchased for £2,246 17s. 6d. from Israel J. Chamberlin Hopkins of 24 Regents Park, London, conveyed by him to Joseph and Thomas Fletcher on June 21st, 1872.

. They bought another plot of 404 square yards area from N. Bramley on June 3rd, 1876, and this, too, might enter into the vexed factory situation question.

Though much of what has been posed is largely supposition and deduction, it can truly be said that when the brothers did occupy their new factory, the profits rose to five figures, and this annual level was maintained till February 4th, 1879, when once more, and for the last time, Joseph took the lead in the greatest adventure of all—and died, to end this truly remarkable partnership. His resting place is only a few yards from the grave of his brother Samuel, near the wall between the Rock Cemetery and Nottingham Forest.

Joseph and Lavinia Ann Fletcher had eight children, four sons and four daughters, and all of them, with the possible exception of Zillah Stella, the youngest, were born at Hyson Green. She may have been born at Heanor, but that is open to doubt.

Their parents appreciated the value of learning, so Mr George Packer, Principal of Holly Mount Boarding and Day School, Clarendon Street, Nottingham, directed the boys' preparatory education, and the Misses Eaton and Winters gave the girls private tuition before and after the family lived at Heanor.

Elizabeth Mary was born on June 7th, 1852, and died from typhoid fever at Heanor, April 28th, 1867. She was buried in the Rock Cemetery, Nottingham, and was their eldest child.

. *Sarah Ann* was born in 1854 and died in 1923 at a Nottingham Nursing Home. She married John Marshall, gentleman farmer, maltster and brewer, son of John Marshall who farmed at Trent Lock. They also had a family of four sons and four daughters, of whom we shall write elsewhere.

Joseph Edward. Of this son, born in 1855, and subsequently a student at Loughborough Grammar School, it could truly be said that a heartbreaking blow in early manhood denied him those sustaining and uplifting delights which give added flavour to man's material successes in life. He married a fine young lady of commanding presence, whose full name and connections could not be discovered. Her christian name was Elizabeth and she worked at Jessops or some similar high-class Nottingham establishment and, seemingly, was never accepted by Joe's family. Their first and only home was on Nottingham Road, near Long Eaton Green, where Elizabeth died ten months after her wedding-day.

After his wife's death, Joseph Edward returned to The Hall and lived there till it was purchased by Long Eaton Council when he bought Morelands.

Morelands was built by Mr Spridgeon, lace machine builder, and there Joseph Edward died on November 21st, 1943, in his eighty-ninth year.

Joseph Edward's business career was outstandingly long and successful in character. By 1874, when only nineteen years old, he and a Mr Bestwick were already established as lace manufacturers in Long Eaton, but this partnership was quickly dissolved and Joseph continued on his own account till 1895.

During those twenty-one years he concentrated manufacture at Whiteley's, Fletcher's and Willatt's factories, and did all his merchanting and finishing in Nottingham where he had warehouse accommodation in Commerce Square and at 38, 40 and 40A High Pavement.

Trent Cycle Works, Long Eaton, which came into being about the middle nineties, with Mr Borebanks as partner, was a notable milestone in Joseph Edward's trading operations.

The old penny-farthing cycle had, by then, become a museum piece, and its successor, the solid, rubber-tyred 'boneshaker' was, as a means of individual transportation, almost outmoded by the increasingly popular masterpiece on wheels—the pneumatic safety bicycle.

The growing number of cycle clubs then added their quota to this form of the country's new road traffic so, as one might expect, Joe took a hand in supplying these machines from Sutton's factory. This venture paid high dividends, so after buying Borebanks out, he

59

accepted a good price offered by Ernest Terah Hooley for the business. The great financier then floated the Trent Cycle Company which, in later years, went into liquidation.

Joseph Edward's last years of activity in the trade [approximately 1899-1910] were spent in Whiteley's factory, Leopold Street, Long Eaton, and Nottingham Lace Market where, with brother Arthur Allen as his manager, manufacturing and merchanting was continued on a large scale until he partly retired from the business.

When this happened, the control of the machine plant and other ancillary concerns were left in the hands of his nephew, Arthur Harry Fletcher, until a slump developed and everything was sold.

Livinia was born in 1857 and married Albert Marshall, a Loughborough hardware merchant whose family were not related to the Marshalls of Trent Lock. For some years they resided at Zouch and had two sons, Arthur and George, and a daughter, Vera.

When Albert died, Lavinia returned home to The Hall, but in her later years she lived with brother Joe at Morelands, where she passed away on December 15th, 1940.

Edward Alfred began life in 1860 at 6 Terrace Street, Hyson Green, and finished with it, still a bachelor, at The Hall, Long Eaton, on February 23rd, 1904, and was buried in the Rock Cemetery, Nottingham. In partnership with his brother George Henry, lace was manufactured at Long Eaton and finished and merchanted in Nottingham at 2 Commerce Square till Alf died.

There are good grounds for believing that one of the Marshalls and George Henry controlled affairs until the business was sold as a going concern and, as recently as 1941, the firm of E. A. Fletcher, lace manufacturers, was still operating at the old Commerce Square address.

Arthur Allen, born in 1862, was destined never to become a master man in his own right. Instead, his father, recognising the vital importance of creating understanding relations between the European market and the Nottingham lace industry, sent him to College Monge, Beaune, Côte d'Or, to learn the French language and customs to fit him to serve the trade in a much wider field. This seat of learning where, by rule, all students wore uniform, was near Dijon, the wine-growing district and whilst in residence there, Arthur Allen spent several of the shorter vacations in the home of a friendly French fellow-pupil. The mother of this boy, and his

60

PLATE 9
LAVINIA MARSHALL holding son ARTHUR

father, Mons. Coulon [agent for Jos. & Thos. Fletcher in France] were always welcome guests at The Hall when visits were made to England to study lace trade technique in and around Nottingham and report progress on the firm's prospects abroad.

This was the atmosphere in which Arthur Allen came to appreciate a choice bottle of red burgundy; esteem the French people he contacted; to love Paris and there be the family business representative after leaving college until his father died, which compelled his return to England.

He subsequently revisited France several times before becoming the manager of brother Joseph Edward's machine plant in Whiteley's factory, Long Eaton.

And then, suspecting a lung spot, Dr Jacobs, the Nottingham chest specialist, sent him to Llanfairfechan Nursing Home, where he died from pleurisy on September 17th, 1912, and left a widow, Ellen [née Tanser of Wellingborough] and four sons and four daughters to mourn their loss.

George Henry, who partnered his brother Edward Alfred in the lace manufacturing business of which George Harriman was manager for many years, was born late in 1863 or early in 1864. He never entered into the bonds of matrimony and died at The Hall, Long Eaton, on the eve of the first World War.

Zillah Stella, the eighth child of Joseph and Lavinia Ann Fletcher, was born in 1865 and attended Miss Winter's Preparatory School, Nottingham, before entering a boarding school at Kegworth for further education. She married her cousin, Allen Gething, second son of James Fletcher, and lived quietly at Grove Cottage, Attenborough, where she died on September 26th, 1946, aged eighty-one. The family grave is in the village churchyard.

The generation of grandchildren added twenty-four twigs to the Joseph Fletcher branch of the Family Tree, but as the offspring of Allen Gething and Zillah Stella Fletcher belong to the James branch of the story, only the senior nineteen are included here.

The first eight are the children of John and Sarah Ann Marshall; the next three stem from Albert and Lavinia Marshall; and of the remainder, eight are the offspring of Arthur Allen and Ellen Fletcher [née Tanser].

Thomas Marshall, a third generation tiller of the soil and a brewer of beer, was educated at Trent College and served in the Transport

Section at Chilwell Ordnance Factory during the first World War. He had no issue.

Evelyn Annie Marshall became the first spouse of Dr Frederick William Bloomer of Long Eaton, who married his deceased wife's sister Laura Elizabeth after becoming a widower. There were two daughters and a son by this first marriage.

Harold John Marshall, by profession an engineer and wheelwright and a great all-round sportsman whose specialities were fishing and shooting, enjoyed a varied, adventurous life. He served in the Boer War with the Imperial Yeomanry, was slightly wounded and, the fighting over, emigrated to Canada to farm government land. After being the proprietor of a large hotel in Rapid City, Saskatchewan, he finally settled down in Vancouver Island, British Columbia.

Joseph Fletcher Marshall died in early boyhood.

Elsie May Marshall served in the nursing arm of the 76th Division Middlesex Territorials, during the 1914-18 war. She married Duncan Ilted Witherington. They reside at Nailsworth, Gloucestershire, but have no family.

Zillah Stella Marshall revels in forms of voluntary work such as organizing National Savings drives. She was Quartermaster [1914-18] of the local V.A.D. and did duty with Civil Defence [1939-45]. Her favourite hobby is making decorative pottery by hand, a craft she studied at the Derby School of Art.

Laura Elizabeth Marshall, a fine water-colourist, was a full-time student at Nottingham School of Art where she gained the Holbrook Prize for the best flower study. She became the second wife of Dr Frederick William Bloomer and the mother of one son and a daughter.

George Edward Marshall soldiered with the Durham Light Infantry in the first Great War [1914-18] and now lives in Bristol.

Arthur Marshall made his début in the business world at the Humber Cycle Works, Beeston, but eventually changed over to lace manufacture.

When Edward Arthur [or Alfred] Fletcher died, he partnered George Henry Fletcher at Commerce Square, Nottingham, prior to the business being sold.

Arthur lived at Morelands, Long Eaton, for many years and is an ardent collector of china and similar antique treasures.

George Marshall emigrated to Canada when quite young and leased government land for farming purposes but died before the allotment was got into working order.

Vera Marshall married Samuel Wood, a cashier with the National Provincial Bank until he retired into private life. They are both keenly interested in horticultural gardening, their chief hobby, at The Crofts, Hepscott, near Morpeth, Northumberland, where they have a small nursery, but no children.

Arthur Harry Fletcher excelled at all sports. The Championship of Peterborough School for two successive years and the Midland Counties Cross Country Championship [1907] Gold Medal, are but two of his many notable achievements.

Harry served his apprenticeship to the lace trade in Eastwood's factory, Long Eaton, and then, in 1908, went to Canada and had farmland in Alberta. He could not settle, so worked his way across country doing coalmining at Bankhead and many other jobs as he approached British Columbia, where he was a lumberjack in the forests of Vancouver Island before returning to England in 1912.

The two years that followed his father's death were spent in uncle Joseph Edward's lace factory. Then came the first World War in which Harry served [the Somme, Vimy Ridge] in France with the Royal Field Artillery, 46th [North Midland] Division—a famous unit. When peace reigned again, he returned to uncle Joe's factory and then married Mabel Smedley, a grand-daughter of an old well-known farming family—the Goodwins of Partney Mill, Lincolnshire.

In Derby today, another up-to-date Fletcher partnership—the Derby Factoring Company—has been established by brothers Harry and Glyn.

Violet Tanser Fletcher married Joseph Launcelot Harriman, an engineer, who was educated at Repton School. They have a son and daughter.

Dolcie Robinson Fletcher, a vocalist of recognised ability, married Harold Taylor, an ironfounder. They have two children—one daughter and a son.

During the first World War, Harold Taylor made many thousands of Mills hand grenades at the Excelsior Foundry, Sandiacre, and in the last fight for freedom [1939-45] he gave excellent service as a sergeant in the Derbyshire Special Constabulary.

Marjorie Emma Hirons Fletcher was married at St Laurence's Church, Long Eaton, in 1917, to William Henry Henton of Attenborough, now a paper merchant in Nottingham, who was granted a commission in the A.S.C., M.T., and served in France and Belgium with the 44th Field Ambulance from May 1915 till after the Armistice [1915-1919]. They have two sons.

Like millions more British women of her age, Marjorie gave valuable voluntary service in both world wars. In 1914-18 she was a V.A.D. [Derbyshire] Red Cross nurse at Long Eaton Auxiliary hospital. During 1939-45 she drove a motorised canteen manned by four ladies, on call at any hour, mostly at night, to feed soldiers on manoeuvres, civil defence workers and civilians. All their duties were outside and they were always ready to answer any emergency call whatsoever.

George Byron Fletcher was educated at Nottingham High School and worked in the lace trade for his uncle Joe Fletcher until war broke out against Kaiser Bill. He then enlisted in the Royal Field Artillery and served as a gunner in France and Belgium. On returning to civil life, he was employed by Rolls-Royce, Derby, and was in their service when he died in 1953. George Byron married Alice Eaton and begat a son and daughter. The Eatons are of lace manufacturing stock and one twig, Mrs H. C. Onion [née Florence Eaton] and her family now live in South Africa. Early in the present century, this first cousin of Alice, then a young schoolgirl, left Britain with her parents. Some years later, after much hard travelling by covered waggon, she and her husband settled on a ranch in Northern Transvaal near the Limpopo River, whose water they drank when their own tanks were dry. Lepoards, flood, malaria and other hazards made life a non-stop adventure of which the uninitiated can learn more from Vernon Bartlett's *Struggle for Africa*.

These pioneers and their two married daughters have reached safer Union harbours and one son-in-law, Mr J. V. Hart-Davis, sports master at Hilton College, Natal, has introduced several old boys, including some in the team now touring England [1955] to Test Match cricket.

Lancelot Fletcher died in early childhood—our only record of him.

Nellie Fletcher, born at Long Eaton on February 27th, 1901, and educated at Western House, The Park, Nottingham, always had a flair for housewifery and gardening. She married Captain Sydney

Barrett Good, son of the Rev. A. B. Good, vicar for many years of All Souls' Church, Radford, Nottingham.

Captain Good, a regular officer of the Indian Army [now Lieut.-Colonel, retired] fought in both world wars [France, India and Palestine] from 1916 until invalided from the service in 1944. Between the wars he served in many campaigns on the North-West Frontier of India, was mentioned in despatches and awarded the O.B.E. As Major in temporary command of the Guides Infantry operating with two Brigades commanded by [now] Field-Marshal Earl Alexander and Field-Marshal Sir Claude Auchinleck, a night attack was made on an enemy hill position in the Mohmand country not far from Peshawar on September 29th, 1935. Dawn found the leading troops of the Guides engaged in a bitter and often hand-to-hand fight for possession of the hill-top. All British officers of the Guides were either killed or wounded and of one hundred-and-forty men actually on the hill, less than thrity answered the roll-call in camp after the cease-fire. Captain Godfrey Meynell, of Meynell Langley, near Derby, was killed winning the Victoria Cross.

This section of our family, which includes a son and daughter both born in India, has settled at Parley Cross, a peaceful Dorsetshire village a few miles north of Bournemouth.

Glyn Fletcher, a Giggleswick School old boy and one-time student apprentice at Rolls-Royce, Derby, served [1939-45] in the Derbyshire mobile section of the National Fire Service and did considerable relief work in London—two of the most dangerous duties on the home front. Glyn now partners his brother Arthur Harry as the Derby Factoring Company. They supply motor accessories and have a wharf on Siddals Road, Derby.

The fourth generation of the Joseph branch numbers fifteen souls, and though its members have not individually figured in the building of the Fletcher House of Lace, they do, collectively, furnish an informative cross-section of wider family associations.

Margaret Evelyn Bloomer completed a sound education at Headington, Oxford, and later left the General Hospital, Nottingham a fully-qualified pharmacist to take an executive post on the staff of Torbay Hospital.

She remained there after marriage and throughout the second World war, but when the National Health Service came into being, she reorganised her department into a central pharmacy for all hospitals controlled by the Torquay District Hospital Management Committee.

Margaret Evelyn married Herbert Fletcher Lunt, but is now a widow and resides at Torquay.

Hilda May Bloomer had private education in Nottingham and at Cheltenham Ladies' College before entering and becoming a State Registered Nurse and Sister at Great Ormond Street Hospital for Sick Children. Then, after a special course of training at University College Hospital, London, she was Theatre Sister there for some years and also became a qualified Midwife.

Hilda May is now the wife of Thomas Hall Rivers, a horticulturalist of Sawbridgeworth, Herts.

John Frederick Bloomer prepared for life at Repton School and on leaving there entered the realm of finance with the National Provincial Bank on whose headquarters staff, Manchester, he now serves.

During the last war, John Frederick, now in his late forties, served in the Royal Artillery from 1939 to 1945 and was commissioned in 1941. He married Edna Rowantree of Barnsley, Yorkshire, and they have one child, a son.

Joan Bloomer, a student at Cheltenham Ladies' College, and trained in pharmacy at University College, Nottingham, became a certificated dispenser at University College Hospital, Great Ormond Street, London.

She married Humphrey Burkill whose interests were then in Malayan rubber plantations, but is now the Warden of Singapore Ornamental Gardens. They have two children—one son and a daughter.

Guy Darton Bloomer was not strong when young so, very wisely, his parents sent him to Mr Sparrow's School for Delicate Boys at Seacroft, near Skegness, Lincolnshire, where he was physically and mentally strengthened for further education at Epsom College, Surrey. Guy then took a course in farming at Devon Agricultural College where he met a fellow-student named Ann Leigh, whom he married. Today, Guy and Ann are jointly interested in a mixed farm, at Willow Grove, near Trafalgar, Gippsland, Victoria, Australia, and have four sons.

Joseph Fletcher Harriman, born May 30th, 1919, attended the County Secondary School, Long Eaton, where he matriculated and passed the High School Certificate examination. By virtue of a Samuel Clegg Scholarship and a Revis Studentship to University College, Nottingham, he became a mechanical engineering student [1937-40].

In November 1940 he was commissioned and posted to the Royal Air Force Volunteer Reserve as engineer officer, to serve at home, followed by three years in the Mediterranean theatre, for which he was awarded the M.B.E. And—thanks to post-war college studies— the letters B.Sc. [Eng.] [Lond.], A.M.I.M.E. and A.F.R.Ae.S. can be put after his name also.

A two years engagement [1946-48] with the National Gas Turbine Establishment, Leicester, preceded Joseph's present appointment to the staff of Rolls-Royce Ltd. Flight Development Establishment, Hucknall, and his recent marriage [March 30th, 1955] to Katherine Robinson of Nuthall.

Dolcie Mary Harriman claims Long Eaton as birthplace; Derby High School as Alma Mater, and the Admiralty, London, as the centre of her Civil Service activities before marrying Kenneth Stilliard. Their home town is Ashford, Middlesex.

Peggy Taylor married Edgar Goodall, and they have three children, all girls. Edgar, who is on the payroll of British Celanese Ltd. and whose works are at Spondon, near Derby, is interested in the production of yarns and the export of woven fabrics for which this noted firm has many markets.

Norman Harold Taylor studied and qualified in medicine after leaving Nottingham High School. Later on, he spent two or three years with a skin-grafting specialist in a military hospital and then served with the Forces in Malaya. He married Doris Cavey of St Albans and is now in practice at Halifax, Yorkshire.

John Fletcher Henton is another of the many family 'twigs' that attended Nottingham High School for Boys. In January 1940 he enlisted in the Royal Naval Volunteer Reserve and served as writer until commissioned in 1942. As ship's radar officer, he saw much naval convoy duty in the Mediterranean, the Far East, and the Pacific that reached overseas to Australia, from which continent he docked at Portsmouth for demobilisation on February 16th, 1946. Since then he has worked with father in the family paper factory.

Robin William Henry Henton is a Southwell Grammar School old boy and did two years' national service in the Fleet Air Arm at Thorney Island prior to entering his father's business, where he is now working.

Marjorie Eileen Fletcher first married a Lieutenant Edwards, a member of the United States Armed Forces, and thereby forged yet another of the many similar family links that help to bind our country to America. This bond did not endure, so she became the wife of an Englishman named Lazzari. They have two young sons, Peter Mark Symington and Simon John Symington, and their home is in Breaston, near Derby.

Joseph Arthur Eaton Fletcher was until comparatively recently a schoolboy, but is now on the staff of F. Perks and Son, builders and contractors of Long Eaton. Since he has no father to give him early coaching may he, as the years go by, succeed in building up a tidy score off his own bat.

Anthony Barrett Good was born in India on September 12th, 1931. When his parents brought their family home thirteen years later they sent him to Trent College to advance his education, and then to Sandhurst to prepare him for a military career.

Today [1957] Anthony is a regular officer [Lieutenant] in the 8th Royal Tank Regiment, part of the Army of Occupation in Germany. His unit occupies Hitler's famous Panzer barracks at Paderborn.

Since leaving Trent College this young officer has made a prominent place for himself in the athletic world in which he has gained a number of varied successes.

At Sandhurst, he broke the swimming record for 50 yards free-style and then captained the regimental team which won the British Army of the Rhine ski-ing championships in 1953.

During the ensuing year he not only became the B.A.O.R. pole-vault champion, but also gained three major successes in his regimental sports—firsts in the pole vault, high jump and 220 yards hurdles.

Anthony, who is a keen soldier and sportsman, will be defending these titles during 1955, so good health and a little good fortune permitting, he should, step by step, follow in father's footsteps up the army ladder. [His achievements in Services Sports have also been remarkable during 1956].

68

Elizabeth Ann Good, like her brother, first saw light of day in India on August 29th, 1935, and returned to England with her parents in 1944. She was educated at St Ronan's School, Duffield, Derbyshire, and Broadgate School, Nottingham, where a liking for tennis, hockey and swimming provided those refreshers so needful to the satisfactory learning of lessons.

Nurses are numerous in our large family, so it will cause no surprise to hear that Elizabeth recently completed a four-years course of general training in nursing under the National Health Scheme at Addenbrooke's Hospital, Cambridge.

A few months ago, my wife and I, the Compiler, met this family 'twig' in the parental home at Parley Cross, where Nurse Good made it plain that she loved her chosen profession.

Joseph Fletcher's great-great-grandchildren—six boys and four girls—are all very young; their days of achievement have yet to come.

David John Bloomer, the senior member of this rising generation, came to life on New Year's Day 1935 and was educated at Mosley Hall Grammar School, Manchester, where he excelled in mathematics. He was awarded a State Scholarship and also gained an open one to Queen Mary College, University of London, where he was in residence for three years.

David John evinced all the skills of a rising tennis star by winning the North of England Championship for Boys under 16 in 1950; the Under-21 Championship in 1954; and by becoming Singles Champion, University of London, in the same year. He also represents Cheshire at tennis.

Peter Henry Burkill and Linda Elizabeth Burkill must ask mother for a romantic story and then, maybe, she will tell them some enchanting tales about older members of the big family to which they and we belong.

Jonathan Guy Bloomer and his three brothers, *Simon Leigh, Timothy Johnson* and *Michael Fletcher*, are a lucky quartette of Bloomers. Their home and playground are part of a farm in the State of Victoria, Australia, so, without any doubt whatsoever, they enjoy sunshine, fresh air, butter and eggs, and out-of-door sports with ponies and dogs to the full.

Elisbeth, Margaret and *Rosemary Goodall* all attended Ockbrook Moravian Girls' School which was established in the mid-fifteenth century and has five hundred years of history within its walls. It is probably one of many similar schools founded by a Protestant sect originated by John Huss of Bohemia. These united brethren were not numerous, but active and earnest. Avoiding dogma as much as possible, the Moravians make piety their religion, so it will be intriguing to notice what effect these principles have upon scholars affected by such kindly teachings.

PLATE 10

SAMUEL FLETCHER

CHAPTER III

THE SAMUEL BRANCH

Contributed by Samuel Billyeald Fletcher

SAMUEL FLETCHER, my grandfather, third son of Edward and Phoebe, born at Heanor on March 8th, 1829, was twice married, had seven sons, and died at Holmdale, The Park, Nottingham, in his fifty-sixth year.

He was a generous man and, to mark their appreciation for this trait, his employees presented him with a personal portrait in oils on his fiftieth birthday.

In 1858, Samuel installed his first lace plant in Abbott's Factory, Hyson Green, married Mary Wood of Calverton, and made a home at Portland House, Southey Street, where his first four sons were born.

Grandfather's venture succeeded but, when security and comfort together seemed assured, my grandmother's death in 1865 severed the root of those great expectations. Nine or ten years later he married Mary Turner, a widow and mother of three children. She bore him three more sons, only one of whom became permanently associated with the lace trade.

In 1874, grandfather moved his plant into Thoroton Works, Thoroton Street, obtained warehouse accommodation in Nottingham at 28 Stoney Street and, two years later, turned the business into a limited liability company with William Longmire as manager.

These developments made a suitable residence nearer the seat of business necessary so, by 1877, the family had moved from Southey Street to 11 Derby Terrace, The Park.

Two years later, Lincoln Villa became their next home, where they lived till the autumn of 1883, when Holmdale became grandfather's last residence in The Park. Incidentally, Lincoln Villa is bounded at the back by Western Terrace and at the front by Pelham Crescent where, from its extensive grounds, a delightful view of the Trent Valley, and beyond, can be enjoyed.

71

It was here that prosperity peak was reached and a continuous struggle with asthma began. Business control devolved upon Mr Longmire, the manager, but this did not work smoothly.

Grandfather's condition deteriorated rapidly and, despite a stay by the sea in the care of his doctor, complications developed and he passed away as previously described.

Exactly when the family interest in, and their control of Samuel Fletcher & Co. Ltd. ceased, is not known, but it is clear that Mr Longmire was manager in 1886, that Mr L. P. Lymbery had succeeded him by 1888 and still held the post eleven years later, so, very probably, 1887 was the year of severance. The Lymberys ultimately bought the business and ran it as a going concern until 1931 when the nameplate 'Samuel Fletcher & Co. Ltd.' disappeared from Nottingham Lace Market.

It is said that the families of Lymbery and Fletcher are related, so if genealogically inclined, it may interest you to know that several of the first-named, who went over to Ireland with Cromwell, settled at Bell Lake, Dunmore, Co. Waterford, and multiplied. They returned to England *en masse* in the 1820's and established numerous lace manufacturing businesses in the Nottingham district and other areas.

All Lymberys, like most Cutts, Fletchers, Hancocks, Jardines and Radfords, loved sport, especially ball games and, with many other local lace families, were prominently associated in the founding of Nottingham Forest football and cricket clubs.

After the Fletchers left Lincoln Villa, Sir John Bright became its next occupant, and it is still the home of this family today.

Grandfather's second wife, widowed for the second time, moved her family from Holmdale into Lynwood House, Mount, Hooton Road, near Nottingham, Forest, but the part this played in the Samuel Branch must be left to a more facile pen than mine to describe.

Edward John Wood Fletcher, my father, and grandfather's eldest son, born May 13th, 1860, had every opportunity in early manhood. He had a complete education which commenced at a private academy near the Arboretum, continued at All Saints under William Gaskell, and finished with three years at boarding school in preparation for the serious part of life.

He joined his father's business in 1876 and from then until 1882 the new member had six years full of golden opportunities to get on in the world.

They were not taken. Dad had a greater love for out-of-doors sports than he had for the 'old firm'. He and his family paid in full for this philosophy in later years.

My father 'followed in his father's footsteps' by adventuring into matrimony and business on his own account simultaneously. He married Edith Kate, eldest daughter of James Billyeald, another family that has traded in lace for over a century.

Their first home was Portland House, which still stands on Southey Street and Bentinck Road corner and there, May 23rd, 1883, I was born, the first of four sons and two daughters.

When I was four years old we were living at 6 Terrace Street, Hyson Green, the home of our common ancestors, and I can just remember the garden layout, the terrace overlooking the lawn, the positions of the fruit trees and the greenhouses where father burned tobacco in battling against insect pests.

The year I was born, father was already an established lace manufacturer in Town Hall Buildings, Weekday Cross, and then— as did his grandfather Edward—he put other irons into the fire.

Two shops, one on Alfreton Road, nearly opposite Thoroton Street, and the other at 11 Radford Road, were staffed and stocked with ladies' haberdashery in an endeavour to wed millinery to lace.

Mother, who before marriage was with U. P. Truman, 8 South Parade, Nottingham, worked very hard, but this attempted marriage between these dainty commodities failed utterly. They were unable to run in harness together. A minor lace trade slump swallowed the Weekday Cross venture and both shops had to be closed down.

Everything was sold to meet creditors' demands and so, by 1891, father ceased to be a private business man. Luckily, he found employment with Pratt, Hurst & Co. Ltd. but this was not a permanent rock and stay, as on the eve of the first World War a major slump blitzed this seemingly indestructible lace firm out of existence for ever.

Father died July 26th, 1927, the day before our son's thirteenth birthday, and mother was laid to rest on the eve of Christmas nineteen years later.

In 1896, I, *Samuel Billyeald Fletcher*, started work at the Nottingham Mechanics Institution, first as library boy and then as clerk.

Under the guidance of the Chief Librarian, Mr John T. Radford, and the Secretary, Mr George Bryan [a one-time lace manufacturer],

I developed a great love for books and an aptness for pen work. These joys, together with the manifold delights to be found on the sports fields and in the countryside, have provided the relaxations so necessary in a busy life.

On leaving the Mechanics, I obtained an appointment with our local Education Authority, whom I served, mainly in Mundella School science laboratories, until I retired in May 1943, after nearly 42 years' service.

I married Dorothy Sophia, younger daughter of James and Elizabeth Ann Shaw of Nottingham and in 1956 we celebrated the forty-third anniversary of our wedding.

Our two children matriculated at the County Secondary School, West Bridgford, now the County Grammar School.

Philip Frederic, the elder one, continued his studies at University College, now Nottingham University, gained his certificate there and in 1938 began teaching at Wilford village school.

He was already a sergeant in the South Notts. Hussars when Chamberlain took up Hitler's challenge, so in the New Year [1940] left England with the 107th [S.N.H.] Regiment R.H.A. for Haifa, Palestine, where they had intensive training prior to taking part in the Western Desert operations against the Italians, under General Wavell.

Fred left the South Notts. Hussars on Christmas Eve 1940 and was posted to G/[R], an operation designed to collect and organise Ethiopian deserters from the Italian *banda* into guerilla units under British leadership to harass the enemy forces over a wide area as they retreated towards Addis Ababa. Between January and October 1941 these guerilla bands made their way there one by one, on foot, from the Soudan. When Fred's force reached its journey's end, the hand of destiny was already shaping the lives of two strangers, then very far apart, but fated to meet. Fred spent five years in this wonderful country which, apart from the short Italian occupation, had never felt a conqueror's heel for three thousand years. He was soon granted a commission and posted to the British Military Mission Ethiopia [B.M.M.E.] commanded by General A. E. Cottam, C.B., C.B.E., M.C., who was responsible for raising and training the Ethiopian army to protect the realm and person of the Lion of Judah, His Majesty the Haille Selassie. A staff of British personnel discharged this heavy, exacting duty, and so the years slipped by— three of them.

November 20th, 1944, was indeed a 'red letter day' in Addis Ababa when, after ten days' travel from Nairobi by plane, road and rail, 1/*Lieutenant Mary Alice Handscomb, Q.A.I.M.N.S./[R]*, younger daughter of James and Mary Louise Handscomb of Upper Maidensgrove, Oxfordshire, and 1/*Lieutenant Nancy Addison, T.A.N.S.*, niece of Lord Addison, M.P., arrived to open a hospital for the B.M.M.E.

For the purposes of this story these fair additions to the Mission staff will hereinafter be mainly identified as Mollie and Nancy.

Mollie had most of her training at King Edward VII Hospital, Windsor, and St Mary Abbott's Hospital, Kensington. She was Nursing Sister [Surgical] at the Elizabeth Garrett Anderson Hospital, London, when in December 1943 she volunteered for service with the Q.A.I.M.N.S./[R]. Five months later she left Gourock, Scotland, for Nairobi and served in No. 1 General, an eleven hundred native bedded hospital. Subsequently, she was sister-in-charge of the ambulance train on the Nairobi-Mombasa run, evacuating and returning wounded from and to the Burma, India and Ceylon theatres of activity. Mollie and Nancy were a great attraction, so we at home were not completely surprised when Fred announced his engagement to Mollie and told us that the marriage would take place at St Saviour's, Addis Ababa, at eleven o'clock on November 3rd, 1945, and that Father Kevin Devenish, assisted by the Rev. Coleman Watkins, would conduct the ceremony.

The church was adorned with lovely flowers, and in the presence of many military and local well-wishers, the nuptial vows were made. Lieutenant Nancy Addison was chief bridesmaid; Colonel G. S. Grey attended the groom; Colonel R. M. Cubison acted as usher, and General A. E. Cottam gave the bride away and was host at the reception held after the ceremony.

An Ethiopian Military Band, conducted by the Master of the King's Music, rendered suitable airs throughout, and this gathering was followed by a Sundowner to regale those guests whose duties forbade their presence at the earlier celebrations.

The honeymoon, a trip to the Blue Nile, was made as part of an armed convoy under Fred's command, taking stores to outlying B.M.M.E. units near Debra Marcos.

Over a decade has passed since this panorama of scenic beauty was witnessed. Meanwhile, the best man has married the chief bridesmaid, the General has entered the Church, and Mollie and

Fred are settled atop of the Chilterns. Their home in Upper Maidensgrove almost overlooks both Henley-on-Thames, the Mecca of the world's greatest oarsmen, and the small Oxfordshire country town of Watlington whose youth Fred now teaches the rudiments of learning.

Mollie avers she has only 'worn the trousers once, army issue or any other male pattern', since her marriage, and that was on her honeymoon, when she put them on back to front—an excusable error under all the circumstances.

Our daughter, *Dorothy Elisabeth*—'Betty' in the family circle—born September 4th, 1923, some nine years after Fred, did not, for health reasons, commence school at Miss Bissill's Private Academy until she was seven. Good progress was made nevertheless. Music, painting, sketching, literature and cooking were her pet subjects. She was also fond of climbing ropes and ladders in the school gymnasium, but shuddered when cutting worms and dissecting frogs during nature lessons.

Betty studied theory and practice [pianoforte] at the Clovella School of Music and, under the direction of Gertrude Baldwin, competed with marked success at numerous Derbyshire and Nottinghamshire festivals and in the Trinity College of Music and Royal Schools of Music examinations.

From 1940 she was a staff member of Nottingham Trustee Savings Bank and then, in 1950, left and married George Owen Selby, of Hubert Durose and Pain, the son of Mr H. Q. Selby of British Railways, and Mrs Selby of Nottingham.

George, Royal Navy 1942-46, served with the Malta convoys and in craft that supported the landings in Southern France and Italy. His main job was 'feeding' the lads holding these 'hot' spots.

The newlyweds decided to go south to enter the service of Wessex Trustee Savings Bank. George is now chief assistant at Winton, whilst Betty, after managing the Christchurch branch for four years, resigned this post in favour of living normally in their own house on Hengistbury Head, one of Bournemouth's natural beauty spots. They now have an infant daughter, Elisabeth Alison.

My brother *Frank*, brewer's clerk, colliery worker, agent, Ministry of Labour and Pensions official, was ever a rolling stone and when World War I broke out, rolled up to enrol in the Royal Field Artillery and served throughout the campaign as a gunner. He was

76

gassed and wounded twice, and was awarded the Mons Star, the Victory Medal, the General Service Medal, the Great War for Civilisation Medal and the Scroll of Honour for services rendered in France and Belgium.

Frank, doing duty as night watchman at Banton's Works, Meadow Lane, just missed being burned alive when Nottingham was bombed, and the place gutted in a few seconds, during the night of May 8-9th, 1941. This terrifying experience hastened his death, which occurred a few years ago.

Frank's family circle consisted of four sons and three daughters borne by his wife, née Ethel Rose Parnham, of Melton Mowbray. Here, in order of seniority, is a small pen-picture of them all.

George Edward, a coal miner since his early youth, served for five years in the Eastwood Branch of the National Fire Service and was awarded the Efficiency Certificate and Civil Defence Medal. He married Selina Godfrey of Eastwood. They have one child, a son, Reginald, and one grandson.

After two years' training in 2357 Squadron [Eastwood and Heanor] A.T.C. he voluntarily enlisted in the Royal Air Force and served six years [1947-52] as a wireless telegraphist, mainly in Malta, Egypt, Palestine and Cyprus. for which he was awarded the General Service Medal, Palestine.

On September 8th, 1954, Reginald was the last direct male descendant to follow his great-great-great-grandfather Edward Fletcher's example of being married at St Lawrence Parish Church, Heanor.

On that date, the Rev. S. R. Futers, B.A., joined him in marriage to Miss Barbara Joyce Tunbridge, daughter of Mr and Mrs D. S. C. Tunbridge, the Rays Arms Hotel, Heanor.

Ethel, second in seniority, gave many years' service to Manlove Alliott & Co. Ltd., the noted Nottingham engineers. There she worked with the late Mr E. L. Kent, the well-known photographic artist who produced the first copies of the Tree so familiar to many members of our family.

Ethel married Reginald Cyril Jolley of British Railways, who did Civil Defence duties throughout 1939-45 at Toton Sidings, the largest of its kind in Great Britain.

Frank, a rolling stone like his father was, in 1939-45, classified unfit for military service, drafted into the National Fire Service

77

to serve five years, full time, as a driver attached to Nottingham headquarters. He did duty 'on the spot' during raids on London, Derby, Birmingham, Coventry, Manchester and other large centres.

During one of the enemy's heaviest visitations on London, fire-fighting appliances from other towns and cities queued head-to-tail from the city outskirts away back to Oxford, awaiting their turn to go in to assist in fighting the flames.

Frank married Margaret Voce of Apsley, Nottinghamshire, and now works for British Road Services.

Harold, brother Frank's third lad, obtained a post in the City of Nottingham Corporation Estates Department wherein he works as stores clerk today.

On August 11th, 1941, called up for military service, he was trained as general armourer, drafted to R.A.F. Bomber Command, No. 61 Squadron [Lancaster Bomber Group] and served in that arm until August 1946. From 1942 he did duty servicing and keeping planes in the air for the 500-1,000 bomber raids on Berlin, Cologne, Essen, Milan, Turin, and all the main targets in Europe.

The women of 61 Squadron W.A.F. fed the men during this hot work and one of them, L.A.C./W. Kathleen Blow, a cook with four years' service, daughter of Frederick Knight Blow and Mrs Blow of Saxilby, Lincolnshire, caught Harold's eye. They were married at Leicester and have a young son John, a bonny red-head and a great-great-great-great-grandson of John Fletcher who lived on Tag Hill, Heanor, in 1791.

May, the second daughter, was born on Christmas Day. She married William Barratt, a fitter at Raleigh Industries Ltd., Nottingham. They have a son, William, and a daughter, Jean.

Percy, the youngest son, was born on March 22nd, 1923, and married Mollie Brough. After completing his apprenticeship as engine fitter at Rolls-Royce, Nottingham depot, he had two years in the Royal Air Force and was then transferred to Derby to assist in the construction of the advanced type of engine demanded by the super-jet age. Percy is an able aeronautical engineer and has been a member of Rolls-Royce Ltd. staff for nearly eighteen years.

Maud, the whipper-in, worked for the same firm as her sister Ethel and then married William Collier of Ruddington, Nottingham-shire, a tool setter at the cycle works belonging to Raleigh Industries Ltd., Nottingham.

In her days of single bliss, my elder sister, the late *Edith Mary*, obtained employment at the Thoroton Works and there found a sturdy ally in tussles with a hard taskmaster [female] in *Allan Cree*, grandfather's one-time engine driver, by then an old man with definitely fixed ideas about what constituted fair play and good manners.

She married John Baines, who had his first taste of army life with the King's Own Scottish Borderers in various parts of India, where the humble 'Tommy' could enjoy a large basket of choice fruits at the cost of a few annas in those late Victorian days.

My brother-in-law has vivid memories of the troops being brought home to Old England in a cattle boat—the good ship *Jalunga*.

He was recalled to the Colours on August 4th, 1914, stationed in turn at Berwick-on-Tweed, Portland [coastal defences] and Edinburgh where, as sergeant-instructor, he finished his army career when World War I ended.

Winifred, their elder child, still a home bird, spent the earlier part of her working life at Players, Nottingham, suffering the soothing atmosphere of that noxious weed, tobacco. Needing a complete change, she entered the service of Radio Rentals Ltd. whose works are a stone-throw from where the later John and Mary Fletcher of Parkfields, Heanor, lived and kept a milliner's shop during the 1850's.

Before the outbreak of World War II, *John Junior*, their son, was a clerk with W. J. Furse & Co. Ltd., Nottingham, and today is a British Electricity Authority wayleaves officer, responsible for negotiating wayleaves for overhead lines across country.

He enlisted in June 1940 and from August 1941 to August 1945 served with the Middle East Forces, Cairo, and in the Deputy Advocate-General [Legal Branch] Department, Nairobi, where in 1942 he met and later married in Nottingham, Chief Petty Officer Gertrude Brenda Greening, whose father was a colour-sergeant in the Royal Marines for twenty-one years.

As was only natural, *Brenda* chose the salty arm in which to serve for nearly six years. This ranged from the Orkneys and Scapa Flow, through the Royal Naval College, Greenwich; Chatham; Sheerness; Shotley and Rosyth, away down to Cape Town and Mombasa. There she was N.C.O. responsible for dealing with the incoming and outgoing mail for the Fleet and Shore Establishments in that area.

John, and Brenda, who is now Clerical Officer, Post Office Telephones, Nottingham, told me this East African on-duty yarn which may thrill the reader:

"When all duties were finished one Saturday lunch-time, a special signal came from a ship carrying five hundred bags of surface mail, stating that many of them had been rifled either by the crew or passengers.

A party of us clambered aboard and found the hold where the mails were stored in a terrible mess. We set to work under the eye of a police sergeant noting the damage.

After labouring furiously for hours [we had a team of six Africans with us] we sat back for a breather on some boxes. One of the blacks lit a fag-end—but it was not till some time later that I noticed the boxes we were sitting upon were labelled HIGH EXPLOSIVES! DANGER!! NO SMOKING!!! I *still* do not know where he threw that match!"

Brenda also says one of her great great great grandparents was reputed to have been one of the last persons to be hung at Tyburn— but whether his offence was sheep-stealing, pilfering bread, or a Dick Turpin act on the king's highway is not mentioned in their family records.

John is now with the National Coal Board and Brenda is employed in another government department.

Hilda May, my younger sister, married Frederic Gale, who served in the 1914-18 war and, when demobilised, kept a shop in various parts of Nottingham.

Edward Robert, gifted at-sight and by-ear pianist and regular soldier [1908-25] also worked as library boy at 'the Mechanics' from 1904 to 1908. At the age of seventeen he enlisted in the Royal Garrison Artillery and, in turn, soldiered in Guernsey, Mauritius, France and Flanders [1915-18], Sierre Leone and Alderney, reaching the rank of R.Q.M.S. before he was invalided out after seventeen years' service. He then secured a post with the Ministry of Labour and continued in their employ until he died five or six years ago.

Ted introduced me, and later, all my immediate family, to the charms of Guernsey where we have had many lovely holidays.

He married a Channel Islander, Margaret Jane Hunt, and they increased our Fletcher stock to the extent of one girl and five boys, of whom *Percy* and *Alan* died in early childhood.

Marion Irene, their eldest child, married Merle Clifford Campbell, an American soldier and a draughtsman by trade. When the 1939-45 war finished she returned home with him to America and they are now happily and comfortably settled at 822 First Street, Kewaunee, Wisconsin, U.S.A., where their house stands almost on the shores of Lake Michigan. They both work very hard for their church and as Marion sings in the choir, the outlook ahead for this small family, which includes a growing daughter, Janice, is full of promise.

Leslie Edward, the eldest of five boys, took up dental mechanics after leaving school and is now associated with Mr McGowan in that profession at Sherwood, Nottingham. Early in the second World War he was posted to Army Dental Command, went overseas, and served as sergeant-mechanic, 162 Mobile Field Dental Unit, British North African Forces. *Joan Edson*, of Plumtree, Nottinghamshire, became his wife and they now live in that village with their three children—Barry, Lesley and Jeremy Alan.

Leonard and *Kenneth Herbert*, the two youngest sons of Ted and May, both did a spell of service in the armed forces of the Crown.

Leonard married a Nottingham girl, Joan Simmons, and was resident-manager at Hilton Shoe Shop, Ashby-de-la-Zouch. They have one child, Steven, and now live in Rotherham.

Kenneth emigrated to Australia some five years ago to enlist in the Royal Australian Air Force and is still serving as a corporal. His wife [née Maureen Wright] accompanied him and their address is 2 Lloyd Street, West Newport, Melbourne, Victoria, Australia.

Leslie Alfred, my youngest brother, died in infancy [1894] and was buried with his great-grandparents, John and Ann Wood, in the Church Cemetery, Nottingham.

Frank Allen Fletcher, grandfather's third son, died just after reaching his majority in 1885 and left no issue. He was also buried in the Church Cemetery.

When grandfather's business passed into the hands of the Lymbery family, his older sons had to make their own way, so from 1887 to 1895, *William Percy Fletcher* traded as a lace manufacturer in Fletcher's Factory and West End Mills, Long Eaton, near Nottingham. This venture was ruined by a trade slump, so he turned over to draughting, designing and card-punching in which he was very skilled. This uncle of mine was also an artist in oils of repute and I have one of his paintings I greatly treasure.

Mid-way between the two world wars he went to Canada and did some designing there, but shortly after returning to Long Eaton, he died very suddenly at North House and was buried in the local cemetery.

Uncle begot two daughters, and a son, *Douglas*, who made the Supreme Sacrifice in the Great War of 1914-18. His elder daughter, *Mary Elsie*, married Richard Bethell Wilson, a barrister who, until his death some few years ago, was secretary to Rolls-Royce Ltd., the world-famous manufacturers of motor cars and aircraft engines. *Geoffrey*, their son, and his mother, now reside at Kirk Leys, Derby.

Flora Marchant, the youngest of the trio, married Reginald Wallis of Long Eaton. They have one daughter, Pamela, born in Toronto shortly before the family returned to England. Today, as representative of a London contracting firm, Reg. travels up and down the country a lot, so he and Flora have settled down at Shirley, Solihull, Warwickshire, a comfortable, central spot, in which they hope to remain.

Pamela, the mother of two young sons, Timothy John and Mark Charles, and her husband, Norman John Payne, M.B.E., a civil engineer and partner in a London firm, are 'at home' in North Wembley, Middlesex.

OUR NEW ZEALAND STORY
by Leslie Walter Fletcher

It is now my turn to describe what has happened before and since my parents and my brother and I left England to build new homes in this lovely country so far from the land of our birth. First of all, my father, Samuel Fletcher, the second of grandfather's seven sons, was born at Nottingham in 1861 and joined the family business in 1874. He spent most of the next ten years at the Thoroton Street Works where his ability to draw and sketch enabled him, by careful training, to become an exceptionally skilful designer and draughtsman. Unfortunately, grasp of business technique did not keep abreast with his artistic attainments, but despite this lack, he was well fitted for the role of master man when grandfather's business passed into other hands.

PLATE 11

THE NEW ZEALAND BRANCH

(See overleaf for names)

Back row: ALEC BOND, SAM FLETCHER AND MRS. SAM FLETCHER, L. W. FLETCHER, F. N. FLETCHER
(*brother-in-law*)   (*father and mother*)   (*son*)

Middle row (adults): H. MURRAY, MRS. H. MURRAY, MRS. ALEC BOND, MRS. MURRAY, MRS. L. W. FLETCHER, MRS. F. N. FLETCHER
(*brother-in-law*)   (*sister-in-law*)   (*mother-in-law*)   (*daughters-in-law*)

Middle row (infants in arms): Little Miss MURRAY, a little BOND, ALISON FLETCHER, ZILLAH FLETCHER, NESTA FLETCHER
(*Frank's youngest*)   (*Frank's eldest and second daughters*)

Front row: MURRAY FULLER, LESLEY ALISON, FRANCES NOEL, ALEC TOPHAM, HAMISH SAMUEL (*all Leslie Fletcher's children*)

Dad was already firmly established in the trade when, on June 16th, 1886, at All Saints Church, Nottingham, he married Julia Alice, the daughter of Frederick Topham, who had lace machines in Adcock's Factory, Gamble Street, and resided at Lindum House, Burns Street, facing the Arboretum. Their first home was on Hope Drive, The Park, near Nottingham Castle, where I was born.

Father's lace manufacturing plant was then in Woodland Mill, Long Eaton; but before continuing this part of my story, I would like to tell you something about Grandfather Topham, whose family are, through a female line, so Cousin Sam says, of Pentrich Fletcher stock.

In addition to his Nottingham commitments, he had a long-established lace manufacturing business in Calais. My mother was born and educated there, and when grandfather brought his family back home to England, she could speak both French and German fluently and was also an accomplished musician. Luckily, Dame Fortune smiled upon father when he avoided the dire effects of a fire that raged through Woodland Mill in the late 1880's. He had just moved his machines into Fletcher's Factory, Peel Street, and remained there four years.

Dad next made use of the West End Mill, Leopold Street, until 1898 and then continued production at Sutton's Factory, Clifford Street where, for depressing reasons so clearly outlined by the Nottingham writer, Hilda Lewis, in her historical novel, *Penny Lace*, which describes the rise and fall of many local lace-makers, he went bankrupt in 1905.

In an endeavour to ward off the evil day, Grandfather Topham gave father four fine 100-inch lace machines which, compared with the then new ones having 192-inch frames, were uneconomic.

Dad was not allowed to sell these old machines and buy new ones with the proceeds, so, after twenty years striving to uplift himself, he had to work for others awhile as a designer and draughtsman.

Whilst these events were happening, the family left Hope Drive and lived, in turn, on Fishponds Drive and Hamilton Drive, The Park, followed by The Limes, Long Eaton, where my brother, Frank Noel, was born on May 24th, 1892. Eight happy years together at The Limes preceded several equally joyful ones at Western House, Attenborough. Treasured memories are wrapped in them all. Then came the business break-up which compelled mother and father to move to Elm Avenue, Beeston, their last home before going to Germany in 1908.

That year Dad went to Plauen, Saxony, as designer and draughtsman to a lace firm whose owner, by all accounts, was British. Mother and Frank accompanied him. Four years later, however, my brother saw World War I clouds beginning to gather over Europe, so decided to join me in New Zealand.

Incidentally, Plauen—known as the Nottingham of Germany on account of its lace manufacture—received shattering attention from the Allies' bombers on April 9th, 1945.

Mother was deported to England when war was declared in August 1914 and was appointed interpreter at the Foreign Office, but Dad saw the inside of Ruhleben Camp as an enemy alien of military age. He was released for a time on rations and under close supervision, to work in the factory, but when hostilities intensified, Dad [accompanied by the factory owner] was confined to camp again till he passed military age [55] and freed in 1917 to rejoin mother in England. Three years later, the whole family was reunited in New Zealand.

There was great joy among us that day, but something else equally stupendous immediately confronted our parents—' to earn their daily bread in the years that lay ahead'. They were in a new country where men and women had to prove their worth, maintain their independence, and by so doing, gain one of life's greatest honours— 'the respect of their fellows'.

The old folk met the challenge manfully and were so respected to the end of the road.

Their first home down here was with us on the farm at Thakara, Levin, where Dad started a vegetable round among the local residents to whom he sold produce drawn from our large market garden.

Mother gave private tuition in elocution, voice-culture, music, singing, French and German to school teachers and other pupils.

Domestic security was greatly increased when Dad became the caretaker of the Borough Council Buildings and St Mary's Church Hall, next door to where he lived. He held these posts till he died.

Strengthened by a stable income Dad, like other Fletchers, could not resist the temptation to have other strings to his bow. He opened

84

a cafe in Oxford Street, Levin, where he made up his own Notting-ham pork-pies—and thereby hangs a tasty story.

A prospective customer spotted half a pie in the window and enquired if that was pork-pie on view—he hadn't seen one since leaving his home-town, Melton, many years ago! Receiving an affirmative, he ate the piece on the spot, took a whole pie home, and called regularly for others afterwards.

Frank and Mona [my wife's sister] managed the cafe whilst Dad continued caretaking and made it pay, but just before the 1930 depression began, the business was sold at a small profit.

And so, through the years, was the flag of independence kept aloft. Mother found refreshment in music, books and flowers, and bowls, cricket and out-of-door friends made Dad's leisure a pleasure.

Mother was laid to rest in Levin Cemetery on July 12th, 1928, and our loved ones were reunited on September 12th when Dad died five years later.

MY OWN EMIGRATION

After leaving Shoreham Grammar School, I started work in 1904 at father's Long Eaton lace factory for 2s. 6d. a week, but not liking this, I went to Ericssons, Beeston, for 7s. weekly, and then had a course in agriculture at Joule's Farm, Bramcote, Nottinghamshire, before emigrating to New Zealand with Fred Rowarth, one of my friends. We left Nottingham on Goose Fair Eve 1907 and stayed with Grandfather Topham at South Norwood, London, until we went abroad.

We sailed from Tilbury on Friday, October 7th, calling at Ply-mouth, Teneriffe, Cape Town and Hobart, Tasmania, and seven weeks later docked at Wellington, Sunday, November 25th—a day I shall ever remember.

Wishing to recover our land legs, we accepted the option to finish the journey to Plymouth, New Zealand, by train, where work in a cheese factory was offered us. Instead, our first jobs in 'En Zed' were on a Hawera two-hundred-acres dairy farm where, for the next seven months, from four every morning until eight at night, we milked thirty cows apiece as *part* of the job.

We then parted company, Fred took on as rouseabout [Aus-tralian slang for odd job man or woman] on a Wairarapa North sheep farm, and I went hay pressing at Rangitiki [Bulls].

85

The right to live and eat was earned by cow banging, navvying, and road building in Wellington; rabbit shooting on North and South Island stations; scrub cutting; sheep farming and cow tending at Mangarou, near where we first landed—and other tough, testing jobs.

Then my lucky star began to rise. I became camp cook at a two-thousand-acres Wairarapa bush station where I had to use open fires and feed a dozen men. My camp chores included killing and dressing meat, cutting fire wood, milking the cow, and baking bread and cakes.

I then had the good fortune to meet my future wife at a dance, and further meetings took place at Christmas and New Year picnics.

By taking french leave to attend the second picnic, I lost the job as camp cook, but gained Jacqueline Murray, a farmer's daugher, for wife. We were married April 2nd, 1913, at Jackie's home in the Waihoki Valley by the Presbyterian parson and our honeymoon was spent sowing grass seed on a burnt-out section of our 192-acre bush farm.

A few months later we sold out and went to Levin to run a 24½-acre land ballot thirty-three years leasehold farm. We farmed here till 1924, when we disposed of our interests so that, during the next twenty-one years I could, in turn, work for the Horowhenna Electric Power Board, whose service I finally left in 1945; the Public Works Authprity, and the Native House Building Scheme.

In 1934 we bought a section at Waitarere Beach, built a cottage and, two years later, left Levin to enjoy the charm and peace of this retreat by the sea.

Today [Jackie was born July 2nd, 1889, and I, May 18th, 1887] we are, as State pensioners, still active in life. She is secretary of the Women's Institute and a teacher in the Sunday School. I am secretary-treasurer of the Ratepayers Improvement Association, and we both revel in the delights of a fruit, flower and vetetable garden. We are also the proud possessors of fourteen grandchildren.

THE YOUNGER GENERATION

Our three sons and two daughters were all born in the North Island, educated at Thakara and Levin and, since their early youth, taken a leading part in athletic pursuits requiring equipment ranging from balls, bats and rackets to water, cartridges and guns.

86

Murray Fuller, our eldest, born at Eketahuna, December 29th, 1913, worked as a storeman and then on a farm till he joined the army in October 1939. He went overseas to Egypt with the 2nd New Zealand Expeditionary Force, January 1940, rose to the rank of Q.M.S. and was discharged in 1945 after five-and-a-half years' active service.

The Rehabilitation Department then allotted him a sixty-five-acres farm, on renewable lease, estimated to carry forty cows able to produce 12,000 pounds of butter fat annually; four sows; eight calves for replacements, and a horse.

In June 1947, Murray married Kathleen Mary McLean, of Scottish farming stock. This partnership has prospered amazingly. They have built a house on the farm; started a young family; invested in motor transport; and, in time, this estate can become their own property.

Lesley Alison, our elder daughter, born at Levin Marhc 18th, 1915, learned something about nursing the hard way as housemaid, cook and general rouseabout at Amara Private Hospital. She then had general training [1935-39], gained her State diplomas and took a maternity course at Masterton General Hospital, and spent another year at Whangerie, North Auckland, before returning to Masterton General as Sister.

Sister Fletcher then joined the Army Nursing Service and, after a year at Waierera Military Camp, was posted to the hospital ship *Manganui* which carried wounded home to New Zealand and medical supplies and personnel back to Egypt. On one such voyage Lesley found her brother, Hamish, among the badly wounded troops and then, after a run to Durban with South African casualties, she was posted to No. 1 Hospital, Egypt, where she met and married Bill Hill in Cairo. They have three young sons, and their home is in Hastings where Bill is secretary-accountant at a printing works.

Frances Noel, our younger daughter, was born February 26th, 1916, on my father-in-law's farm in the Waihoki Valley. Her favourite hobby at school was fashioning and trimming ladies' headgear so, on leaving in 1932 she became, in the employ of a local milliner, a practised expert in this decorative art. She married Corporal Keith Davies, a cabinet-maker who, after his discharge from the New Zealand Air Force and return from the Pacific Islands, began building in 1945 in Levin on a large scale and established a thriving business—K. Davies Ltd.—of which Frances is one of the directors.

They have built their own factory and have two daughters of middle school age.

In 1953, Frances and Keith flew to England to witness the grandeur of the Coronation of Her Majesty the Queen and see some of the glories of London for the first time. They also enjoyed short stays with members of the family living in Beeston and West Bridgford, where the opportunity was taken to watch the Test Match between England and Australia at Trent Bridge.

Our travellers then glimpsed the splendours of France, Switzerland, Italy, Holland and Belgium during a tour which included visits to Paris, Montreux, Lucerne, Milan, Naples, Sorrento, Rome, the Isle of Capri, the Hague, Brussels, the Battlefield of Waterloo and the Hook of Holland.

After a few more days in the Motherland, the globe-trotters left Liverpool by boat to cross Canada *en route* for home—and what a story they had to tell us when they got back again!

Hamish Samuel. This country was in the grip of industrial and agricultural depression when our second boy left school to start work in a grocery stores. Three years later he was apprenticed to a local master joiner, but only half this contract had expired when he enlisted in the Forces.

He had been overseas but a few months when he was very severely wounded and taken prisoner at the Battle of Sidi Rezeg by the Italians, who left him and other casualties in Bengazi hospital 'as not worth shifting to Italy when they retreated'.

The South Africans found them there so, that Christmas, Hamish was one of the six badly wounded En Zedders who, from their hospital beds, were able to radio messages of greeting to their kin at home. We heard him!

As already mentioned, Lesley discovered him homeward bound on the *Manganui* where, after six months in hospital, he made a substantial recovery and was fit enough to take a post at Weraroa Boys' Training Farm as temporary woodwork instructor. Twelve months later he took a course at the Seddon Training College where he was awarded his teacher's diploma and appointed games master and handicraft instructor at Rogolai College, Wellington.

Recovery completed and future security assured, he married Dorothy Smaille and built a house overlooking Lyle Bay, where a car is a prime necessity to carry a growing family around.. Some of the trips in it are associated with the delights of cricket, at which sport Hamish was a near-test-match standard exponent when the 1939-45 war began.

Alexander Topham, the youngest of our flock, born July 18th, 1920, has been a printer and seeker after news all his life—so far. He began his association with the presses as an apprentice printer's devil and as the years passed, became a master printer in the town.

His military baptism was voluntarily undergone in the Manawatu Mounted Rifles. Then, after twelve months' further training in our Regular Army, he went overseas with reinforcements for the 2nd New Zealand Expeditionary Force and the 8th Army in Tripoli. From there, he took part in all the fighting that surged into Sicily, through Italy, and was granted a commission before the end was reached.

Ultimately, he reached his final self-declared objective—England —and traversed some of the Trentside haunts that father once knew so well before returning home to pick up the broken threads of normal life and marry June Benning.

Today, Alec is president of our branch of the Returned Soldiers Association, proprietor of Levin Printing Works Ltd., printers, bookbinders, stationers, and publisher of *Levin Weekly News*.

My personal story ends here. The journey was hard at the beginning; but in the ending, New Zealand has given me and mine many blessings to count and be thankful for.

Frank Noel has, in many respects, had experiences similar in pattern to those of his brother.

After leaving Shoreham Grammar School he, too, worked for father in Long Eaton and with him in Plauen, but jobs of any kind were very acceptable when he joined Leslie in New Zealand.

Whilst serving with the Dinks Rifle Brigade in France during the first World War he was awarded the Military Medal and then, at forty-seven years of age, he went overseas in 1940 with the New Zealand Expeditionary Force to help in the common cause against Hitler.

Frank married his sister-in-law, Mona Murray and became a local farmer, but could not settle on the land so, in turn, he worked for the Electric Power Board at Levin and Hastings. Further employment was then found in a Hastings freezing works until he and Mona returned to Levin where their three daughters, Alexa Zillah [April 3rd, 1920], Nesta Christina [April 21st, 1922] and Alison Murray [July 9th, 1925] were born.

Levin, where Frank worked as a practical joiner, has been their home town ever since and, should you give them a call, you can admire their beautiful garden, usually aglow with flowers and rich in fruit and vegetables.

Zillah, the eldest daughter, had her hospital training at Palmerston North; a course in midwifery at Kawa Kawa; and became a fully qualified Sister. She married Robert William Pattison, an electrician, who served with the Royal New Zealand Air Force in the Pacific. They have a son, Ian Robert, and a daughter, Margaret Jean, and their home is at Russell in the Bay of Islands, North Auckland.

Nesta was secretary of a local building firm until she married Lester Baker, a partner in a Levin joinery factory, in which locality the young couple reside, and have one child, Kara.

Alison teaches at Levin Primary School, where she is the sports mistress and also specialises in general infant training.

Frank has recently retired but has been enjoyably busy with bits and pieces ever since. He can now please himself [and Mona] so they, too, are in safe harbour, at the last.

SAMUEL FLETCHER'S SECOND MARRIAGE

Contributed by Mary Barbara Fletcher

This portion of the chapter concerns the lives of the children of Samuel Fletcher's second marriage—three boys, Arthur, Bert and Fred, who at the time of their father's death were aged eight, six and four.

In the year following the death of Samuel Fletcher at Holmdene in 1884, his widow removed with her family to Lynwood House, Mount Hooton Road, where she remained until her death in 1899.

During their father's last illness the two older boys were sent to boarding school and they continued there until they went to the Grosvenor School, where they all completed their education with the exception of Bert, who spent two years at Nottingham High School for Boys.

90

The two older boys grew up at Lynwood House with their half brothers and sister. Both of them became keen members of the Nottingham Rowing Club and ardent philatelists, a hobby which lasted throughout their lives. Arthur was also very fond of cycling and covered much of the country round Nottingham on his penny-farthing bicycle.

The first break in the family circle came when Frederic, the youngest boy, left home to join the Training Ship *Conway* prior to serving in the Merchant Navy.

After leaving school, it had always been expected that the other two boys would follow their father's footsteps and enter the lace trade, so arrangements were made for Arthur to start his training with the firm of Dunnicliff & Smith, and for Bert to join Messrs Birkin & Co., Broadway, Nottingham, where he stayed until his retirement fifty-three years later.

It was a great grief to both boys when their mother died and the home at Lynwood had to be broken up. With Frederic away, Arthur and Albert went into rooms at Edwalton, but Arthur's heart had never been in the lace trade, so not long after his mother's death he emigrated to South Africa where he joined his brother Fred who had left the sea and was looking for a job in Durban.

In due course, Arthur obtained a post with the E.R.P. Gold Mining Company near Johannesburg, where he became assistant manager and remained until he retired in 1953 after fifty-one years in office—the longest service of anyone with E.R.P. Mines since its inception.

As soon as he had an assured position his fiancée, Kate Poyser, a Nottinghamshire girl, joined him and they were married shortly after her arrival in South Africa. He established a home in Boksburg where his family, two boys and two girls were born, and he remained there until his wife died shortly after the celebration of their Golden Wedding.

During the first World War he fought with the South African Rifle Brigade in West Africa [rank, warrant officer] and for his services rendered there holds the 1914 Star and two other medals.

He was much too old to take an active part in the second World War, but both his sons were in the thick of it throughout all those anxious years.

Victor, company sergeant-major, South African Survey Brigade, served in North Africa, Egypt, Syria, Palestine, the Caucasus, Sicily and Italy. After the war was over he found it hard to settle down again but finally made a home for his family in Cape Town.

Richard, the younger boy, a sapper in the South African Artillery, also served in Abyssinia, Egypt and North Africa and had the misfortune to be taken prisoner at Sidi Rezeg after his unit, the 5th Engineers, had been reduced to thirteen unwounded men. He was sent to Italy and then to Stalag 344 in Silesia, and was one of the noble band of prisoners who survived the endless 800-mile trek through snow, under the most appalling living conditions, to a point near Frankfurt, where they were surprised by the Americans as they were about to be driven still further from the Russians.

After spending a week in Birmingham with an aunt, he came to stay with his uncle Bert in Nottingham and took part in V.E. Day celebrations and also attended a party given in his honour. During his stay, he saw many places of interest in and around Nottingham, and also visited Lynwood House where his father spent his boyhood. He then returned home and shortly before becoming an established accountant, married Beryl McKenzie. They reside in a house of their own just outside Johannesburg and have two children, one son and a daughter.

Arthur's two daughters are both married and have families, so when their mother died in 1953 he gave up his Boksburg house at Blue Sky and made his home with *Mary,* the younger one, at Wychwood in the district of Germiston.

During this time, *Bert Fletcher* had traced a very different course; he stayed in Nottingham and settled down in the lace trade so, for a few years, his life was somewhat uneventful. In 1905, he became engaged to Grace Wilson, the second daughter of Thomas Wilson of Park Road, Lenton, and a few months later he was sent to New York to help to establish a wholesale supply depot for Messrs Birkin & Co., lived there for almost a year, and returned home largely Americanised in outlook.

He married in 1907 and, after living on Castle Boulevard for a time, moved with his wife and small daughter to Claremont Gardens, Sherwood Rise, where they stayed for over twenty years.

His trip to New York was a forerunner of almost annual visits to the United States and Canada, to which he travelled on all the famous boats of the Cunard Line. He also visited Paris quite frequently and, on several occasions, attended the race meetings at Auteuil and Longchamps to observe the use of lace in the gowns of the period.

These activities were naturally curtailed during the 1914-18 War so, being medically unfit for service in the Forces, he joined the Special Constabulary.

Directly after this war ended, the lace trade went through a very bad period indeed, so, in the autumn of 1927, Bert started off on a world business tour and followed part of the route taken by the Queen and the Duke of Edinburgh during their Commonwealth Tour of 1953-54. After calling at Madeira, he went on to Cape Town, Durban, and finally to Johannesburg where he stayed with Arthur and his family. The two brothers had not met for over twenty-five years, so the hours were many that they spent talking over the old days in Nottingham. He then moved on to visit all the chief towns in Australia and saw the famous Jenolan Caves on his way to Sydney, where he spent Christmas.

From Australia, the next stage of his journey took him to North Island, New Zealand, where he visited many places of especial interest, including the wonderful Thermal Springs of Rotorua and the Waitomo Caves. He was particularly intrigued by the Maori villages and customs and brought back many souvenirs of their work.

After making a call at South Island, he journeyed on to the Fiji and Hawiian Islands and thence to the United States and Canada where he completed his tour among old friends and new ones. He sailed for home in the spring of 1928 having been away nine months.

During the 1930's Bert made fortnightly visits to London in an endeavour to improve the firm's export trade, and in 1931 moved his family to 48 Cyprus Road where he spent the rest of his life.

The second World War had barely finished when he underwent a very serious operation which unfitted him to carry on his business, so he retired after fifty-three years' unbroken service with Birkin & Co.—an outstanding and probably unequalled record in Nottingham Lace Market.

For his remaining years he was happy doing as much gardening as he was able and many summer days were spent at the Trent Bridge county cricket ground, but his health gradually failed and he died in January 1952 at the age of seventy-three.

Bert's only child was a daughter, *Mary Barbara*, whose chief interest lay in music. After taking her earlier music examinations and completing her education, she studied at the Stockwin School of Music and became a fully-trained music teacher, but for a period did very little teaching.

During the second World War years she acted as warden-telephonist, helped with a mobile canteen which served troops in camps and on gun sites near Nottingham, and held a position in a general store. When the war was over she accepted an appointment at Mountford House School where she had been a pupil as a child.

Her other special interest lay in Girl Guiding. She worked in various branches of the movement before becoming, in turn, district secretary and Trefoil Club member—a department for Guides who have given up active work for the cause.

After her father's death she and her mother stayed on together at their home in Cyprus Road, Nottingham, where the family had lived for over twenty years.

After leaving the training ship 'Conway', *Fred*, the youngest of Samuel Fletcher's seven sons, had an adventurous life. In his early days at sea, the ship in which he was serving caught fire and was burnt out, but he managed to escape on a raft. His family had given up all hope of seeing him again, but he calmly walked into Lynwood House some months later.

After being in the Merchant Service for some years, he left the sea and went to South Africa where he joined his brother Arthur.

During the Boer War he was in charge of a naval battery and also formed part of Kitchener's bodyguard. In the Natal Rising he took part in hand-to-hand fighting with the natives and the bayonet he used was given to his brother Bert.

In 1914 he was on a supply ship which was blown up in the Southern Pacific, but once more his luck held and he was picked up unconscious and later landed at Nelson, New Zealand.

During one of his trips from Australia in the first World War, he met his future wife, Ivy Halloran, who was a passenger on the same boat. She and her mother and sister—Australians from Sydney—were coming to England for a holiday. She and Fred became engaged and were married in 1917.

For some years after his marriage, Fred remained in the Merchant Service and then he retired and went to live in an Oxfordshire village. However, at the time of the Abyssinian campaign, he once more felt the call of the sea and was put in charge of a supply ship, standing by at Haifa. There he contracted a tropical germ which the doctors were unable to combat and he died some months later at his home in Thame, Oxfordshire.

In the December before the second World War his wife returned to her people in Sydney where she lived with her sister until her death in 1953.

Something must be said in conclusion about the fate of Lynwood House. It was privately owned for many years after the Fletcher family left in 1899 but during the last war [1939-45] it was taken over by the military authorities. It was during that period that Bert Fletcher took his nephew Dick to look at his father's old home and was distressed to see how badly it had been treated. However, the house is once more private property and after being completely restored has become a hostel for our University students.

PLATE 12
THOMAS AND ISABELLA FLETCHER

CHAPTER IV

THE THOMAS BRANCH

Compiled from family notes and those of other contributors

Thomas, the fifth son of Edward and Phoebe Fletcher, was born at Taghill, Heanor, Derbyshire, on August 28th, 1830, and died in his prime on August 5th, 1880, at North House, Long Eaton. He took Isabella Litchfield, daughter of John Litchfield, farmer, of Epperstone, Nottinghamshire, to wife, who bore him three sons and four daughters, none of whom were connected with the lace trade after their father's demise for very long.

Thomas, a man of foresight and uncanny judgment of a bold enterprise laid, in partnership with brother Joseph of The Hall, much of the foundation on which Long Eaton's name and fame were built.

This partnership, which lasted nearly twenty years, is fully described in the Joseph Branch of this story so, to avoid needless repetition of detail, I will content myself with saying here that the distinguished part Thomas played in the trade began around 1860 when, as a Lenton resident, he had lace machines on his own account at Hyson Green, probably in Abbott's Factory.

Two years later, he and brother Joe were firmly established together, so whilst the elder member was living at Parkfields and doing the firm's business at Heanor, Tom the younger, folded his tent at Lenton and, in 1865, moved into Long Eaton to become an ornament of the lace trade as he lived a full and unselfish life for the good of his fellows. This is what those who knew him well have to say about his outstanding services to the causes he loved and in which he believed.

George Fletcher of Long Eaton, the oldest surviving grandson of Edward and Phoebe, contributes this graphic pen-picture:

"I was only five years old when uncle Thomas Fletcher died, and so have little personal recollection of him, but I can remember his funeral quite well.

All business was at a standstill. Everybody in Long Eaton seemed to be present to pay the last respects, and so dense was the crowd that I, being so young and new to the district, lost my way going home."

"As chairman of the local School Board, he was largely instrumental in the building of our first board school and for many improvements in other public services. Never was a man more respected by the residents of Long Eaton, rich and poor alike.

Grandfather Edward's business at Hyson Green employed so many of the family that, Thomas being a good draughtsman, began to map out his own career unaided. He obtained a situation with a Mr Bush who had some lace machines in New Tythe Street, Long Eaton, and soon became manager of the plant. Not being satisfied with his prospects in this business, he decided to launch out on his own account, so gave notice to leave.

Mr Bush, recognising his worth to the business, told him he could have a machine or two in his factory and still act as manager for him. This he did with such outstanding success that, eventually, he bought out Mr Bush altogether. As uncle Tom's business grew, he built Fletcher's Factory near the railway, which some years after his death was burnt down.

His initiative and drive were tremendous. He commenced to finish his productions with the view of making Long Eaton a buyers' centre for lace. And what a tragedy it was when Uncle died so comparatively young. He had decided to give a party to commemorate his fiftieth birthday, to which every man, woman and child in the town was invited. Acre Close was to be made into a gala ground. Teas, various other refreshments, roundabouts, and sports were among the highlights to mark the half-century of a gentleman revered by all classes. But this was not to be. Fate dealt a generous soul a shabby trick. Thomas Fletcher attended a farm sale on one of the ducal estates and inhaled a putrid smell which developed into typhus fever and an early death. And so this great birthday gathering had to be cancelled."

Sam Truman, a historian of repute, made this deservedly eloquent tribute to Thomas Fletcher a few years ago in the local press, when he wrote about Old Landmarks of Long Eaton:

"Memories of Long Eaton recall that to the west o' the Green was a field known as Haycroft Close. A thorough-going native of Long

Eaton would pronounce it as 'Akad Cloose'. This latter pronunciation probably conforms more closely to the ancient rendering and meaning. It was a meadow and part of an adjoining farm across which, from a point near the Palace cinema, to another spot near the Scala cinema, ran a footpath connecting with Lovers' Walk and Dockholme. At either of the points mentioned, there was a rather ramshackle stile and through the gaps in the hedge that bounded The Close, Long Eaton youths and some of its seniors made their way. To reach the hedge, one strided across a foul ditch. The waters in it rose in the higher lands of Wilsthorpe. They were further fed from a spring in the Vicarage grounds, borne under the canal, and finally disappeared near Oxford Street.

The water was more than offensive and, as industrial and house property grew in the 'West End' of the town, an ever-increasing number of the local inhabitants took exception to its provocative influence.

But why all this about a ditch that many now alive never saw? Simply because, as a consequence of neglect, The Close fell into the builders' hands and on it three roadways were laid out—Regent Street, Oxford Street and Fletcher Street. The last-named is foremost in our minds now because it answers to the name of one of Long Eaton's most noteworthy sons—Mr Thomas Fletcher of North House, though I hasten to say that it was not to commemorate him that this thoroughfare was so named. Another branch of the Fletcher family owned the land and perhaps inscribed that designation to the street.

To speak of Tom Fletcher, as he was universally and affectionately called, I have to rely on the voracious testimony of those who knew him, worked with him, and were employed by him.

Impressionable youth takes in more than the seniors imagine and hero-worship, like measles, is the malady of youngsters.

Making every allowance for that, one is proud to remember that at home and at school, impressions were made that linger through these seventy-odd years, that when he was spoken of, esteem was heavily tinctured with affection. That is the public man's chief reward.

He died on August 5th, 1880, at the age of fifty years. I, though then but ten years old, do well remember the funeral in the churchyard.

99

We, of High Street Board School, were on holiday, and fittingly so, since I learned later that he was one of the most inspiring spirits in its creation.

Some impressions were made that day that all the years between have failed to efface. Our parents were there; the entire village seemed to have turned out; and the grief was genuine, the more to be noted that strong men sought to cloak it.

Tom Fletcher held the premier position as lace manufacturer in the district and was co-head of a very prosperous business.

His foresight was such that he turned to the finishing and dressing of his product and shrewd men have averred that if he had been spared, Long Eaton might well have become the centre of the English lace trade.

He brought to bear a rich personality on all movements that made for a prosperous, contented and progressive community.

I am not concerned to debate the question whether he was, or was not, born among us, or if, as some others, he chose Long Eaton for his enterprises.

Apart from a memorial stone in Mount Tabor Church and the simple inscription on his tombstone, Thomas Fletcher has no other public tribute that I can recall.

After all, we have our day and cease to be. Time is ruthless in its process of erasure of all traces of valiant spirits. Perhaps it is as well!

Few, maybe, who have followed what has been said will remember Thomas Fletcher personally. None will begrudge a tribute paid him by one who was reared by folk who spoke of him with an added something to respect, and deplored that he was called to cross the fateful river with Old Charon the Ferryman so early in life. Happy, however "to have reached it without the loss of half his faculties and half his friends". So spake two well-informed authorities of the fine qualities and sound character of Tom Fletcher, our kinsman!

In the short space of eighteen months, the Reaper not only destroyed the rock-like partnership between Joseph and Thomas, but in one fell swoop also severed an artery that fed life-blood to the social, cultural and industrial vitals of Long Eaton town.

This devastating blow immediately opened a gap in local family associations which was never effectively bridged, as only one son was, for a short period after his father's death, associated with the merchanting of lace in any respect.

Charles Edward, the eldest, and the one lone son who tried to keep Dad's industrial nameplate bright, had a very brief connection with the lace curtain trade at New Tythe Street Mills, Long Eaton, and died, without issue, before reaching the age of thirty. He lies at rest in the vault at Long Eaton Church, where all members of the family except his brother, George Arthur, are buried.

Both *Anne* and the *first Isabella* died in childhood, and *Thomas* passed on in his early 'teens.

Alice Eliza, the second daughter of Thomas and Isabella Fletcher, came to a very sad end. She married a tea broker named Doar, in the trade at Newcastle-on-Tyne, and died there in child-bed with her two children [twins]. They were all brought to Long Eaton for burial and were laid to rest in the churchyard. Many relatives, friends and other sympathizers were present to pay the last respects.

From time to time the name Doar appears in connection with local activities—golf is one of them! Where does it belong? Is the local bearer of the same root stock as the tea broker?

By all reliable accounts, *George Arthur*, the youngest son of Thomas Fletcher, had very little taste for the lace trade so, after his father died, preferred to live in comfortable privacy at Aslockton Hall, Nottinghamshire.

He married Kate Plackett, née Tabberer, widow, of Breaston, near Draycott, Derbyshire. She presented him with three sons—Lance George, Thomas Charles and John Tabberer—who all looked elsewhere than in lace for a means of livelihood.

When George Arthur died at Aslockton, his mother thought he ought to be buried in the family vault at Long Eaton with his father, sisters and brothers, but the widow could not consent. She laid her husband to rest in the General Cemetery where a wealth of old famous Nottingham names grace the stones.

Some of you may still be wondering what became of *George Arthur's* boys and their families.

Well, *Lance George*, the senior of the trio, has had a long, notable career on the stage, and during the second World War played a leading part amusing and entertaining His Majesty's Forces at home and overseas.

Extracts taken from a London letter dated March 23rd, 1946, are full of human feeling: 'I am married and have one daughter, Vera

Victoria, who is the wife of Robert Rowe, cashier at Coutt's Bank, Strand, London, W.C.2. They have one child, a daughter, Jean.

As my parents died when I was very young, I know very little about myself and can't even trace my birth certificate or find out where I was born. If you—or any other member—can furnish me with these details I shall be more than grateful. For these reasons alone I should very much like to have a copy of our Family Tree when it is issued. Yours sincerely, Lance George Fletcher.'

The Compiler has nothing more up-to-date to tell you—but what relevant information can *you* convey for Lance George and so help a 'twig' of the clan know and respect himself the more?

News of *Thomas Charles*, second son of George Arthur, is scanty to a degree. The sum total to say can be expressed in thirty-one words: 'He is married, has a son Nicholas by name, was in business in Derby at one time as a haulage and removal contractor, and in 1946 was a resident of Brighton'. Wherever he may be now, we hope happiness and comfort is his lot.

In sharp contrast to the little we know of Thomas Charles, much more can be said about the yougest of these three brothers, *John Tabberer Fletcher*, who can look back with excusable pride upon 'something attempted, something done' in the Navy, Army and Police Force of our country.

An important step towards making good use of life was taken when he married Dorothy Henderson, daughter of the Reverend Henderson, minister of Castle Gate Congregational Church, Nottingham, and begat a son, John David, and a daughter, Pamela Margaret Catherine. Incidentally, the Rev. Henderson was also the father of Roy Henderson, the noted Nottingham singer and chorister.

Captain John Tabberer Fletcher served with distinction overseas during the 1914-18 war and was awarded the Military Cross.

Something unusual happened to all the members of this small family when the second World War broke out.

'Father rejoined the Army and was posted to the Royal Navy as Lieut.-Commander, North Sea Patrol; mother and daughter both enlisted in a Women's Service unit; the son served in the Royal Air Force'.

They all answered duty's call but, sad to relate, *Flight-Lieutenant John David Fletcher* was killed in the air in 1944.

PLATE 13—FLETCHER GOLF AT CHEVIN, 1923

Standing (left to right): H. W. ASTLE-FLETCHER, J. L. LITCHFIELD, F. R. FLETCHER, J. E. FLETCHER (nephew), J. L. FLETCHER,
J. T. FLETCHER, T. FLETCHER

Seated: J. E. FLETCHER (uncle), Mrs. J. T. FLETCHER, F. W. C. FLETCHER, R. W. FLETCHER

In front: C. H. FLETCHER, P. M. FLETCHER (MRS. AYRE)

Photographer: J. W. S. FLETCHER

John Tabberer's career in the Nottingham Constabulary between both world wars, and after the second one, was equally meritorious.

It is rumoured that he was a village 'bobby' at Scarrington, near Aslockton, when he joined the Force, but whether this is true or not is of little consequence in itself. What is of account to record here is that when the time to retire was reached a few years ago he had become an Inspector, Headquarters Division, Nottingham City Police.

At one time he was known as 'Captain John Fletcher, the Nottingham Bird Man' and his comments in the local press about the feathered tribe were interesting features and were read over a wide area. Fanciers up and down the country recognise him as an authority on, and a first class judge of cage birds, which he has exhibited with marked personal success over the years at various shows.

He still lives in the Sherwood district of Nottingham, but the present whereabouts of Lance George and Thomas Charles and their families is, at present, still unknown.

Mary Isabella, the youngest of Thomas and Isabella Fletcher's seven children, married Dr. Dickson of Long Eaton. They had three daughters, namely, Alice Isabel, Violet, and Margaret Irene McEndoo, none of whom married. Violet died in early womanhood, but Alice and Margaret built themselves a bungalow at Toton where they lived together for many years.

They were fond of caravan holidays and toured much of the country in their own motor-drawn house-on-wheels till the outbreak of World War II put a stop to these delightful trips. Both girls then found work of national importance to do at Chilwell Royal Ordnance Depot between 1939 and 1945. Margaret's death severed this long sisterly partnership, so Alice is now the sole surviving representative of this section of Thomas Fletcher's branch of our family.

JAMES LITCHFIELD

Since the male line stemming from Thomas Fletcher has completely severed its connection with the lace trade, it devolved upon the late James Litchfield of Attenborough to represent this branch in the industry.

'Jimmy'—as he was affectionately hailed by many who knew him well—was a nephew through his father and Mrs. Thomas Fletcher,

103

who were brother and sister. He has supplied many valuable notes towards this story.

Let me, the Compiler, describe James Litchfield's long association with the manufacture of lace in his own words.

'In 1913, after leaving school-mastering, I joined the firm of W. M. and R. Cook who, with a plant of nine or ten machines, were then trading as lace manufacturers in a factory in Bennett Street, Long Eaton.

From that I drifted quietly—and, I think, successfully—into my present position at Beeston, having first made a start on my own in the Harrington Mills, Long Eaton'

Very modestly put; but you should also, I think, be made to realise that this almost apologetic mention by Mr Litchfield of part played, covers a great many years of unflagging activity and notable achievement by him in the best interests of the trade.

The proof that these interests have had wider than mere family associations can be found in his booklet *Lace: The Fabric of Romance and Nottingham* which he compiled for the 1924 British Empire Exhibition.

This widely-written work is a mine of information concerning the development and progress of Nottingham and its industries since the days of the cave-dwellers, to those more enlightened times which saw the founding of Nottingham School of Art, the Art Museum, and University College, where students had facilities to learn much more about craftsmanship, good taste, theory and practice.

Improvements in lace-making and the building of lace machines are a special feature, but the blazing acts of the Luddites in the 1830's and the growth in prosperity locally on coal, iron, cycles, engineering, hosiery, light clothing, wicker and basket, tobacco, fine chemicals, printing, and other staple trades are also dealt with in this work of art, which is tastefully illustrated.

Pride of place, as frontispiece, is given to 'The Old Lacemaker' industriously weaving the right threads between the appropriate pins, as she sits in the lamplight making pillowed lace.

Other interesting inclusions are a bijou copy of the famous painting, 'May Morning, Nottingham', by Arnesby Brown R.A.; views of the Textile Gallery and the collection of lace and early machinery housed there in the Art Museum, Nottingham Castle; diagrammatic designs of divers choice laces; a portrait of John

Heathcoat, a Derbyshire worthy, who invented the first bobbin-net machine in 1809, and similar relevant illustrations.

Historical works dealing with the lace trade are, unfortunately, both scarce and rare on the material side, so it is as great a privilege to claim the author of *Lace: the Fabric of Romance* as a member of our family circle, as it is to report that, at nigh four score years, he was still active at Beeston in business and in his home at Attenborough.

EDWARD FLETCHER

Edward was the fifth son and sixth child of Edward and Phoebe Fletcher, and was born at Heanor, July 24th, 1832. He moved with the family to Hyson Green and died there shortly afterwards on October 19th, 1850, and lies at rest with his parents in St. Paul's Churchyard.

PLATE 14

ADA JANE, LADY JARDINE

CHAPTER V

THE JAMES BRANCH

Compiled from notes supplied by Sir John Jardine, Bart.,
and Alfred G. Merryweather
Supplemented by extracts from the
'Fletcher Collection of Family Letters'

JAMES, the sixth son of Edward and Phoebe Fletcher, first saw the light of day at Heanor, Derbyshire, March 31st, 1834, and died at Radnor House, Arboretum Street, Nottingham, September 12th, 1910, in his seventy-seventh year.

Much of his 'teens, and most of his early manhood, were spent in the factory at Hyson Green learning the arts of lace-making under the watchful eye of his father, before the establishment of a business, and marriage, launched him into the seas of life on his own account.

James had two spouses. His first, Eliza Eley, was a sister of Mary, who married his younger brother Robert Fletcher.

Eliza Fletcher bore ten children. Three—William, Hiram and Mary—born September 17th, 1869, were triplets, and they all died within half-an-hour, an hour, and one hour-and-a-half of their birth respectively. After bearing one more child, Blanche Lucilla, she departed hence at the early age of forty-one, December 12th, 1874, and lies at rest in the Rock Cemetery, Nottingham, with her husband, James, and her eldest son, Henry Edward, her daughter, Florence Lavinia Sheldon, and the triplets.

James' second helpmate was Harriet Ann Batters, a lady of culture and refinement. She presented him with one further addition, a daughter, Annie Clarissa who, through the unrivalled knowledge of Fletchers of bygone days was, upwards of sixty years later, a rock and stay and a mine of valuable information when our ancestral grave in St Paul's Churchyard was restored, the Family Tree was compiled, and this story came to be written.

May I, 'S.B.F.', the principal concerned with these efforts, be allowed to pay this tribute to her memory.

An old Nottingham reference book records that James Fletcher entered the trade as a lace agent and manufacturer in 1860, and that his machine holdings were situated in Outgang Lane, New Radford, a district then almost rural in character. The same authority lists 6, Shakespeare Villas, Shakespeare Street, Nottingham [1860-71] as the first home of James and Eliza Fletcher, and all their children except Blanche Lucilla, were born there.

Subsequent residences were 64. Bilbie Street [1872-75], where Blanche Lucilla was born and her mother died; 19 Larkdale Street [1876-84]; and Radnor House [1885-1910], into which he moved with his second wife and family to end his days.

James Fletcher possessed many of the fine qualities found in a shrewd business man of high character. He believed in laying good foundations for future building of all kinds, and, almost above everything else, he believed that keeping one's pledged word, for good or ill, was a sacred obligation.

The first outward signs of his early mounting prosperity did not become visible until 1869 when, needing much more space to house additional machines, he moved his holdings from Outgang Lane into Whitehall's Factory, Wollaton Street, where they remained ten years, and obtained warehouse accommodation in Nottingham Lace Market on High Pavement for the next seventeen years of merchanting.

By this dual arrangement, he combined 'the arts of making with the skills of salesmanship' to greater advantage in trade and reputation.

These were 'the days of grace in lace'. Figuratively speaking, the amount needed by the dressmaker to trim a damsel's ballroom frock would have completely ringed the dance floor confines she and her cavalier cavorted upon.

They were also the days when the thriftless masters and men smoked big cigars as they drove to work in hansoms if they felt like it, or—if they felt more like it—to the races on the Nottingham Forest, where they were often 'out of pocket both ways'.

James Fletcher preferred to invest his capital and profits in something tangible so, in 1879, his entire machine plant was transferred from Nottingham to Long Eaton where, in Fletcher's Factory [1879-1888], Peel Street, he concentrated all lace-making production. This policy still obtained when his holdings were removed to Orchard's

Mills [1889-1902], Bank Street, just before Fletcher's Factory was destroyed by fire.

In course of time, changes in warehousing were necessary so, as an integral part of the overall plan of improvement, 24½ and 26 Stoney Street [1887-91]; 2 Broadway [1892-99] and Riste's Place, Barker Gate [1900-02] became, in succession, the firms seat of trade in Nottingham Lace Market.

The lace trade was at the peak of prosperity in this district during most of the latter half of the nineteenth century, so great skill and craftsmanship, hard work, and non-stop production of the right materials combined to cope with the ever-rising flood of orders that reached James Fletcher & Co. from the home and overseas markets.

Ladies of almost all ages and races loved lacey lingerie and other garments made from these dainty fabrics, which were the flair of the fairer sex and the snare of the men.

Nearly every housewife contrived to display the finest lace curtains at her front room windows, and delicate veilings were always to be seen on special occasions such as weddings and christenings.

Attractive lace mob caps were the indoor headgear of our grandmothers and other elderly womenfolk upwards of fifty years ago, but the vogue was relatively short-lived. They made the really old look older still and the younger ones old-fashioned before their time, so out of production went the mob cap for ever. The end of the century and dawn of the twentieth slump was about to begin its fell work.

Slowly, but inexorably, Nottingham lace curtains disappeared from almost every window in the land, and dresses, gowns and underwear made entirely of, or heavily trimmed with lace, ceased to be worn overnight when length line for ladies' attire was first shortened after the Boer War. This new style hit lace hard.

Then James Fletcher was called to his Maker and, in the twinkling of an eye the scene was changed and the stage set for his children to add their achievements to those of their father.

Henry Edward, his eldest child, died October 17th, 1875, aged fifteen years, so had little chance to add to these laurels.

However, when Ada Jane married Ernest, son of John and Julia Jardine, a link with this notable family of lace machine builders was forged.

John Jardine Ltd., known the world over for the excellent quality of its constructions has, for upwards of a century, been directed either by the father or the son, who did not retire till they died, or by the grandson of that name, who is still serving on the board of directors.

All types of lace machines, including Levers, Go-through, Rolling Locker, Double Locker, Curtain, Machlin, Veiling and Warp machines, with all the necessary accessory machinery, have been built and delivered to firms in England, Scotland, Austria, Brazil, Canada, Chili, Denmark, Egypt, Finland, France, Germany, Holland, India, Israel, Italy, Japan, Mexico, Portugal, Spain, Sweden, Switzerland and United States of America over the years.

A goodly number of most patterns were supplied to Edward Fletcher's eight sons who, one by one, became manufacturers in the trade and installed machines in their factories.

This is how the local press described one such *'believed to be misadventure'* in Derby over fifty years ago.

ENTERPRISE IN ACTION

"The story of the forty-seven lace-making machines at the works of William Fletcher & Sons [Derby] Ltd., of Nottingham Road, is one of outstanding enterprise in face of predictions of disaster.

In 1900, when eleven of the first twenty-four machines ordered by the late Mr William Fletcher were installed by John Jardine Ltd., Nottingham, Jardine's Lace Machinery Register records: 'Mr Fletcher took a bold and what was considered by many people, a perilous step when he ordered the machines'.

PROPHETS PROVED WRONG

It was said 'that the machines were too wide; that he would not get men to work them; that the goods could not be dressed that width; that production would be extremely small—and that the lace would be bad'.

But in spite of the prophets, the company's 47-strong plant of 224-inch wide lace machines, the biggest in the country, is today playing an important part in enabling the firm to keep pace with the post-war [1939-45] revival in the lace industry.

This revolutionary departure in lace production was a triumph for the makers—*but what of the builders*, three of them, whose almost human machines turned possible success into reality.

Coming events began casting shadows before them when, 'on the eighteenth day of June, in the year of our Lord One thousand eight hundred and thirty-nine, Thomas Jardine of the town of Nottingham, jeweller, did apprentice John, his son [aged fourteen years] to Charles Lees of the said town of Nottingham, clock and watch maker, to learn his art and with him after the manner of an apprentice to serve from the date hereof until the full end and term of seven years . . ."

The original indenture, signed and sealed in the presence of the three contracting parties, gave witness to divers undertakings between them. What emerges today, however, is the main reason why Jardine constructions have always operated with precision.

The art and craftsmanship built into the most delicate of intricate machines, has bubbled in their blood for at least four generations.

JOHN JARDINE THE ELDER [1825-95]

When Kate O'Brien, an Irish lady, believed to hail from Dublin, married Thomas Jardine, she endowed their descendants with a lively outlook on life which, allied to healthy enterprise, transformed seeming over-venturesome risks into outstanding industrial successes with uncanny regularity.

. Therefore, when the end of forty years' strenuous endeavour was reached, it was no surprise to find that their son John had laid the main foundations on which John Jardine Ltd., with factories at Chelsea Street, Deering Street, Arnold Road, Basford and in Calais, still stands today.

Exactly how long John Jardine remained interested in the art of watch and clock making after completing his apprenticeship mid-way through 1846 is not clear. By 1855, however, and probably earlier still, we do know that he and his first partner, Stephen Bates, were building lace machines at their factory in Grant Street, New Radford, and also, that he had married Julia Foster.

Their first home was in the precincts of The Park, an oasis-like retreat in the very centre of Nottingham industry, that has housed three generations of this family almost continuously.

John Jardine parted company with Stephen Bates about 1872 when, needing more space, he acquired a factory in Raleigh Street where an engineer named Hooton became his partner.

111

Incidentally, a few years later—1879 to be exact—his son Ernest, with a Mr Ball as partner, established a cycle works in Raleigh Street also, but output ceased there in the early 'eighties.

The partnership with Mr. Hooton did not endure. Both men were distinctly individualistic so, very wisely, they went their own way. Today, over seventy years later, John Jardine Ltd. and William Hooton Ltd., Great Eastern Street, Nottingham, are both prominent rivals, but friendly competitors, in the engineering world.

ERNEST JARDINE [1861-1947]

When Ernest, son of John and Julia Jardine, was born at Nottingham in 1861, a sound education, with a knowledge of languages, was recognised as a prime necessity by thoughtful industrialists of the day.

The advantages of such a course were plain to John Jardine so, stage by stage, his son's education began, continued and was complated at Mr Gregory Porter's Preparatory School, Balmoral Road; the Nottingham High School; and the Lycee Imperiale, St. Omer.

Attainments garnered from these seats of learning, reinforced by ten years [1884-94] practical managerial experience, were valuable assets when, in his early 'thirties, he assumed control of John Jardine Ltd. in 1894 in the stead of his father.

The many responsibilities that ensued were courageously borne for over fifty years and, in the bearing, he served his fellows faithfully. These services were many and varied.

Parliamentary Service

As Mr. Ernest Jardine, he sat as Liberal-Unionist Member for East Somerset 1910-18.

Glastonbury Abbey

One of his most generous actions was to buy this ancient abbey and subsequently hand it over to the Church of England.

Created Baronet

In 1919 he was created a Baronet. The act of bestowal must have been almost the proudest moment of his life when his public services and philanthropy were so recognised.

Other Distinctions

Honours and distinctions, well and truly deserved, included

112

PLATE 15

Above: EXPORT. 60 tons of Go-through Lace Machines: one week's production 50 years ago

Below: PRODUCTION. The heart of production of the Go-through Lace Machine to-day

Chevalier of the Legion of Honour; High Sheriff of Nottinghamshire 1929-30; and Justice of the Peace for the City of Nottingham.

Nottingham Forest Football Club

As a young man, Ernest Jardine was one of the earliest members of the Forest, played for them as an amateur, and was president of the club for over thirty years. He loved sport and encouraged it generously where it was most needed.

The Champion of Industrial Freedom

Good taste and modesty preclude any further mention of the distinguished services he rendered during a long, busy life.

Nevertheless, if tribute to his championship of the private employer's right to be 'master in his own house—of business, was not paid, this story would be manifestly incomplete.

Agitators never worked their will in his factories, and wickedly hard accusations were levelled against his good name. When Sir Ernest died, however, some of his most bitter critics have lived long enough to realise that the greatest, and the last, fighter for the cause of honest private enterprise has passed from our midst and left much lesser men bewildered on what, nowadays, *is* a field of battle.

JOHN JARDINE THE YOUNGER [1884——]

John, the eldest child of Ernest and Ada Jane Jardine, was born in Nottingham on October 3rd, 1884.

After a preparatory course at the Grosvenor School, Nottingham, he went to France [Tours and Paris] and Germany [Frankfurt and Heidelburg] to be educated.

He joined the firm in the early 1900's and was managing director for a period of nearly thirty years before taking over full control when his father died in April 1947.

During his tenure of office, the engineering industry's resources were twice geared to meet the demands of world war, and reorganised to supply the needs of peace—a weighty burden that John the Younger bore successfully in the best family traditions.

Much of his leisure has been absorbed in serving and giving pleasure to others, so it will not be out of place to mention some of his many interests here.

Helping those who help themselves

Thrift, whereby men and women insure their future obligations, prepare for a rainy day, or just save to make the most of a golden opportunity to improve their standard of life, has always had his wholehearted support.

Many years of service on the Board of Governors culminated in Sir John being appointed Honorary President of Nottingham Trustee Savings Bank. He also has an interest in the Royal Insurance Company, of which he is the local chairman.

Other Honorary Appointments held in the interests of local public service include:

   Served as High Sheriff of Nottinghamshire, 1932-33.

   Appointed Justice of the Peace for the City of Nottingham, 1928.
   President of the Lace Machine Builders' Association.

   President of the Nottingham and District Property Owners' Association.

His Military Career.

During the peaceful days that followed the South African War, young John Jardine, like many of his generation, prepared himself to serve in war with the Robin Hood Rifles and the North Somerset Yeomanry.

When the Kaiser threw down the gage of battle and started the *First World War in* 1914-18, he served as Adjutant, 2/1st South Notts. Hussars; O.C. [Captain] 2/1st Notts. and Derby Mounted Brigade Signal Troop; O.C. [Major] 1st Mounted Division Signal Squadron; O.C. [Lieut.-Colonel] G.H.Q. Signal Company, British Salonica Force and Army of the Black Sea; and was awarded the British War Medal 1914-18, the Victory Medal, and the Territorial Force War Medal for services rendered in that campaign.

The Second World War, 1939-45

In this upheaval, John Jardine the Younger, as Honorary Deputy Commissioner of the Middle East Commission of the British Red Cross and the St. John War Organisation, was responsible for providing equipment such as mobile X-ray units, ambulances, travelling cinemas and all kinds of hospital stores and amenities to all medical units in the Middle East Command. This included Egypt, Lybia, the Soudan, Eritrea, Palestine, Syria, the Lebanon, Cyprus, Malta and Aden. Supplies were also sent to Greek and French colonial units.

'For services rendered in this theatre of hostilities he was awarded the 1939-45 Star, the African Star, the Defence Medal, and decorated with the Order of the British Empire [Officer], the Order of St. John of Jerusalem [Commander], and the Order of the Redeemer [Greek].

JOHN JARDINE LTD.—ITS FUTURE STATUS

As a rule, each succeeding generation strives to leave the family business in a sound condition for the one to follow. Sir John has made these high endeavours but, having no son to inherit, and wishing to ensure a safe income for his two sisters, recently sold the group of Jardine family businesses to Hardwick Industries Ltd. Heavy death duties might have made it difficult to adequately continue as a family business operation.

Sir John retired from *active* business in 1951, but at the request of Hardwick Industries Ltd. still remains a director in an advisory capacity. May he enjoy to the full the greater leisure he so richly deserves.

Outwardly, this family business will continue in name, but when Sir John finally retires, perhaps to his cottage, Oaker End, near Matlock, to enjoy the delights of Derbyshire, all connections between the James Fletcher Branch and the lace industry, both in the direct male line, and indirectly through the female side, will be severed.

Edna Winifred, elder daughter of Ernest and Ada Jane Jardine, married twice, first to Augustus Fortington, O.B.E., and secondly, to Harold Cutler Whitman, an American. She resides, in turn, at Bedford Honour, Bedford Village, New York, U.S.A., and Longbird Cove, Tuckerstown, Bermuda.

Mrs Whitman is a Member of the British Empire, and has one daughter by her first marriage, the Hon. Mrs Nadia Kinnaird, who lives in south-west London.

Iris Gwendoline, their younger daughter, married John O'Connell. She has three children—John, Patricia and Jean, of whom both girls are married.

Her elder daughter, *Patricia*, married a cousin who served in the R.A.F. and was killed during the second World War.

She has one son, Nicholas, and they both live with Mrs O'Connell whose home is The Dogs, Wincanton, Somerset—that lovely part of England where some of the best cider can be enjoyed.

115

Jean, the sister of Patricia, married Colin Thompson, Assistant Curator of the Scottish National Gallery. They have one child, a daughter, Jane, and their home address is Anne Street, Edinburgh.

With one or two exceptions, there is not much of account to record of James Fletcher's other immediate descendants.

Allen Gething, the second son, managed his father's plant of lace machines in Orchard's Factory, Long Eaton, and manufactured there on his own account till he died suddenly—and tragically.

A complete sportsman, he made Attenborough, his abiding place, famous for its village cricket.

It was a day of days when the locals, reinforced by Uncle George Fletcher and his son Allen of Long Eaton, faced Notts. Castle, complete with Jimmy Iremonger of Nottinghamshire and England fame, on the green opposite the old village inn.

Jimmy, boon companion of Allen, jokingly promised to knock him out of the ground but failed to do so. Allen spreadeagled Jim's wicket but not until he had hit the bowling to all parts of the field and notched well over a hundred runs.

Allen Gething's marriage to Zillah, his cousin and youngest daughter of Joseph Fletcher, began in colourful romance and ended in painful tragedy. Their home, Grove Cottage, standing on the corner of the lane near Attenborough Church, was blessed with five children. Three of them—Allen, Zillah and Claude—have survived their parents. Sad to relate, father and a friend were instantly killed by a passing train one night whilst walking on the line from Beeston.

Allen, the eldest of the quintette, is married and has one son, Jack, and a daughter, Sally, but no other news of his family is available.

Zillah, the elder daughter—now Mrs Scotson—says that her late husband had patents in many parts of the world. They travelled extensively and visited many notable places of interest in lands across the seas, including Australia, New Zealand, India, China, Japan, and most of Europe. She is now back on Trentside at Oldbell, The Strand, but a stone-throw from the home of her childhood. She has no children.

Claude, the second son, has lived in Attenborough for many years and made the well-kept garden which surrounds Grove Cottage an ever-recurring delight to the eye of the passer-by. We cannot tell you whether he is married or still living in single blessedness.

116

Dorothy Gething, the younger daughter, and *Eric Joseph*, the fifth child, both died young, and were buried in Attenborough Churchyard, where their mother and father were also laid to rest.

Florence Lavinia, James Fletcher's second daughter, married Joseph Sheldon, proprietor of a general merchant's store at Heanor. He retired somewhat early and removed to Burton Joyce where the family settled and became well known.

Two sons, namely, *Briddon Fletcher*, who subsequently spent some time in Canada before returning to England, and *Gilbert Edward*, of whom little is known by the writer, were born to them.

Their mother died in 1899 at the age of thirty-five and is buried in the family grave which lies in the Forest Road side of the Church Cemetery, Nottingham.

Her two sons received much of their education from a Mrs Cullen in the village school, and some years later, the younger one, so I am told, died at sea of a tropical disease. Whether he was a naval man, or just an emigrant sailing to a distant land, is one of those family near-mysteries I am unable to unveil.

Briddon Fletcher Sheldon, the elder boy, always liked the open air and sunshine, and spent a number of years abroad trying 'to make hay' in that direction out of farming.

Briddon married twice and was left with three children from each union [five girls and one boy] to mother and father as best a man can until his elder daughters were old enough to lend a hand, in turn, as each older one married. All three elder girls are now married, and the eldest, *Dorothea Mary*, has raised him to the status of grandfather twice at least, and further additions to the Tree may have occurred since.

Shortly after the last World War, I got to know and met Briddon on Trent Bridge cricket ground, Nottingham, and how this came about could best be told by his sister-in-law, Mrs N. E. Kirk, or her husband, of Trent Lodge, Annesley Park, Nottinghamshire. Their story would convince you that truth *is* stranger than fiction. At that time Briddon was, and still probably is, doing well on Norman Farm, Wyverstone, Stowmarket, Suffolk.

Beatrice Eliza, James' third daughter, was born June 3rd, 1866, and in the spring of 1896 married Thomas Haddon, a merchant on the Manchester Corn Exchange, who then lived at Heaton Mersey.

Beatrice met Thomas whilst staying with the Goodall family at Walsall. They had one child, Roy, who was educated at St Cuthbert's, Worksop, one of the noted Woodard Schools, where other members of our family had their education in later years.

In the late 1920's he left England and settled in New Zealand where, as late as Christmas 1944 he was living at 198 Forbury Road, St Clair, Dunedin.

Cecily Hartshorne, the fourth daughter, died unmarried and, as previously mentioned, William, Hiram and Mary all died on the day they were born.

Blanche Lucilla, the tenth and youngest child of James' first marriage, married Christopher Goodall, a wholesale coal merchant, who had strong family connections with Walsall, and lived at Solihull, near his Birmingham office.

Their only child, *Pilot-Officer Alan Fletcher Goodall,* R.A.F. was killed in France during the second World War, and a widow, a daughter, Maralayne, and a son, Peter, were left to mourn his passing.

Blanche resided in Torquay for several years and died there towards the end of 1950; but where her grandchildren, who lived with her, now are I am unable to say.

JAMES FLETCHER'S SECOND MARRIAGE

Annie Clarissa, the only child of this union, married Alfred George Merryweather, whose father and grandfather, both named Henry Merryweather, founded H. Merryweather & Sons Ltd., nurserymen and specialists in roses, fruit trees and shrubs, in Southwell, just over a century ago.

These pioneers made their names a household word when they succeeded in developing and marketing the Bramley Seedling apple, and this—in the words of Alfred Merryweather, the present head of the firm, a Justice of the Peace and member of Southwell Parish Council for many years—is how it all happened.

"Briefly, it was raised from a pip sown by Mrs Bralesford and her daughter in the early years of the nineteenth century, and the tree, which still exists, grew in a garden eventually owned by Matthew Bramley. A few trees were grafted from it, but not till the late

118

PLATE 16
ALFRED AND CLARISSA MERRYWEATHER

'fifties or the early 'sixties did my father first learn of them. He soon realised that there was not an apple of its type in commerce nearly as good, so decided to try to put it on the market and give it a name.

He asked Matthew Bramley if he minded and he said he did not— but it must be called by his name; so though he is dead and forgotten these seventy years, his name lives on."

Eventually, Henry Merryweather junior sent sixteen apples weighing sixteen pounds to the Fruit Committee at Chiswick, and the fruit received a fine certificate of merit. So was the Bramley Seedling, previously but a local wonder at Easthorpe, introduced to fruit lovers and growers of the world.

Should you ever look in at Brinkley Nurseries—120 acres of them —you will find Alfred Merryweather and his two sons grappling with an ever-growing problem—'satisfying the needs of customers who cherish Bramley Seedlings, Merryweather damsons and lovely roses—and like to grow their own.'

THE FIRM AND ITS FUTURE—ANOTHER CENTURY HENCE

At the close of one century of activity one is tempted to speculate a little about ownership in the years that lie ahead.

Luckily, *Henry James*, the elder son, a continental trained nurseryman and ornamental landscape gardener, not only has five children, but three grandchildren also, whilst the younger one, *John Fletcher*, has five olive branches to his credit.

Since five of these Merryweather 'twigs' are of the male kind, the question of possession should present no difficulties for some generations to come.

Father and son both saw military service. In the 1914-18 War, Corporal Alfred Merryweather, Royal Garrison Artillery, was wounded near Ypres, after which he did duty on the Rock of Gibraltar. His son, *Sergeant John Fletcher Merryweather*, H.A.A. Regiment, Royal Artillery, had six years' service [1939-45] and fought in North Africa, Normandy, Holland and Germany. His unit, 284 Battery, 'D' Troop, 90th H.A.A. Regiment R.A., B.L.A., was part of the Allied Forces spearhead to enter Belsen Concentration Camp, where the conditions under which very many thousands of prisoners had *existed* and *died* were so wickedly horrible. John sent a description of the awful sights, as he and his comrades saw them, home to his parents. Copies of this letter, entitled 'To any who may wish to learn of the Germans', were sent to members of our family and my copy is before me as I write.

The cruelties inflicted, which included slow death by torture and other similar satanic devices, are unfit to retail here, but those who doubt their authenticity may call at my home and read, mark and learn about their devilry for themselves.

RELATING TO A COAT OF ARMS

Some time ago, a cousin of Alfred, secured the grant of a Merryweather coat of arms from the College of Heralds and sent reproductions to members of that family.

Alfred very much doubts the right to entitlement and says "The most suitable decoration to be borne on *his* family shield would be an apple with a rose stuck in it."

Other family names it would be fitting to mention here are *Wood*, so prominently associated with several main branches, including my own and that of Merrywether [minus the *a*] of Lincoln which, for upwards of a century has been noted for the manufacture of fire engines and other fire-fighting appliances.

Limitations of space and other claims forbid, so I will conclude this section by referring to *a Guiding Honour* accorded the third daughter of Henry James Merryweather, reported in the *Nottingham Evening Post* issue of June 1st, 1953. This should interest the very young ladies of our family.

"*Karen Merryweather*, of the 1st Southwell Girl Guides, has been given the 'Queen's Guide' award, the highest honour that can be bestowed upon a member of the movement.

The first recipient in the Southwell Division, she was invested with it by Lady Starkey, County Commissioner for Nottinghamshire. Karen also had the further honour of representing the Division at our Queen's Coronation."

Elizabeth Fletcher Number Two.—This, the eighth child of Edward and Phoebe Fletcher, born at Heanor November 12th, 1835, had no longer span of life than her elder sister, as she also died in infancy on December 6th, 1836, and was buried at Heanor.

PLATE 17
HENRY AND CATHERINE FARNSWORTH

CHAPTER VI

THE CATHERINE-HENRY FARNSWORTH BRANCH
Compiled by 'S.B.F.' from the 'Fletcher Family Letters'

CATHERINE, the second daughter and ninth child of Edward and Phoebe Fletcher, was born at Heanor, May 4th, 1837, and on July 19th, 1858, she celebrated her majority year by marrying Henry Farnsworth, the son of a Codnor baker.

For many years they lived at 248 Alfreton Road, Nottingham, near the Board School, where they brought up a family of eight sons and three daughters of whom only one daughter, Kate, and two sons, Arthur, and Frank the youngest and the only one to have issue, outlived their parents.

They, Henry and Catherine, passed away January 9th, 1915 and April 12th, 1921 respectively so, when Grace Elizabeth, only child of Frank, died March 5th, 1945, and her father went to his rest a few years later, there was nobody left of this branch to contribute to our family story.

Therefore, my task is a near impossible one—'that of making bricks with very little straw'—but, nevertheless, I will try to add a few Farnsworth ones to the Fletcher edifice we storytellers are building.

My earliest recollections of aunt Kate, as my mother called her, belong to my schooldays, when I was unaware that my grandfather Samuel Fletcher was her brother—which fact I learned nearly half a lifetime later.

She was a kindly old lady and had the habit of waylaying me as I dashed round the corner of Caulton Street eager for half-an-hour in the school playground before the afternoon session began. Her *modus operandi* always followed the same plan as, after asking how mother was, the real reason for intercepting me was voiced—it was "What have you had for your dinner, my lad?" Details given, a tuck-in was enjoyed and off I ran to school with little time left to play but feeling a lot better inside.

Aunt Kate, who was equally motherly to my sisters and brothers, was a martyr to asthma and when she was laid to rest, 'Better reign

121

in grateful hearts than over nations' would have been a fitting epitaph to inscribe upon her tombstone.

Henry Farnsworth, aunt Kate's partner in life, was born February 20th, 1838, and those who knew him well describe him as a tall, quiet, dark-complexioned gentleman of a studious nature and having religious leanings. For some years he was a clerk in the warehouse of Fletcher Bros. [Joseph and Thomas] and his son Frank often described to me in detail some of the healthy balance sheets his father helped to prepare.

On the occasion of one of my delves into Heanor Parish Church registers some eight years ago, the wife of the verger [Mr Farnsworth] said that enquiries about the Codnor and Loscoe Farnsworths had reached them from the archivist connected with the L.D.S. Temple, Salt Lake City, Utah, whose Genealogical Library is one of the finest in the world.

Some months later, two missioners from the Temple called at my house. By the time Elder and Mrs Albert C. Walker had left, I had learned that his backroots were in Bingham and that Mrs Walker's family, the Sheppersons of Radford, built much of Derby Road, Nottingham, including the street bearing their name.

So does the unexpected frequently stem from believed-to-be relationships and connections—they are the surprises that spur the searcher on.

Both Henry and Catherine Farnsworth lived to a ripe old age, but the next generation, with two or three exceptions, all died in their youth or early middle life.

Frederick William, their eldest child, was born July 7th, 1859, and died July 16th, 1864, and according to his brother Frank, was buried with his grandparents, Edward and Phoebe Fletcher at Hyson Green; but there is no record of this on the tombstone of our ancestors in St Paul's Churchyard.

John, the second in seniority, was born April 19th, 1861, and died December 11th, 1908, in his forty-eighth year.

Joseph, the third son, born March 23rd, 1863, died in infancy, May 20th, 1863.

Edward George, another son, born March 12th, 1864, passed away December 14th, 1886, nearly two years after attaining his majority.

122

Phoebe Ann, named so in compliment to her Grandma Fletcher, born January 10th, 1866, enjoyed life till her middle teens when the spell was broken and she was laid to rest September 28th, 1881.

Samuel Fletcher. Opposite the name of this son there is the simple record, 'Born January 27th, 1868' followed by three tragic words, 'Lost at sea'—but when, where or in what circumstances I am unable to tell you.

Thomas Purcell. The latter part of his christian name has a distinctly musical flavour, but whether this son favoured the art in any way is another of those hidden mysteries which now cannot be uncovered.

Thomas Purcell was the twin brother of Samuel Fletcher, and passed hence towards the end of his forty-first year, November 26th, 1908.

Arthur, the eighth of these eleven children was, by all accounts, the only member of the Farnsworth family to have any practical connection with the lace trade in which he was a draughtsman. Before and during the earlier 1890's Arthur worked for his cousin, Samuel Fletcher of Attenborough in Long Eaton and, in his service, also taught younger workers the art of lace draughting. The archives record his birth date as January 28th, 1870, and that he lived with his parents and sister Kate at 248 Alfreton Road for much of his life; but whether he died there on November 24th, 1945, venerable in years, is not stated.

Kate, the second of the three daughters, was born February 24th, 1872, and, as did her mother, fought a good fight against asthma which, along with its near kin, bronchitis, has been the scourge of nearly all the main branches of our Fletcher family. Gentle in nature, she never married, and died on Empire Day, May 24th, 1938.

Grace. There is not even a wisp of straw with which to make a single brick to lay on behalf of this little girl who, born August 24th, 1874, died at the tender age of seven, September 29th, 1881. Seven has ever been the writer's lucky number, but brought little good fortune to this wee lass.

Frank, the youngest of them all, a retiring, conscientious type of man was, I believe, the only Farnsworth of that group to marry and have issue—one daughter, Grace Elizabeth, who pre-deceased him. Her date of birth was February 21st, 1912, and, as girls always will, became in due course engaged to be married and made preparations for the happy day. Sad to relate, a lingering illness made marriage out of the question so, when she ceased to suffer at the early age of thirty-three, there were two silent witnesses to blighted hopes—her self-made bridal dress and treasured bottom drawer.

Frank, the father of this luckless maid, was born February 21st, 1877, and married Minnie Tollinton, who departed this life August 27th, 1942. For many years he worked for himself as a joiner, cabinet-maker and undertaker at various addresses, the last being 173 Stanley Road, near the present High Pavement Grammar School.

Among the many funerals he directed were several family members including those of my father and mother.

As the years passed by, cousin Frank felt very lonely so, very wisely, he returned to the bench and worked at his trade in a Nottingham government factory till he entered the City Hospital to die there about seven years ago.

OTHER FARNSWORTH ITEMS

When combing old Nottingham Directories, the names of Mrs Kate Farnsworth, of Burton & Farnsworth, fancy drapers [1913-36], 233 Radford Road and Joseph Farnsworth, warehouseman [1914-28] caught my eye. Are they in any way related to the principal subjects of this chapter? Perhaps *you* can tell me!

124

PLATE 18

THE DRAYCOTT FLETCHERS

Family of ROBERT and MARY FLETCHER. née ELEY

CHAPTER VII

THE ROBERT BRANCH

Based upon notes contributed by the late Hiram Fletcher,
Mabel Elsie Taylor, the Draycott Fletchers, Fred Fletcher,
and other members of this branch

ROBERT FLETCHER, the tenth child and seventh son of Edward and Phoebe, was born at Heanor on March 30th, 1839, and died at Long Eaton on August 4th, 1894.

He was already an established lace manufacturer at Hyson Green, Radford, when, in his twenty-first year, he married Mary, the daughter of Henry Eley, at the Wesleyan Chapel, Heanor, on July 21st, 1859. This union was blessed with three sons, who all grew up into the lace trade, and three daughters, born in the following order: Jane Phoebe, Robert William, Edward Henry, Mary Ann, Betsy Lavinia and Hiram Richard.

Robert Fletcher had no desire to travel afar or to be closely associated with any form of politics or local government. Rather was he attracted to, and fascinated by, the diverse creations produced from his machines in West End Mill, Long Eaton, where he and his sons manufactured lace till the beginning of the present century, and the comforting delights of The Elms, which were more in keeping with his homely tastes. There, in his hothouses, he found quiet relaxation and food for mind and body, growing grapes, figs, tomatoes, and other delicate dessert fruits.

On Christmas mornings he invariably invited the local Salvation Army band into The Elms to play selections on the lawn, and afterwards regaled its members with mince pies and pork pie—and beer for those musicians who preferred that form of cheer. The band always led off with 'Christians awake', which cousin Elsie thought was lovely.

Robert Fletcher died at The Elms, intestate, whereupon Robert William, his eldest son, refused to take any personal advantage from this situation and immediately made all his brothers and sisters equally secure with himself in their father's estate—an epitaph to character indeed!

We, who are the descendants of Robert Fletcher, find pleasure in the knowledge that our old home is again in kindred hands and that a young surgeon-dentist and his family belonging to a junior main branch of our large clan are now there, in residence, at The Elms.

My mother, *Jane Phoebe Fletcher*, ventured into matrimony early in life and was left a widow with one young daughter—myself—to nurture at the age of thirty. She married Samuel Henry Smith, the son of Henry [and Hannah] Smith, mine host at and owner of The Old Cross Inn which stood in the Market Place, Long Eaton. They made their first home in Lime Grove nearby.

Father was in lace, mostly as a manufacturer, apart from one month's work only at the Westminster Bank which provided the wherewithal to buy a brooch for his mother, now one of my treasured possessions.

He was very fond of cricket, dogs, game shooting and similar sports, but his early death limited the pleasure and thrills gained therefrom, though on one memorable occasion burglars broke in and stole all his guns.

After father died, mother remained in Long Eaton until 1920 and then moved to 111 Musters Road, West Bridgford, where she resided until her death.

Mother was cast in similar mould to the cowboy of story-book fame. As he did, she was always ready to try everything at least once. She loved sport, was keenly interested in politics, and for a time was chairman of the Long Eaton Women's Conservative Association. Her many other, varied recreations and pursuits included ice and roller skating, cycling, swimming, croquet, and bridge, in all of which she was adept.

It is quite true to say that mother did indeed enjoy her life to the full until she passed away in 1934 in her seventy-third year.

I, *Mabel Elsie*, the only child of Samuel Henry and Jane Phoebe Smith, have little in the way of professional experiences to look back upon, but since coming to live in West Bridgford in 1919 I have been very interested in the British Red Cross and to this day am still acting as honorary chauffeuse for this well-known society.

126

During the 1939-45 World War I also drove for the Hospital Car Service; assisted in occupational therapy at the hospitals, and served as chairman of the street groups of the National Savings movement. In June 1945 I [and many others] received an invitation from the Lord Chamberlain to attend the Royal Garden Party which His Majesty gave at Buckingham Palace to mark his approval of work done in the cause of national thrift.

Since then I have been a member of the Musters Ward Conservative Committee, and three years ago they elected me life honorary vice-president for services rendered.

During the year 1954-55 I also acted as Chairman's Lady to Mrs Cora James, Chairman of West Bridgford Urban District Council for her year of office. It was a wonderful experience and I enjoyed every minute of it and all the duties it entailed.

May I now tell you a little about my helpmate and partner. I married Joseph Whalley Taylor, the son of Joseph Whalley Taylor of Hull, a sea-captain in the passenger service of the Wilson Line. Our first home was in Briar Gate, Long Eaton.

My husband worked as a lithographic artist until he decided to enter the lace trade in conjunction with an uncle, a Mr Rowland Hill, whose factory was in Long Eaton.

Soon after the first Great War broke out, he was commissioned, posted to the King's Own Yorkshire Light Infantry with the rank of lieutenant, and saw active service with that unit in France and Italy until his discharge in 1919. The rigours of war shortened his life which, I am grieved to say, came to a close a year or two ago.

Robert William, the eldest son and second child of Robert and Mary Fletcher, first came to the notice of the Compiler through the agency of old Nottingham Directories which listed him as being established as a lace manufacturer at West End Mill, Leopold Street, and in residence at 40 Derby Road, Long Eaton, from 1889 to 1899 inclusive.

A few years later, possibly by the beginning of 1895, he had become the controlling influence in his late father's business, then styled R. Fletcher and Sons for which, just before the first World War [1914-18], the self-same books of reference gave Victoria Mills, Draycott, Derbyshire, as the source of the firm's lace production. Maybe 'R.W.F.' also moved house at this juncture from Long Eaton to The Hall. This pleasantly situated residence is still home

127

to his two daughters, Katherine Mary and Margaret Gething; the focal point of memories for members of the widely-scattered Robert branch, and by those who claim to have seen them, the repository of a fine collection of Fletcher photographs and paintings.

'Uncle Will', as we affectionately called him, was ever ready with help for those who badly needed it. Mother often spoke of him as her rock and stay when my father [Mabel Elsie's] was taken away from us so very early in life.

He married Mary Shepherd, who bore him two daughters and two sons, from whom have stemmed three grandsons—Marcus William, John Harold and David Robert—and three grand-daughters— Elizabeth Mary [now Mrs Peter Setchell; Jean Macdonald [now Mrs Henri Garnade] and Patricia Ann [now Mrs Edward Owers].

Five great-grand-daughters—Susan Mary Setchell, Dorothy Rosemary, Sarah Margaret, Gillian Mary Astle-Fletcher, and Célene Ann Garnade—and three great-grandsons—Brian Peter Setchell, Anthony Robert Garnade, and Marcus Robert Astle-Fletcher— have still further increased the stock of this branch of our family.

Uncle Will was very proud of his 'finely balanced' family, and almost equally so of the choice wall-fruits cultivated in the gardens of The Hall.

He did an immense amount of political work in the cause of good government in conjunction with his friend and close collaborator, the late Sir Robert Doncaster.

Local administrative service had always been one of his most concentrated studies. He was a member of the Draycott Parish Council for twenty-five years, and for twenty-two of them he was the chairman until he retired from office in 1934.

In 1912 he was elected to serve on both the old Shardlow Board of Guardians and the Shardlow Rural District Council, and in 1929 was appointed vice-chairman of the latter body.

Robert William Fletcher was undoubtedly a man of parts for, during the first World War not only was he a member of the local committee concerned with the administration of the Prince of Wales' Fund for the relief of dependants of soldiers and sailors on active service, but also served as chairman of the Advisory Committee to the Shardlow Tribunal. In January 1927 he was made a Justice of

128

the Peace, and nearly eleven years later [December 1937] he and his wife celebrated their golden wedding.

Katherine Mary, the elder of his two daughters, served as a V.A.D. nurse in the 1914-18 War and did Red Cross and A.R.P. [air raid precautions] work in the last one [1939-45].

She is an active worker for the Church as a member of the Parochial Council; for the Women's Institute as president of the Draycott and Wilne branch; and for commerce as a director of the Draycott Hosiery Company Ltd.

Margaret Gething, the younger one, served with the Red Cross and Civil Defence [A.R.P.] throughout the second World War [1939-45]. Today, the vice-chairmanship of the Derbyshire Federation of Women's Institutes movement and leader for the British Red Cross Society are her main preoccupations for service.

She excels at golf and for several years represented her county as a member of the Derbyshire team.

Frank Robert, the elder son, has not remained in the lace trade, but through the medium of the Draycott Hosiery Company Ltd., a changeover to the manufacture of this commodity at the Draycott Mills was made—a wise decision by those responsible for this particular Fletcher family concern. Hose in one form or other is a near necessity for the whole population. All lacey productions are, by comparison, in limited demand.

He married Ida Mary Macdonald and, by all accounts, both husband and wife serve their fellows both religiously and well.

Frank served as a Councillor on the Shardlow Rural District Council and was also Chairman of the Draycott Parish Council for a number of years until his retirement from office in 1954 through pressure of work.

During the 1939-45 War he served as chief air raid warden. Nowadays, membership and the treasurership of the Parochial Church Council occupy much of his leisure, but when he feels the need of, or has the time for a little personal relaxation or pleasure, he tills the garden attached to his Draycott home, or enjoys a spell of county or test match cricket at Trent Bridge, where many members of the Fletcher clan foregather.

For her part, Ida brings an immense influence for good to bear upon the surrounding community through her activities within and without the precincts of Wilne Parish Church.

Their three daughters served their country during the 1939-45 War. *Elizabeth Mary* worked as a physio-therapist in war hospitals; she is now living in Malaya where her husband is a District Officer in the Colonial Service.

Jean Macdonald served in the Women's Auxiliary Air Force in the Meteorological Department.

Patricia Ann worked on the land.

Harold William, the younger son of 'R.W.F.', one of the principals of the Draycott Hosiery Company Ltd., married Muriel Wallet Astle and then, by Deed Poll, changed his name to Harold William Astle-Fletcher, by which hyphened style of surname this section of our family is now known.

During the first World War he went on active service with the Universities and Public Schools Battalion, was later gazetted to the Sherwood Foresters, and afterwards attached to the Machine Gun Corps. He rose to the rank of captain and adjutant and was mentioned in despatches.

Harold was very severely wounded, and this misfortune was undoubtly the main cause of his death at the age of fifty-six some three years ago. His two elder sons served in the second World War [1939-45]. *Marcus William*, who is a scientist and holds a B.Sc. degree was a 'back room boy' *John Harold* joined the Royal Artillery in 1944 and later went to India where he was commissioned and attached to the Royal Indian Artillery with posting as captain.

Some of our cousins may like to know that Harold's widow, Muriel Astle-Fletcher, resides at Cedarville, Breaston, Derbyshire, and that two of their sons, Marcus William and John Harold Astle-Fletcher and their families live at The Elms, Draycott.

Edward Henry. We are indebted to Fred Fletcher, of Blean, Whitstable, Kent, for his father's part in the story. Here is what our kinsman has to tell us.

My father, Edward Henry Fletcher, the second son of Robert and Mary, was born in 1864 and, in due course [approximately 1889] entered his father's family lace business and subsequently married Emma Jane Preston, who is still living.

They had five children—Robert Preston, Norman Edward, Fred, Eric and Nora, born in 1886, 1888, 1890, 1892 and 1896 respectively.

Mother and father made their first home in Lime Grove, Long Eaton, and later built and moved into nearby Highfield on the

130

Derby Road where our growing family resided for many years.

'We five' were all born at Long Eaton and were given good educations—a lasting benefit. My brothers Robert and Norman began their learning at Tottenham Grammar School and finished at Loughborough Grammar School, as did Eric and myself. My sister Nora attended Loughborough Girls' High School. We were all boarders and were all also associated with the lace trade until 1916 when the family firm was wound up.

After the 1914-18 War my father ran a poultry farm at Selston where he died in 1920 as the result of an accident. Since then, my mother has lived most of the time in Combe Martin, North Devon, with her daughter Nora.

Last year [1955] at the age of ninety, having been blind for a number of years, she had cataracts removed at Exeter Hopital and now, her sight restored, lives a full and active life with a great sense of humour.

My three brothers and I had to start afresh after returning from the war, but though nothing outstandingly great has been achieved, we have all made good and lived full, active lives.

It would seem that the call of the land was in our blood for, loving nature and animals, we all made for the country rather than the town. Both mother and father were extremely clever with their hands and this delightful and useful trait has been passed down the line and is very noticeable in most of their great-grandchildren today. There is a saying that 'a Fletcher can make anything except money'.

Father was, in his day, one of the few who could 'make' his car go, and was probably the first man in Long Eaton to own one—a 3/4 h.p. De Dion of 1900 vintage.

In 1914, *Robert Preston*, my eldest brother, and his wife [née Dorothy Palethorpe of Nottingham] had only just begun housekeeping at Fernbank, Attenborough, Nottinghamshire, when the call to arms to the fit and willing was sounded. Rob was one of the many who heard it and left his own lace business at 5 Warser Gate, Nottingham, in other managerial hands whilst he served throughout the war as a gunner in the Royal Artillery and had a rough time.

Since he left the lace trade in 1922 [approximately] Rob has lived in the Cotswolds, Lyme Regis and Dawlish until finally settling in Taunton, Somerset. From these lovely spots he has travelled much of the West Country, in which district the farmers have long regarded him as an expert in agricultural and feeding stuffs, his trade today.

Rob delights in music, particularly the violin, and also has two daughters—Doreen Stanger [Mrs Robert Smythe]; Barbara Jane [Mrs Douglas Steer]; a son, Robert Edward [married to Marie ——?], and six grandshildren—Robert and John Smythe; Michael and Heather Jane Steer; and Ann and Ian Fletcher—to add further brightness and interest to his life.

During the second World War, Rob's son joined the Royal Navy as an able seaman, and rose to lieutenant, and his son-in-law, Douglas Steer, served with the Royal Marines and reached the rank of captain. To all enquiring friends, Rob's full address is Hill Crest, West Monckton, Taunton, Somerset.

When the Great War of 1914-18 broke out, my elder brother, *Norman Edward*, tried very hard to get into the Army, but was rejected on medical grounds. During the years 1920-22 [approximately] he merchanted in the brown from 4 Fletcher Gate, Nottingham, but after the post-war lace slump he too left the trade and went on to the land. After a time so occupied in this country, he migrated to Canada in 1923 under the Harvesting Scheme then in force and managed to pay a visit to his uncle Hiram and aunt Emily Fletcher then living in Prince Albert.

The following year [1924] he moved on to New Zealand and tilled the land there until his eyesight failed. After several years of complete blindness the cataracts were removed and contact-lenses fitted, sompletely restoring the sight.

Brother Norman married a New Zealander named Margaret, and though I know he has greatly missed the family live contact, I feel sure that he and his wife have been very happy together in New Zealand. They are now living in Christchurch and have a family of two sons—Eric and Gordon—and a daughter, Hazel, their eldest child, now Mrs Robert Park and the mother of a young son of her own, *Grant Robert*.

Eric, the youngest of we four sons, was barely twenty-two when the Kaiser threw down his challenge to the free nations. After some preliminary O.T.C. training as an infantryman at Nottingham, he was commissioned, posted to the Royal Army Service Corps, and served in Ireland during the rebellion with that unit. He was then seconded to the Royal Flying Corps, suffered the loss of his left leg

132

in France in 1917, and was invalided out with the rank of captain to spend the next five or six years in and out of hospital.

My brother was then able to accept a succession of posts, mainly with the petroleum companies, one of which, with Gulf Oil [Great Britain] Ltd., he has held for the past twenty-four years.

In 1932, Eric married Irene Gay-Price, a professional musician who taught at a Louth girls' school where she was held in great esteem by staff and pupils alike, as was most noticeably shewn when she passed away last year [Easter 1955].

Their only child, Peter Gay, born in 1936, had, at the early age of eleven, firmly made up his mind to 'follow in mother's footsteps' and take up music as a career. He was educated at Cranleigh. After taking his A.R.C.O. with distinction at the age of seventeen, and L.R.A.M. a year later, he was granted a scholarship to Jesus College, Cambridge, and is now reading music with marked success.

In 1939, Eric again found himself in the Royal Air Force—this time as an armament officer. He finished his service in 1947 as flight-lieutenant of an aerial torpedo unit, and is now in residence at Glendale, St Mary's Lane, Louth, Lincolnshire.

Since leaving boarding school mid-way through the first World War, *Nora*, our only sister, has lived a quiet but very full life during which she has done the best job of us all—that of looking after our dear mother. She also renders a great deal of church and social service; is a clever needlewoman; an amateur painter; a keen gardener; an animal lover; and very gifted in many forms of constructional ornamental productions.

For some years she maintained a small private school in Combe Martin in which she taught and cared for young children of folk compelled to travel abroad for divers responsible reasons.

You will learn from the Family Tree and I, *Fred Fletcher*, am father's third son. You may also like to know that I married Mary Margaret Lees of Oldham, a graduate of Girton College, Cambridge. We have four children, all of them girls, and as three of them have been married for some years, my wife and I are now living in active retirement at Red Lion House, Blean, Whitstable, Kent.

My first World War service began in R.N.A.S. Armoured Cars, a part of the combined force that made the first historic landing in Gallipoli, and ended in France where, as a commissioned officer posted to the R.A.S.C. attached to the Royal Artillery, I was wounded in June 1918.

It is said that 'every cloud has a silver lining'. My own hovered over Devenport Military Hospital where I met a V.A.D. nurse, Mary Lees, and married her.

Between the two world wars I commanded a Squadron of the Legion of Frontiersmen and, as Lieut.-Colonel, I was in command of the Canterbury Battalion Home Guard during the second one. In the days of my comparative youth, I worked as an engineer and manager for Shepshed Lace Manufacturing Company at Peckwash Mill, Derby, until 1925. I then connected with oil in Yorkshire and Lincolnshire, in which I dealt until we moved to Canterbury in 1934.

Our family hobbies include music, gardening, poultry-keeping and animals generally. We have a musical ensemble of two violins, viola, 'cello, double-bass and piano. Since we are seldom able to get all together now, we play in various orchestras.

In 1954, we moved from the house on the outskirts of Canterbury to a four-hundred years old one at Blean, three-and-a-half miles distant, and half-way to Whitstable. I mention this for historical reasons, as this area was the scene of the last military encounter on this island—'The Battle of Blean Woods'—in which the central figure, an imposter in the guise of Sir William Honeywood Courtenay was, in fact, John Nichols Thom, son of a Cornish publican. Local historians describe this last armed clash thus. 'In early morning of May 31st, 1838, Constable Mears approached Courtenay to serve a warrant for his arrest, was shot dead by pistol, run through by sword after falling, and then kicked into the dyke and left. Then, at 8 a.m. he administered a sacrament in bread and water to his followers. About noon of the same day, one hundred of the 45th Foot [now The Buffs], commanded by Major Armstrong, encountered Courtenay and his band of similar strength in Blean Woods where a scene of shocking slaughter ensued, during which Lieut. Bennett stepped up to Courtenay and called upon him to surrender but was immediately shot dead by the madman. Thereupon, a private nearest to the officer levelled his piece and killed Courtenay himself on the spot. Courtenay's band suffered many casualties. The wounded and killed were taken to the Red Lion Inn nearby, and the captured to Maidstone Gaol.'

Courtenay was the complete rogue. He stood for Parliament in 1832 under his assumed name and title, failed, and after many discoveries of frauds, was detained in Barming Asylum for four years, and on release settled in Blean Woods claiming to be the Second Messiah.

Our present home, Red Lion House, once an inn, contains a 'priest hole' where fleeing, defiant clerics from Canterbury hid from the Queen's men. It stands on nearly five acres of land, all very neglected in the past, of which we have let four acres of meadow to a farmer. My wife looks after the greenhouse and flower garden and attends to twenty hens, so a plentiful supply of eggs and an occasional bird for the pot are assured for the house.

The vegetables, fruit, lawns and shrubs occupy most of my leisure at home, whilst the chairmanship of the Canterbury Orchestral Society and visits to Roehampton Hospital about my war-wounded leg fill up much of the remainder.

I believe my own proudest memory is the reading of the lesson from the pulpit in the nave of Canterbury Cathedral at the 'Stand Down' service of the Home Guard in 1945.

The most spectacular memory is that of the visit of King George VI the Queen and Princess Elizabeth to the Canterbury Cathedral Service of Thanksgiving for its preservation throughout the war, at which I was given a seat in the choir almost opposite the Royal party. A beautiful incident of this gathering is, I believe, worth recording.

On reaching their places near to the High Altar, the King stood gazing around at the wonderful splendour, seeming to forget to bend to offer his private prayer. The Queen gave him a little nudge and they all went down to their knees in reverence together—truly a remarkably homely incident!

There is very little of note to record concerning our own offspring. Most of them are young in years and their days of great achievement have yet to come.

Dorothy Ada, our eldest daughter, is a trained nurse and an ambulance driver. She married Arthur Reynolds Carter who served as a gunner in the Middle East for four years during the second World War. They have four children—Christopher Paul, Andrew Hamilton, Helena Mary and John Reynolds.

Margaret Helen, late of the W.R.A.F. [Meteorological Department] married Captain Ken Harris of The Buffs, who was killed in action [1945] whilst serving with the Sudan Defence Force. He left no issue.

135

ʼ: Margaret is now a professional musician with a special affection for the violin and piano.

Winifred Nora, our third daughter, staff member of the Inland Revenue and a part-time worker in the National Fire Service, is, as yet, unmarried.

Audrey Joan, our youngest, and her husband, George R. Fleck, also served in the National Fire Service.

The needs of three young children—Anthony James, Robert Gordon, and Timothy—and the claims of a smallholding, occupy most of their leisure when George is not away from home travelling for Spillers.

Robert and Mary Fletcher were blessed with two other daughters, both of whom are now widows but still living, one up in the broad acres of Yorkshire, and the other one down in glorious Devon.

Mary Ann Eley, the elder of this pair was, when young, a truly marvellous ice-skater and also played a skilful game at tennis, at which sport quite a number of the Fletcher fair sex have distinguished themselves over the generations.

She married Herbert Lunt, a quiet and rather retiring type not fated to make old bones. They had one child, a son, whom they named *Herbert Fletcher*, probably in a vain endeavour to perpetuate the nomenclature of both sides of their family.

This young man of scientific leanings was delicate from birth, and though he lived to marry Margaret Bloomer, she was left a widow with no children to remind her of her loss.

His mother has lived in quiet retirement for upwards of thirty years at Min Avon, Oxlea Road, Lincombe Hill, Torquay, and hopes to celebrate her eighty-fifth birthday on Empire Day, 1956.

Betsy Lavinia, the youngest daughter, married Harris Begbie Abbott who, until his death, was the proprietor of a very flourishing furnishing business in Leeds, now no longer a family concern. They had three children—a daughter, Ann Mary, who became the wife of John Darley, and two sons, Robert William and Geoffrey Fletcher, who have both embraced the bonds of matrimony.

The Abbott family have long had close ties with the Masonic Craft through the late Harris Begbie, his father before him, and his two sons, who represent the third generation in this brotherhood of fellowship.

136

Robert William worked as a chemist until he joined his younger brother, *Geoffrey Fletcher*, who owns two garages in Leeds, one of which is known as 'The Spot'.

Betsy Lavinia still resides at 228 West Park Drive, where, without doubt, she makes a great fuss of her only grandchild, *Robert Fletcher Abbott*.

Hiram Richard. It is with a feeling of admiration and privilege, and a real sense of responsibility that I, the Compiler, take up my pen to record what can rightly be said concerning this, the youngest child of Robert and Mary Fletcher—a man of outstanding character, and an independent one.

In early life he was by trade a brewer in the service of Hooleys, an old, well-known Nottingham family firm, and, as with most men who appreciate a glass of good beer, especially one of their own brewing, Hiram was by nature a kindly, tolerant and generous soul. In support of this testimony, let me remind you, the beneficiaries, that during the second World War he spent a small fortune on those lovely parcels sent home to cheer up his kinsmen. Every one of us who valued the thoughts that prompted these rare gifts will remember him gratefully and revere his memory.

Towards the end of the last century he married Emily Lunt and settled down with her at 30 Albert Avenue, Lenton Sands, to brew beer for a few years. In the summer of 1903, however, the urge of the wanderlust in their blood took them to Canada, which lovely, spacious country became the land of their adoption until they both died in Victoria, British Columbia—Emily on December 9th, 1930, and Hiram quite recently on March 13th, 1956, at the age of eighty-one years. They had no children.

Many Fletchers of Hiram's day and generation have crossed the Seven Seas to build anew and lived very lonely lives in consequence. In one of his many letters to me from 1482 Dallas Road, Victoria, British Columbia, dated April 3rd, 1946, were these revealing words: 'It will be forty-three years this summer since I arrived in Canada, and during all that tme I have not *seen* or *heard* from a kinsman, outside my own family, of course, with one exception—Norman Fletcher, son of my brother Edward, who visited us in Prince Albert in 1922. We never heard from him again'.

In that year [1922] Hiram and his wife adopted the widow of an old friend and her little boy, Bill. This kindly act was a great blessing in disguise as, shortly afterwards, Emily was taken ill and was in and out of hospital until, in 1926, Hiram decided to gratify her wish to move from Prince Albert to Victoria, British Columbia. The doctor gave her but a few days to live and though he also said she might die on the train nothing untoward happened, so in this lovely island retreat Caye nursed her through the remaining years of her life.

After Emily's death, Caye and young Bill stayed on to look after Hiram's welfare whilst he tilled his garden, explored the island in his car, enjoyed his game of golf or fished for salmon from his motor launch in the Sound. Gardening was a chancy pastime since 40 to 75 m.p.h. off-sea winds frequently scattered the sown seed into divers profitless places.

His salmon catches, too, experienced more 'downs' than 'ups' during the next quarter of a century as large numbers of commercialised boats ruthlessly ousted the amateurs from the Brentwood waters, a world-renowned fishing ground.

His first year of sport there [1926] yielded 545½ pounds of this choice fish, but during the last one [1953], after which failing health caused the sale of his launch and gear, every single salmon cost him ten dollars each to land.

To underline their great esteem for this 'retired from active service' member, the annual meeting of the Clover Point Anglers Association Incorporated elected him president, with acclammation, for the twenty-first time of office.

Hiram took pride in being the most westerly situated living 'twig' of the Fletcher clan and whenever Big Ben struck 9 p.m. in London [heard in British Columbia around mid-day] he drew himself a tankard of his own home-brewed with which he toasted and drank to the health of 'The Family' back at home. May I suggest that love for one's ain folk never really dies!

His mail to me over the years contained much that has been both intimate and interesting concerning his life. In one letter [quoting] he said: 'My grandfather, Edward Fletcher, your great-grandfather, constructed a lace-frame which would use thick threads and fine ones together in the making of lace. My father and brother Will both told me of this and said grandfather would have made a fortune if he had patented his invention. He delayed doing so, but copyists did and thereby profited substantially'

138

On another occasion, when commenting upon the time and trouble it must have taken to compile the copy of the Family Tree sent to him by his nephew, Frank Fletcher of Draycott, he added a finishing touch of pungent 'H.R.F.' humour.

Said he: 'Do you want an interesting job? If so, try to find out for me exactly who Ben Fletcher was and where his family sprang from. He was Governor of New York in the time of William of Orange and Mary, a typical Fletcher, very hot of temper and autocratic. He was hanged for his associations with Captain Kidd. I had a biography of him which was left behind at Prince Albert when we left. A boiler blew and destroyed everything I had in storage.' This is the he-man pattern of research task one does—or busts! I have not embarked upon it as yet!

Hiram stories about his great strength, tough constitution and healthy appetite are legion. So may I add a new true one of my own to the collection?

My first World War Q.M.S., then an elderly man by military standards, and a once-upon-a-time very fine tennis player, apologised [you know how warrant officers do this to other ranks!] for asking me a surprising and personal question.

'Are you related to the Fletchers of Heanor and Long Eaton who make lace?' On hearing my affirmative, he recalled with glee the tennis tournaments the Heanor section organised and the suppers enjoyed at Long Eaton where, as he put it, the host, Robert Fletcher, 'carved helpings of cold beef that hung over the sides like tarts on plates'.

A local clergyman, a frequent fellow-guest, always insistently voiced his inability to eat his portion, whereupon 'R.F.' said, 'Never mind parson, pass up your plate; I'll put two or three more slices on it and it will do for our Hiram'.

All the pictures I have seen of him are evidences of his Samson-like qualities, but in 1954 his health began to give real cause for anxiety. This deterioration increased throughout the following year during which he had a succession of very bad falls, but stood up after them again and again to fight for the continuance of life. Ultimately, all resistance was of no avail. He had to give in to the inevitable, so in saying good-bye to Hiram here, I think it fitting to tell you a little of what Caye [Mrs D. E. Hocking] said to my wife concerning those last few days on earth among us.

March 28th, 1956. 'Your cousin, dear old Lenkie, was a resolute but very considerate man. Despite his great and ever-increasing weakness, he would not hear of me calling in the doctor, nor could I persuade him to go into hospital until the last resort. After a week there he seemed to be getting better and the doctor said he could return home, perhaps tomorrow.

He smiled as he talked hopefully of the coming spring, the warmer weather and a recovery of strength. Little did I realise it then, that this was to be the last time I should hear him speak. The next morning he was unconscious when I reached the hospital where, at 3.30 in the afternoon this very dear one, who had been both father and mother to me and mine all these many years, passed peacefully on'.

So spake his friend in need as she paid richly deserved tribute to a family character that brings this chapter of our story to a close.

SAM AND MARY SELINA BRITTLE

PLATE 19

HENRY FLETCHER

CHAPTER VIII

THE HENRY BRANCH
LIFE ON A SOUTHERN RHODESIAN FARM
By Sarah Elizabeth Fletcher

THE Boer War of 1899 was indeed the answer to the prayer of young Henry Hooton Fletcher who, at the age of twenty-seven, had found disappointment in life. His career as a lace designer in his father's business did not appeal, so he was glad of the opportunity to migrate with his family to Georgia, America, later returning to England again where he was married and indulged in photography.

The loss of his wife and child again disillusioned him and re-awakened his wanderlust. The doctors having advised him to go to a warmer climate for a chest ailment, he eagerly joined the forces which were sent to South Africa in 1899.

The Boer War was raging with all the fury which was possible in those days and life was very trying for the women while their husbands were on commando. One of these was Sarah Weihmann who ten years previously had married an officer of the regular Boer army of the name of Karel Cremer.

When hostilities started, the women and children were left on the farms while the men joined the Boer forces. The natives took advantage of these conditions and were a constant menace.

On one occasion, Mrs Cremer fired at a night prowler in self-defence, and on investigating the following day the culprit was found under a krantz where he had died of the gunshot wounds.

Their house was situated between two kopjes and at one stage, fighting with cannon from one kopje to another, where the foes had established themselves, lasted for a week. Mrs Cremer and her family took refuge in a stable constructed of strong granite stone, only narrowly escaping whizzing shrapnel when she was forced out to bake bread in her Dutch oven.

A neighbour, on being molested by natives, who demanded a good meal including turkey, reluctantly provided it, but poisoned the lot when she served the coffee. She put 'something' in it!

141

Towards the end of hostilities matters deteriorated rapidly and the women and children were compelled to move to nearby towns. Many went to concentration camps, but Mrs Cremer, who today at the age of over eighty-six, still shows her independence, set up a small café in T'Banchu. This place was well patronised by the British troops and she first met Harry Fletcher, my grandfather there, who had firmly made up his mind to settle in South Africa.

Mr and Mrs Cremer had become estranged when she persistently refused to go to a concentration camp, and on his return from Ceylon, where he spent three years as a prisoner-of-war, they were divorced and she married Harry Fletcher in 1906. They settled on a farm in the T'Banchu district.

Four children were born to them and in 1912, at an age when most people have settled down in life, Harry Fletcher was again seized with the urge 'to see around the bend' [his own words].

A friend offered him a position on a farm in Southern Rhodesia, which he eagerly accepted. His wife and children remained in the Orange Free State while he went north to explore and send back a favourable or otherwise report. He loved the carefree Rhodesian life and in two months' time his family followed.

My grandmother had misgivings about starting life again in a new and comparatively untamed country. Wild animals roamed about freely and a certain Major Shaw, sensing her fear, exaggerated matters by telling her that native piccanins [juveniles] were tied in a little hut ten yards from the house to attract lions so that they [the lions] could be shot.

A certain tribe of natives had the custom of filing their teeth into sharp points, and when Major Shaw informed her that these natives were cannibals, she and her children seldom left the house.

Malaria was rife and shortly after their arrival, most of the family was stricken by it; cure was slow and uncertain, as malaria drugs were unknown.

Orchardson, the friend from whom Harry Fletcher had taken the Rhodesian position, owing to shortage of cash, relinquished his farming interests in Rhodesia and returned to the Orange Free State. My grandfather, determined that he would conquer the hardships confronting him, accepted a contract to plant a citrus estate in the Magoe Valley. A permanent position was later offered but it was declined as that part of Rhodesia was then a veritable death trap because of malaria.

142

Another offer was made to him by a farmer at Norton to run his farm on a percentage basis. This was accepted but times proved very difficult; both owner and occupier were short of capital. The nearest water was three miles away and road communications were few and far between. Not seeing the object of battling on another man's property, my grandparents decided to secure a farm of their own under a new land settlement scheme.

An Italian, Graccio, called at the homestead for a cup of tea on his way to Salisbury and told of an unoccupied farm adjoining his, four miles from the Beatrice gold mine.

The necessary transactions settled, the family, fired with optimism, set out on a sleigh for their new home, the only movable assets being a wheelbarrow, a few tools, one cow and the very necessary furniture.

Fortunately, labour was plentiful and cheap, so by sheer hard work and determination they managed to get a footing on the farm.

No roads existed; neighbours were few, and the new settlers were forty miles from the nearest town. Roads were made by chopping trees wherever they wanted to go, and even today there is proof that this line of least resistance was followed.

Grandfather had the good fortune of being given the managership of the adjoining farm while the owner went to the first Great War, so with a steady monthly income matters improved. A better home was built and stock and implements purchased.

The children had reached school age and a problem was solved by establishing a small farm school. A teacher was provided by the Education Department and many of the neighbouring children attended. My grandmother adopted five other motherless children to swell the school numbers and kept them until the father re-married.

Circumstances still further improved and the farm was showing a small profit and a good herd of cattle had been reared. Grandfather Fletcher, like so many other Rhodesians, wished to get rich quickly and turned his interests to gold mining. This venture turned out a costly failure, the herd of cattle being disposed of to pay expenses. Later on, the mine was given out on tribute and a steady income was received for two years. Unfortunately, the company turned down the option of purchase and so the mine has been abandoned.

In 1935 my father, Harry Fletcher the Third married Jeanette Sharp, and as his father was getting on in years, he was given to

143

understand that he had to carry on and see that farm 'Cavan' was kept for future Fletcher generations.

Grandfather left three sons and two daughters, and the sons, who love the farm life, will see to it that this wish is fulfilled as far as is humanly possible.

Harry the Third, after being demobilised in 1946, took over the farm and decided on tobacco as a main crop. Two years of growing Turkish tobacco proved a failure. The first crop of Virginia tobacco was grown in 1948, but Grandfather was not given the pleasure of seeing it turn out a success as he died early in 1949.

Tobacco growing depends a lot on the seasons. When these have been favourable it has turned out a very profitable crop to grow, but in other years when the rainfall is very high, only expenses are recovered. Unless the farmer has some assistance, he can never take a holiday.

Seed beds are sown in early September and the grading of the previous year's crop usually keeps on until October when the auction sales close for the season. In this hot climate beds have to be watered at least four times a day, and this has to be supervised closely as the results of the season depend largely on the plants produced.

When the rains set in, usually early November, the plants are transplanted into fields, and in another two months' time reaping commences. The leaves are picked and tied in bunches of three on thin poles and hung in the barn to cure. Heat is produced by a furnace and flues, and in about seven days' time at the temperature of 160 degrees Fahrenheit the tobacco is cured, and after conditioning with steam is ready for baling. Later, these bales are opened again and the tobacco sorted into different grades to be sent to the auction floors for sale.

Maize is grown for native rations. Apes and baboons prove a menace to this crop. A guard has to be on duty continually to drive them off, and being of a sly nature they usually sneak in unobserved. The farmers annually organise a big baboon hunt and kill off hundreds when they leave their old haunts to torment some other farmer.

Cavan Farm is bisected by a large river. Another river without a bridge flows between us and the main Salisbury Road. During the rainy season, we are very often marooned for two weeks to a month, and when we really have to go to town, oxen or the tractor pulls the

PLATE 20
MR AND MRS JOHN VERNON, JUNIOR
née MARY ELIZABETH WILLIAMS

car on to the main road—that is when the rivers have subsided but still too deep for the car to cross.

Farming is becoming more mechanised every season, and the natives who prefer skilled labour in towns are replaced by machinery. A certain number, however, will always be required for tobacco growing.

The natives—or Africans, as they prefer to be called—are indeed presenting a problem. With the Federation of Southern and Northern Rhodesia and Nyasaland; the rapid advance they have made in the last fifty years and outnumbering the 200,000 Europeans by six million, and with tens of millions more in surrounding territories, makes us ponder on the survival of the white race in South Africa. Will recent events in Kenya influence Africans in other areas?

OUR AMERICAN STORY

By Helen Mary Vernon, née Brittle, of Dallas, Penn., U.S.A.

MARY Selina Fletcher, wife of Sam Brittle, was my mother. She was the daughter of Henry Fletcher and his wife Elizabeth Hooton Fletcher.

There were eight children born to my parents. One, a four-year-old, died and lies buried in Attenborough churchyard. The rest all attained adulthood.

We have had no further deaths among the childern of my parents until a tragic accident took the life of my brother William Fletcher Brittle in 1951.

Mother and father have both passed away, but there remains six children—two sons and four daughters—all married, and at this time of writing [September 21st, 1954] have added to the family tree eighteen grandchildren, who in turn have already increased the third generation by twenty-nine members, two of whom are married, making a fourth generation of two more children, being the great-great-grandchildren of Mary Selina, of whom I am writing. This should be her story.

I remember my grandfather Henry Fletcher very well. After Grandma died he lived in Long Eaton with his two daughters, and as he loved to walk, would stroll over to spend Sunday with us.

Some of my brothers and sisters and I would know Grandpa was coming in time for Sunday mid-day dinner and would go to meet him, generally sighting him somewhere near Toton.

We used to go to Attenborough Parish Church on Sunday morning, but the best part of the morning was meeting Grandpa and going home with him proudly in tow.

'What's your Mama got for dinner today?' would be answered with 'Roast beef and Yorkshire pudding' or 'Leg of lamb and mint sauce', and sure enough one of these tantalizing aromas would be issuing out of the kitchen and dinner would be ready when we reached home where Grandpa would have the honoured place at our table. After dinner, Grandpa must have his nap and we children scattered for the afternoon.

Mother would then stir up a batch of tea cakes, sometimes with currants or raisins and often shredded cocoanut, which would emerge from the oven, hot and delicious, in time for tea, with many cups of the scalding-hot beverage for Grandpa, and usually some of the left-over cold meat from dinner with mother's famous apple chutney. [I wish I had that recipe.]

Then, if the weather was nice, Mother and Dad and some of us children would 'walk Grandpa part way home'.

Came the day we had all looked forward to as long as I can remember.

Ever since I was a very small child I used to listen entranced to Mother and Dad's talk of America and never tired of looking at some small souvenirs they brought back with them.

Grandpa and Grandma and their children had gone to America years ago. They bought a place near Atlanta, Georgia, and Mother and Dad went there too.

It was in Atlanta that my brother William Fletcher was born. He was our first real American.

Some time later Mother and Dad returned to England and Grandpa and the rest followed, settling once more in Long Eaton where the family was all busy in the lace trade. Grandma died a few years later.

My father planned for the time when he would return to America, but it was not until my fifteenth year that we finally got back.

I shall never forget the thrill of crossing the Atlantic and landing in New York. To this day the thrill remains.

My father came to America to work for Marshall Field & Co. as a lace expert in their plant at Zion City, Illinois. The lace factory had been taken over by Marshall Field & Co. when it, and the whole village of Zion, went into bankruptcy after the death of John Alexander Dowie.

There were already a few English families living there and working in the mill. But we were really the pioneers.

Zion City is forty-two miles north of Chicago, and lies along the shores of Lake Michigan. In the days when we arrived there, the town was not well developed. Wooden sidewalks and dirt roads, no electricity [except in the mill], no proper sewers or water works, *were* the order of the day. But we had arrived and there was work to be done and a job for everyone.

Dad and the two eldest boys immediately began working and we established a pleasant home.

Always we were longing for Grandpa to come and make his home with us but he died before those plans could materialise. Mother was heartbroken when she heard the news about his death. All this time she was in constant communication with her brother, our uncle Harry, whom I vaguely recollect. Years later I felt I knew him very well through reading his letters to mother and hearing him discussed so frequently.

My brother Bill was wild to join Uncle Harry in Africa. The photographs of wild animals and the descriptions of his farm were thrilling to each of us and his letters were read and re-read many times. We also wondered about his new family and later his daughter Mary, our mother's namesake, wrote to mother on various occasions.

We were settled in our new home and making many friends. Living in Zion City in those days was not the pleasantest experience. There was much that was downright disagreeable about it, but we all managed to create a good life out of what was available.

Zion City originally was established by Dr. John, Alexander Dowie, a self-styled 'Prophet' to be a place of refuge from the worldly affairs in life. He preached a gospel of his own, made thousands of converts who put all they had into what was to be a self-sustaining community, with a huge Tabernacle as a place of worship, community industries of all kinds to support the population, a school where Biblical subjects were the chief teachings, and a curfew bell which tolled at 6 a.m. to start the day and at 9 p.m. to end the day in prayer. Services at the Tabernacle were the only

147

social activities allowed. No dancing, no card-playing, no theatres or amusements of any type were to be indulged in. Above all, no smoking. The eating of pork, oysters, and some other foods were strictly forbidden, and as a major part of the basic religion, healing by prayer or 'Divine Healing' excluded all doctors.

There was a law against smoking and the use of intoxicating drinks; also the wearing of certain too-revealing dress for the women and girls.

In spite of all these restrictions, Mother and Dad managed to bring up their children in a very happy and congenial home, making many friends with the other 'outsiders' who did not follow the teachings of Dowie and his 'Twelve Apostles'. In fact, we made friends with many of the old Dowie sect and to this day some of them remain our dearest acquaintances. Their disapproval of our way of life has not endured through the years.

In time, our house in Zion City became a centre of attraction for many of the young people. With three young men and three growing girls it was bound to be a lively spot.

Mother and Dad were fun-loving and ever-young at heart. The winters in Illinois are very severe—lots of snow and bitter cold weather. We had to create our own fun.

We had a large house with a double parlour opening out of a hall-way on one side, and a dining room on the other. There were sliding and folding doors between, which could be opened, making one very large room, and we children could always take our friends home for an evening of fun, any time an occasion arose, and indeed there were many such occasions.

The boys and Dad bought Mother a piano for a surprise birthday present. That piano got more pounding than any instrument I ever heard, before or since. Mother could play very nicely and the children were in turn given music lessons, but music did not take very well in this family. No one had time or inclination to sit and practice scales and lessons. But there was always someone who could play the instrument while the rest would sing song after song, making more noise than harmony.

Then we would dance. Many a rug we wore down to bareness and Dad would be coaxed into buying a new one to replace the old worn threadbare household article. That would usually occur when a wedding or a special party was being held and he would say 'You

148

kids have got to stop dancing in here, you'll ruin this new rug just like the old one'.

We never stopped. Mother would say 'Let the children have their fun, rugs can be replaced', and our parties went on and on.

This house had a basement with a very smooth concrete floor, divided into three rooms but all opening together. What a wonderful place to roller-skate on a wet Saturday or Sunday! All the neighbourhood young used to come in.

Dad made his own wine. In one section he had a barrel of rhubarb wine, perfect. He had been sampling it and left hanging on the spigot a little tin cup. One of the young boys, son of a deacon in the church, too freely imbibed of this wine, helping himself to a cupfull any time he roller-skated by the barrel. Soon he was wobbling all over the place and falling down. We decided to take him home, whereupon he fell into a deep sleep, with loud snores. His mother, becoming alarmed, about her son's condition came over and got Mother to look at 'little Harry' and advise her what to do. Mother took one look at his flushed face, heard his horrible snores and smelled his breath. Finally, she looked at the boy's mother and said 'I believe your Harry is drunk'

What a flood of abuse was let loose on poor Mother. No drink had ever been into Mrs D's house and evidently the charge was untrue. But it was true. Harry *was* drunk, and that little episode almost broke up a beautiful friendship.

Dad and the boys each had a horse. They were all saddle horses, and also could be driven, hitched to a surrey or buggy. Mother used to drive Dad and the boys to work and fetch them home. Summer evenings and week-ends we'd saddle the horses and ride far and wide. Our favourite ride was down to the lake. This was a road that was really only a wagon trail, so we'd pound down this track, yelling like Indians, until we were brought up short by the deep sand on the beach of Lake Michigan.

On Saturday night it was the custom to go to Waukegan, the nearest 'real' town. There the men would gather for a drink, while the women would shop and the young folks went to the movies.

All this time, the lace trade and business at the mill was flourishing. Everybody had plenty of money and spent it freely. The men used to have champagne parties and gay times.

When automobiles came in, our horses were sold and we had a

car. Then we began to range further afield and found plenty of other interests outside of the narrow confines of Zion City.

Then 'bang' went the mill! Some labour agitators' came in and stirred up enough trouble to cause a strike. The mill was operated non-union, as our Marshall Field had never put up with strikers and so refused to negotiate.

This was the beginning of the end so far as making lace was concerned in the Zion mills. The strike was never really settled. Some few went back to work on the old terms but most of the men left Zion and got jobs in other lace plants which were all in the Eastern parts of the States, a thousand or more miles away from Zion.

Our two brothers moved away, first to Philadelphia and then to Rhode Island where most of the lace plants are today. Dad did not leave.

By this time all of us were grown up and several married, so Dad and Mother sold the house they had bought in Zion and moved to Kenosha, Wisconsin.

The boys became tired of living in the East, so decided to move back and be near their own folk. We were always a very closely-knit family.

Then came some depression in the lace trade. Dad was already out of it, and the two boys followed suit. They each got in their own business and never went back into the lace trade.

This would be the end of 'the Fletcher family history of lace' as far as the descendants of Henry Fletcher is concerned, except for this writer. I am still with it and will be until my husband's retirement. It was while my brother was in Philadelphia that he met John Vernon, who now enters this story.

He had completed his apprenticeship in the drafting room at Walter Sampson's in Ruddington, Nottinghamshire, England, and came to Philadelphia to take a job at Bromley's.

My brother Bill was on the verge of returning home, when he heard that a new draftsman was required at the Zion Lace Mills. He persuaded John Vernon to write applying for the job. He did and got the job, came out to Zion and worked there as draftsman and designer for sixteen years.

John came to the house with a letter of introduction from Brother Bill, and that was the beginning of our present relationship.

150

Dad and the rest of the family found much in common with him and Mother recalled the fact that Grandpa and Mr Sampson used to shoot together in the Old Country.

I remember many hares and pheasants that came to our table via Grandpa's or Mr Sampson's gun. Hunting and fishing were a very common sport everywhere around Zion and over the border into Wisconsin. All our men carried guns in the season and fished all summer.

John Vernon fitted very well into our family and when we were married, that brought one member of the Fletcher family back into the lace trade. That is I.

Our lives went along in a fine manner until the depression of 1929-31. I'll never forget that 'Black Thursday' when the stock market crashed and fortunes were wiped out overnight. The lace trade was completely ruined, but it was not until 1931 that the Zion Lace Mills were abandoned and John Vernon had to look further afield for another job.

We had two children and had built ourselves a house and were expecting to live in it to the end of our days.

When it was announced that the mill would cease making lace, most of the machines were torn down, destroyed and junked. Two of them, however, were sold to a firm in Lehighton, Pennsylvania, by which time John had established a nice little business of his own doing drafting for the trade. I sent out his letters and helped in the reading off and the figuring of his drafts.

It was much too difficult living in Wisconsin when all his work was a thousand miles away, so when the opportunity occurred to take a steady job as draftsman for Penn. Lace Co. we decided to come East to be nearer the place of business. It was hard to leave our lovely little house and my parents, sisters and brothers behind, but John was a trained draftsman and did not want to change his occupation, although he could have had a partnership with any one of my three brothers, each of whom had a different form of trade. John, the eldest, has a business in Kenosha, Wisconsin, comprising a restaurant, bar and recreation rooms. Bill, the one that was accidentally killed, was a driller of wells, and Walter, now living in Illinois, is a builder and contractor.

We moved to Lehighton in 1932 and stayed there eight years. A better opportunity then took us to Bridgeport where we remained

151

until we came to Dallas, Pennsylvania, seven years ago. We are now beginning to look forward to retirement. The lace trade has been very good to us and we have no complaints against it.

Our two children are now married and settled in their own homes, and John and I are right back to where we started, just the two of us still making lace—but without doubt, the very last members of the Henry branch having connection with the art.

Our son graduated from M.I.I. in 1951 with a degree in chemical engineering and is doing 'research and development' at the Lago Refinery on the Island of Aruba in the Netherlands West Indies. We spent Christmas with him a year or two ago, and hope to go again.

Our daughter finished high school and went to Columbia University in New York. She is a registered graduate nurse and is married and has three children—two girls and one boy, who bears the name David Fletcher Blank.

Byron Blank, our son-in-law, is also with a branch of Standard Oil Co., as is our son, John. Byron was recently assigned to a job in Sumatra, Indonesia, where he is comfortably housed with his wife and family. Their letters are the bright spot in our week. Then we also have twenty-five reels of coloured movies which have been taken during the voyage across and in their new home, so we can see the children in their daily activities and note their growth.

Our son John writes regularly, so we can readily visualise his home and surroundings because we saw it all when we visited the island.

Upwards of three years ago my husband and I were flying over the Atlantic on our way home after a visit to England. We met many of the Fletcher clan and enjoyed every minute of our stay, and heard that a book was to be compiled with contributions from various members of the family.

We spent some happy times with mother's youngest sister, Sarah; we call her 'Aunt Pat'. She lives in Weston-super-Mare. Most of the time we stayed with my eldest sister who then lived in Beeston. From her house we toured the countryside in her car and were taken to see what should have been 'old familiar places' but nothing looked the same and I was utterly lost. That which one remembered at fifteen is not at all like what one sees years later in actuality.

My eldest sister was married and preferred to stay in England when the rest of the family came to America. This branch of the family is getting bigger and bigger. We used to have family reunions when Mother and Dad were with us in the house they built. I've seen 35 all eating together at extra tables set up, but now, with Dad and Mother and Brother Bill gone, the heart has gone out of the old home. Just Bill's widow lives in the house alone, the place that holds so many happy memories—sad ones, too, of course.

If the family could all return at the same time there would be many more than the thirty-five mentioned. New marriages among the grandchildren and many new babies are building up the score. Why, there are already two new babies, making my brother John a *great*-grandfather, and he not much over sixty.

This is the fourth generation since Henry and Elizabeth Hooton Fletcher came to America the first time.

Shortly after I received a copy of the 'Fletcher Family Tree' some very pleasant friendships were formed with other members of the family. One of them was Percy Fletcher. His wife wrote to me and we discovered we were not too far away from each other to prevent visits. We were in Bridgeport, Connecticut, and Percy and his wife were only about fifty-five miles away living in Middletown, Conn. We exchanged many visits until we moved away from Bridgeport.

It is not purely coincidental that at the time we first met Percy Fletcher he was employed by the same concern that offered John Vernon the opportunity to move to Dallas and be their chief draftsman in their [at that time] brand new mill. The lace trade in the United States is comparatively small and sooner or later the men meet the men from all of the mills. We are continually running into some of the old crowd who went to Zion and I am quite used to being introduced to someone who, before the conversation has proceeded very far, will say 'Why, I knew your father and brothers years ago'.

One old man, aged eighty-three, whom we met in Bridgport, claimed he had his first job with Grandfather Fletcher and knew and well remembered uncle Walter Hooton and several others I've heard Mother mention.

Another dear woman was made known to us, all on account of the Family Tree. She was Annie Mullis and a half-sister of Percy Fletcher. She also wrote to me.

Then, one summer, my husband and I were going back to Kenosha for our annual visit. Father had died, but Mother was still in the old home with Brother Bill and his wife and daughter, then a girl almost the same age as my daughter, Dorothy. We always spent part of our summer with Mother even though it was a thousand miles each way.

This time, of which I write was to be a quick trip for us and a chance to see our son John who had just previously enlisted in the U.S. Navy and was attending Radar School at Great Lakes Naval Station, through which we must pass to reach Kenosha.

Upon studying the road maps and planning our routing we saw that by making a small détour we could go through Ravenna, Ohio, the home of Annie Fletcher [Mrs Mullis].

It was late afternoon when we rolled into Ravenna, but not long after we found Annie and only intended to step in and say hello, then goodbye, we were in such a hurry to reach Kenosha and Mother.

But we reckoned without Cousin Annie. I had dropped her a line saying we'd step in to see her, and there she had been waiting on her front porch for hours until we finally arrived. So we were royally welcomed.

Cousin Annie's husband had been dead a few years and she was there making her home with her son Percy Fletcher Mullis and his wife and small daughter Nancy.

Cousin Annie seemed so much like Mother I felt I'd known her always. She insisted on us staying overnight, which we were happy to do. We had already driven over five hundred miles and were quite weary.

The next day, Sunday, Percy and Mary his wife talked us into spending Sunday with them and try for an early start on Monday, when the week-end traffic would be much less.

Before we did get away, Cousin Annie had decided to travel with us to meet her other unknown cousins. So we piled her, bag and baggage, into the car and took her along with us.

Mother was delighted to see the daughter of her uncle Dick and her own cousin. They talked and talked all day and far into the night.

Most regretfully, John Vernon had to get back to his job, so after a week we announced the date and time of our departure for home. By that time Mother decided she might as well come to Bridgeport for a visit at our house, so once again we piled the two old ladies, bag and baggage, into the car and started the long trail back.

Cousin Annie reluctantly disembarked at her son's house in Ravenna and we continued on our way home with Mother as our dear, dear guest for the rest of the summer.

During these truly happy days, the joy of reunion with Cousin Annie was re-lived again and again. These two old ladies cherished the meeting so much that it was soon plain to John and I that another one was already planned to take place at Ravenna when Mother returned to Kenosha.

Here a little conspiracy developed on my part. I felt it quite inadvisable, owing to Mother's health and the distance she had to travel, to have her again meet Annie on her way home. So, three months later, we saw Mother safely seated in a parlour-car fitted with a lower sleeping berth of the non-stop express train to Chicago; and as it pulled out of Bridgeport, we left for our home wondering whether each of these two newly-discovered cousins would stay put in their beds that night. It terrified me to think of Mother six hundred miles away from me and still another five hundred miles to go to reach Kenosha alone and on her own.

Later, I learned from Mother the train had by-passed Ravenna in the middle of the night as it rushed with her, happy and safe at rest, towards home, so the first was also their last get-together.

I hope to be forgiven for spoiling their hopes of being together again, but their age and infirmity compelled me to circumvent their plans. They are now both at their 'final destination'. They did not outlive each other very long.

Since that time Percy Fletcher's wife has passed on and the last we heard was, Percy had gone to stay with his step-son, the son of his wife Ethel by a previous marriage. Thus ends the acquaintance with this branch of the Fletcher family.

The next ingathering was the arrival here in Dallas of Rhona Fletcher Hallford, who drove over from Toronto, Canada, to spend a few days with us. Her husband, Murray Hallford, brought Rhona here as part of his holiday trip. We expect to see more of Rhona and we are planning to drive to Canada in the near future.

My husband and I have come a long way together since the early days when first we met in Zion City. We have travelled considerable distances, but I really believe we are not moving any more until he retires from the lace trade. We live in pleasant surroundings and John's work is among congenial people.

Our son John did not want to follow in his father's footsteps. We saw him through four years of high school and four years of university training in chemical engineering and now he is completely equipped to take his place in this field of engineering. His father and I went to M.I.I. [Massachussets Institute of Technology] to be present at his graduation and learned he had been accepted for Lago Oil Company, a subsidiary of Standard Oil Company, to fill a position on the engineering staff at the refinery on the island of Aruba. This is a small island in the Carribean, off the coast of Venezuela, a tropical isle set in a lovely blue sea. The living conditions there are excellent as we discovered when we went for our visit. We flew the round trip to England the year before. Distance is no barrier these days! It's all a question of 'air hours'.

Son John has made splendid progress, so much, he came back to the States to marry and take his bride back to the island to live. Our daughter Dorothy, with her husband and three small children, bravely took off into the unknown and are now making their home in Indonesia.

This branch of the Fletcher clan must all be 'tarred with the same brush', the same as Grandpa and many more of his relatives. They 'love to wander'.

Mother often talked to we children about one of her uncles who dashed off to California during the 1849 Gold Rush. What became of that one? I hope it all comes out in the book, together with something interesting concerning those Fletchers who went to Russia, and Mother's brother Harry and his family who have lived for so many years at Cavan Farm in Southern Rhodesia.

Mother and Marie Hooton were first cousins and small girls together in Long Eaton, where it was first noticed that Marie possessed a voice of great promise. Her musical career subsequently became almost a legend in this branch of the family.

It has frequently been stated that Grandpa and Grandma were a great influence in the starting of this 'bird of song' in its flight. Grandma often said 'Mary Hooton has a voice as powerful as a man and should be trained as a singer'.

As before remarked, my Grandpa's sister Betsy married Walter Hooton and Walter Hooton's sister Elizabeth married Henry Fletcher. These two marriages created a double relationship which

156

probably explains why these Fletchers and Hootons were more closely knit than some of the other members of our family.

I still well remember being taken many times to spend the day with aunt Betsy in Long Eaton and waylaying Uncle Walter on his way home from the station after visiting Nottingham Lace Market. He always put his hand deep into his pocket to make believe he'd lost all his money, but always miraculously found a penny 'for his little snakes wif wings'—his pet name for me. It was derived from a dried up old rattlesnake, saved by Mother from her Georgia [Atlanta] days, and which I could not be induced to touch, calling it a 'snake wif wings'.

The story goes that Uncle Charlie, Mother's youngest brother, who died young, killed that rattlesnake in the garden of her Atlanta home and so saved her from its poisonous fangs. She stood near the vegetable plot with her apron full of cucumbers when the snake gave its warning rattle.

There are rattlers in the crevasses and rocks on the mountains which surround Dallas. My son John brought one home last summer when he was here on furlough. It had thirteen rattles, but the one I remember best had at least 'a thousand' according to the story I used to recite to Uncle Walter.

Speaking of Dallas, I should like to tell you a little about its characteristics. It is one of the few places in the United States that has a lace and textile plant as its only industry. The factory is new and modern, and besides making lace, also weaves all kinds of tricot, using nylon and dacron, and other synthetic yarns, in making beautiful designs and fabrics.

Dallas is not really a town but a country village nestling in the hills which are a continuation of the Pocono Mountains. These mountains are a chain east of the Alleghanies and eventually run into the Blue Ridge mountains of Virignia. The scenery is very beautiful. Many, many forests and hills are well-wooded at the top. It is said 'For grandeur go west to the Rockies, but for beauty Pennsylvania has it'.

There are lakes and swift mountain streams well stocked with brown trout and those 'speckled beauties' which are so wary and hard to hook.

'Thar's bars in them hills' too, and herds of wild deer, game of all kinds, including wild turkeys, pheasants, grouse and woodcock, and others too numerous to mention.

157

Everyone—well, practically everyone not on crutches—gets a hunting licence that includes a permit to shoot one deer per licence and takes to the woods in season.

It's bang - bang - bang throughout the hunting season, and it's a poor hunter who doesn't bag his deer to share with his neighbours and friends. Rabbits are a pest and a nuisance. All winter I get very attached to these rabbits and throw out food for them. It's amusing to sit by the window and watch them frisk around, especially on a moonlight night when the snow lies deep on the ground.

Comes spring and it's another story. All tender new shoots are fodder to these little destroyers. Young tulips just breaking ground are their special 'tit-bits'. That's the way I'm repaid for my winter feed. Swear I'll never put out another carrot or cabbage leaves, but still it goes on.

Dallas seems rather isolated and 'off the beaten track', but it's not really. We lie between Scranton and Wilkes Barre, far enough away to be clear of those coal-mining regions. There's no passenger train service except a freight train once in a while. Bus service runs hourly and we have an airport less than twenty miles distant.

I really think every family in this village has its own car, some of them more than one. Automobiles are not counted as luxuries but rather as necessities.

The school bus, paid for by the taxpayers, travels around and picks up the children at designated spots. Free transportation is provided if the school is more than a mile distant. Since most of the small district schools are being abandoned, consolidated schools are replacing many of those in the outlying sections.

The small shopkeeper has just about vanished. One 'supermarket' and all your shopping is done under one roof. 'Self-service' is the motto. Take a wire basket on wheels and wander up and down the aisles filling it with the provisions you want as you merrily wend your way through the store, greeting friends and neighbours engaged on the same errand. You pick out your own fruits, vegetables and meats already wrapped in cellophane, and after a complete absence of grab, the whole load is paid for at the 'check out' counter.

There is poverty and distress as in other countries, but it is not apparent here in Dallas. Everybody groans about the taxes and I am teased unmercifully but without malice about our aid to and 'Bundles for Britain' and our Lend-Lease program.

I can retort, 'Yes, but look what the Lace Mill has done and is doing for Dallas'. So we maintain friendly relations in spite of or because of everything that has gone on between our two countries.

Our American citizenship is a privilege and means a great deal. I would not sacrifice it or give it up for anything, but there is a warm spot in my heart for the land of my forebears.

An interesting item caught my eye one day. I see and hear of my friends claiming to be descendants of famous personages. My sister's husband, Edward Palmer Drake, claims to be descended from Sir Francis Drake. How come? I don't actually know!

But the one item that intrigues me was discovered by chance when other friends of mine were telling me of their ancestry and said, 'They came over on the *Mayflower*' which landed at Plymouth in the year 1620 bringing the Pilgrims.

If everyone making claims for that ancestral voyage were strictly true that old *Mayflower* would have had to be as large as the *Queen Elizabeth* and carry thousands upon thousands more passengers and crew instead of the original 24 women and 78 men.

Listed as a member of the crew on that historic and memorable voyage was one Moses Fletcher. I wonder what became of Moses? I'd like to believe his blood flows in our veins whether or not he had to flee England for his religious liberty, or if he had to escape for the heinous crime of stealing a sheep or a loaf of bread.

Many British imports are filling the shelves of our shops these days. 'Trade not Aid' has been a slogan these last few years, and laces are being shipped in, in large quantities.

We have to compete with Britain for our own customers. Higher production costs, with our much higher scale of wages and our higher standards of living, which we do not care to see reduced, sometimes makes this competition somewhat difficult.

Lace weaving is looked upon as a highly skilled trade and the auxiliary workers all share in the high wages paid.

It was extremely interesting to visit the Fletcher Lace Factory at Derby and to be escorted on a tour of the plant by members of the family who own and operate it and still manufacture lace, though in a more modern and up-to-date manner than the original lace men.

Buy lace, wear lace—there's nothing lovelier—and be proud of the family who have kept the trade going these many years!

PLATE 21

WILLIAM FLETCHER

CHAPTER IX

THE WILLIAM BRANCH

By George Fletcher of Long Eaton.

UNCLE Bill was born at Heanor on March 12th, 1842, and was never a master man in the lace trade, but as a young man worked a machine for my grandfather. Rather early in life, he had a stroke which left him with a useless leg, so he purchased the Railway Inn at Long Eaton and appears to have made good, as he spent many years in retirement and left a goodly fortune, half of which was divided between his surviving brothers and sisters, whilst the other half went to his wife.

Uncle Bill, my favourite of them all, was in early manhood a fine figure of a man. Around five feet ten inches in height, robust of build, good looking, dark and clean-shaven, a fourteen-stoner, and as hard and tough as chilled steel.

He was a grand cricketer, a great fisherman with rod and line, and a brilliant boxer who could have been matched against all-comers in the country but for his father's intervention. Grandfather Edward stood for peace, hard work and healthy enterprise, but did not countenance fighting.

It has often been said in the family that Uncle Bill gave sound thrashings to Bendigo, Champion of England, before this famous pugilist gave up strong drink to lead a religious life, and that he also taught King Edward the Seventh the elementary lessons of self-defence. Where and when these notable events took place is not known today, but I can well believe them to be true.

Boxing was his favourite life-long hobby and pastime. He had a few prints and accounts of all the principal prize fights and, as a youth, I often sat with him to read and study them.

One of Uncle Bill's greatest delights was to teach the young idea how to use the gloves, and that's how I learned a great deal about the art. These lessons bore fruit later on when I won a local competition against all-comers. It has been a comforting thought that, thanks to my teacher, I could defend myself in an emergency.

From the ruggedness of boxing to the delicacy of plying a fishing rod is a steep leap. Nevertheless, instinct, anticipation, timing and swiftness of action are common requirements if one is to become truly expert in either of these arts. Uncle Bill had them all so, as in boxing, he not only figured prominently in the contests of his day, but also aroused the interest in, and real love for angling in others which is a far greater success than personal triumphs.

He was indeed a great fisherman, and during my school holidays, or in other leisure hours, we had many outings together near Long Eaton. I used to carry his tackle to the waterside and stay with him all day. My age was then about twelve, and having little interest in the actual fishing, I got tired and fidgety, so when Uncle wouldn't pack up and start for home, I amused myself by throwing pebbles at his float. He took it all in good part and though he had his way and made me stay, I still remember him with affection as a grand boyhood pal. He lit the spark within me that led to infinite pleasure with rod and line in my later years.

We went here, there and everywhere on these country jaunts. On one occasion he took me to a cricket match at Shardlow, so we drove to Trent Station to catch the train from Nottingham.

Old Dick Daft of Nottinghamshire County Cricket Club fame saw us on the platform and invited Uncle and I to join him in his carriage. They immediately began to talk about cricket and I heard Mr Daft say 'You know, Bill, you are the only bowler who ever bowled me round my legs'. What better testimony to ability could be desired!

Uncle Bill must have been a power in the game, since not only was he Cambridge Town C.C. professional for several seasons, but also played for Cambridgeshire when the local club did not require his services.

All who follow the sport of 'Willow the King' know that Cambridgeshire gave two immortals to the game—Tom Hayward and John Berry Hobbs, of England and Surrey; so Uncle surely accomplished something of note by representing so famous a county cricket nursery.

He married Selina Clay of Hyson Green, and I believe the wedding took place at St. Paul's Church, almost facing the entrance to Terrace Street.

When they were host and hostess of the Railway Inn, it was a real treat to call there for a friendly drink and rest as one listened to the yarns of the old-timers of the town as they chatted to one another about the good old days and the [perhaps] not so good new ones.

Uncle Bill died on February 25th, 1904, and Aunt Selina on May 8th, 1906, at the age of sixty-two and sixty-four years respectively. They were both buried in Long Eaton Cemetery, and I am really concerned about the state of neglect of their grave today, where I recently found the headstone lying face downwards on mother earth.

Since Uncle and Aunt had no children, the Clay side of their family were the chief mourners, so I cannot say who is now responsible to do anything to remedy this regrettable condition of things.

This is all I can tell you about a very fine forebear; but I hope that what I have written here will make *you* feel a little prouder of the stock you have stemmed from.

PLATE 22

THE HOUGHTON BRANCH

Back row: ERNEST WILLIAM; Mother, *née* MARY FLETCHER; MABEL NELLIE; PERCY HERBERT; LILIAN MAY; WALTER HENRY
Front row: Father, HENRY DRURY HOUGHTON; ARNOLD EDWARD; Mrs ARNOLD EDWARD HOUGHTON
In front: GLADYS MAY, Grand-daughter

CHAPTER X

THE MARY-HENRY DRURY HOUGHTON BRANCH

Contributed by Walter Henry Houghton [son],
assisted by Gladys May Lees.

HENRY Drury Houghton was born at Mapperley, Derbyshire, on March 5th, 1854, and died at Carrfield Avenue, Long Eaton, on January 12th, 1939. His father, Aaron Houghton, formerly a mining engineer, came to Long Eaton as an architect and surveyor in 1868 when his son Henry was fourteen. He apprenticed him to Messrs Joseph and Thomas Fletcher, and he was trained in their draughting office.

In the meantime, Mary Fletcher, the last of the family left at home in Terrace Street, Hyson Green, was looking after her old father, Edward, and after his death, came to Long Eaton with enough of the old home furniture to furnish two rooms which she rented with Mr and Mrs Banks who lived just opposite to us in East Street. Her two brothers, Joe and Tom, put her in charge of the mending room, where she made a host of friends by her kindness and consideration.

One evening, brother Tom sent a message by Mary to Henry Houghton which brought about their first meeting and the beginning of a friendship. This ripened rapidly, and they were married from Samuel Fletcher's house in Nottingham when Henry Houghton was just twenty, and their first son, Arnold, was born four days before his father was twenty-one.

Soon after completing his apprenticeship he became head draughts man to his brother-in-law Samuel Fletcher for whom he had the highest regard and often said he was one of the very best men God made. This must have been true, for my father never praised you if you did well, only if you did the almost impossible.

A year or two later [1877], on hearing that Father wanted to start on his own as a lace manufacturer, Uncle Sam offered to go equal shares with him, as partner, in the new venture, which was launched at Radford, Nottinghamshire.

Father kept his full-time job with Uncle Sam, did his own draughting at home in the evenings, and put his new patterns on during his dinner hour.

When Mr Orchard built a large factory in Bank Street called New Mills, our small plant was removed to Long Eaton [1881] and Uncle Sam generously let Father buy his share, so he had the business as sole owner, and in the first week the plant made 50 per cent. more racks than the usual Nottingham total. Incidentally, Father was considered one of the finest 'top bar' draughtsmen in the trade and soon built up a good business.

In 1900 it was turned into a limited company with Father as managing director and Arnold and Walter, his two eldest sons, as directors. Three years later [1903] H. D. Houghton & Sons Ltd. purchased the business and plant of James Fletcher, a step that compelled a further move into Albion Mills to meet expanding trade demands. There, Levers lace, Swiss embroidery and plain nets were manufactured until Father's death when, soon afterwards, the machinery was sold.

Henry Houghton was, at the tender age of fourteen, the organist at the Baptist Church, Long Eaton, and when Tom Fletcher and J. Orchard bought a large organ for the Methodist Church, he was persuaded to play that, which he did for over twenty years.

Father was also a very fine musician and composer, and became conductor of the local choral society when Dr Gower left Trent College to go to Zion City, Utah, U.S.A. He was a man of strict integrity, with a stern regard for duty to the community, which six years' service on Long Eaton Urban District Council bears witness.

He also took a great interest in the British Israel World Federation movement and the science of astronomy and lectured extensively on both subjects in many parts of the country. We once went to examine the North Wales iron and manganese mine and when Father bought a big parcel of £1 shares for 30s. and some at 35s., each he was made a director. We were, however, soon alarmed by the quarrelling in the company, so I advised him to sell his holding for which he was offered 30s. each, but he refused, saying 'it was wrong for a man in a position of trust who had inside information to do so.'

The shares dropped to 2*s*. 6*d*. each, whereupon Father doubled his holding. By the outbreak of the 1914-18 War they had risen to £1 so, on selling out, he made a good profit from the whole transaction.

My father was ever ready to quietly help others in distress. One of the first jobs given me on starting work was to go with an old man who repaired our brass bobbins to pay off the bailiff in possession at his house, whilst on another occasion, he provided work for a young Castle Donington farm lad who was in trouble with the police for taking the cook's ring off the window-sill as he was passing and hiding it nearby for a lark for which he was given seven days in prison.

Many years afterwards I saw Arnold and our foreman talking to a stranger in the factory and as I got nearer, the stranger—actually the ex-farm lad who had become a prosperous musical instrument dealer and successful local preacher—turned to me and said 'Yes, this is the young man who used to throw stones at my backside when I was weeding his father's garden'.

At Christmas-time for many years, we distributed a lot of five-shilling pieces among the many poor old people needing good cheer in our neighbourhood.

My mother was very fond of fancy work, particularly crochet, needlework and tatting. She made us all a pair of tatted doilies before she died nearly fifty years ago. I still have the pair she made me, as I also have grandmother Phoebe Fletcher's small silver tea-spoon bag, a quaint little article made of net and tassels with an inside bag of close material.

Mother was indeed an excellent bread-maker and would often take a loaf along when visiting her brothers and sisters, whereupon the first one to greet her would rush off to circulate the news 'that we've got Aunty Mary's bread for tea today'. Incidentally, I, your Compiler, wonders what else they had to reinforce the 'staff of life' for I've often been told 'that *all* Fletchers *were*, and still *are*, keenly appreciative of the finer culinary arts.

She also often regaled we children with tales of Grandfather Fletcher and her life at Hyson Green with him and the rest of the family.

Apparently, when he first started in the lace trade he was very unfortunate with his partners, and one day when he was away, they sent some men [probably Luddite rioters or sympathisers] to take

167

out the insides of the machines. Fortunately, two of his elder sons were at work there, and one of them, picking up a large wrench, threatened to 'brain' the first man that touched the machines, so they all quickly left the factory.

This brought all the trouble to a head and destroyed the partnership, to leave Grandfather in sole possession of the business.

Mother once went with her father to pay a bill for silk, to an old friend Mr Froggatt; the bill was £1,000—a very large amount in those days. 'Now, Edward', said Mr Froggatt, 'take this cheque back and buy another machine; it will be a great help to you and I'll never ask you for the money'. But no, Grandfather preferred to settle the bill and go on quietly with the machines he had.

He wasn't always pleased with some of his sons who liked cricket more than work and was very glad when the two most promising of them both scored a duck in the annual 'Colts' match against the County at Trent Bridge.

In later years he told some of his sons it was time they got married and set up homes of their own. 'Dad', said Uncle Will, looking his father in the face, 'I won't leave the old ship while ever there is a rag of sail left on her'—a reply that quite disarmed and mollified the old man.

He was especially fond of little children and always kept a tin of sweets under his chair for those who visited him. This, together with many other stories about his lovable qualities, made some of us regret we were born too late to know him.

When Mother was a little girl at home, a bull that was being taken to slaughter became wildly infuriated by the smell of blood, broke loose and ran madly through Hyson Green, finally running down a passage into the Fletcher garden, where it was shot. Mother saw this happen through the window and was afraid of cows ever afterwards.

We spent many never-to-be-forgotten holidays at Uncle John's at Heanor. One day, when I was about four years old, chased by an angry uncle, I sped down the drive with his stick, but becoming frightened, threw the stick over the metal railings into the field which surrounded the house. Uncle caught me just as his favourite horse ran up to the fence, and threatened what he would do if I did not get him the stick. By then, I was much more afraid of uncle than the horse kicking me, and was soon over the fence and back again with it.

168

Some years later Mother took Arnold and I to Heanor Wakes and to see Uncle John again. Uncle George Fletcher and two of our cousins were there too.

As we were coming away after enjoying the fun of the fair, Uncle John took a bag containing nearly one hundred three-penny pieces out of his pocket and gave us one each. We youngsters felt in clover.

Our roots will be easier to follow if I state that my grandfather Aaron Houghton was twice married and had four sons and one daughter by his first wife, and two sons [H. D. Houghton was the eldest] and five daughters by his second—twelve children in all.

My father was married twice and had four sons and two daughters by his first wife Mary aforementioned. All his sons worked in the family lace business, and all the six children, except the eldest, are alive today.

Arnold Edward Houghton, the eldest of the family, was born on March 1st, 1875, and died March 30th, 1944. He, too, married twice, first to my mother, Annie Elizabeth Fritchley, of whom I, Gladys Mary Lees, am the only child, and then to Elsie Schofield.

Father was very fond of tennis and such fine contemporary exponents of the game as Grenville Morris, the Nottingham Forest and Welsh International footballer, John Heathcote, Denholm Davis, the well-known painter, and others of like repute, constantly played on our home courts.

He was salesman for H. D. Houghton and Sons Ltd. for their Levers lace, Swiss embroidery and plain net productions, the only firm in the country who made these three distinctive types of goods at that time. He afterwards left the firm and went into partnership with his brother-in-law, William C. Rhodes Gregory, as silk merchants in Nottingham, in 1922.

As *Gladys May Houghton,* my bent lay in the direction of painting in oils and I was also tempted to earn my living professionally as a singer, but, preferring a home instead, I married Norman Lees, whose father was General Manager of the Newstead and Blidworth Collieries. My husband has a post in the Clayworks Department of the National Coal Board.

We have had two children; the first died at birth. Our daughter, *Ruth Elizabeth,* is studying occupational therapy and may go to Oxford in pursuit of further knowledge of this subject.

You may be interested to know that our home lies in the midst of the Byron country, and that Robin Hood's Stables, cut in the solid rock, are only a few yards from the house.

I, *Walter Henry Houghton*, have been both Director and Secretary of H. D. Houghton and Sons Ltd. for fifty-six years; Managing Director since 1939 and, in the words of my niece, am the most travelled member of our family, having visited many parts of the British Isles, America and Canada, besides Norway and other European countries.

I married Margaret, the eldest daughter of Mr Francis Reddish of Ilkeston, Director of J. B. Lewis and Sons, hosiery manufacturers.

She was the president of the Friar Lane Blind Club and is still remembered with great affection by them for her tender sympathy and kindness. She died soon after our removal to Worthing, where I am now living. Her epitaph—'The friend of the poor, the lonely and the blind'—is in the Book of Remembrance at the Brighton Crematorium.

Mother was very fond of my paintings, a hobby I have kept up for about seventy years. I still work half my time at pastel drawings and oil paintings of flowers, grown in my own garden and my neighbours', where I can go and pick any blooms I require.

Lilian May Houghton was a good pianist and is noted for her artistic work, especially her needlework. She passed several important examinations in music, but had to relinquish her studies because of her mother's ill-health.

She married Alfred E. Start, a lace manufacturer of Long Eaton and Sandiacre, but had no children. Many years ago they made their home at Hempton, seven miles from Oxford in the Cotswolds, where Mrs Start, now a widow, still resides.

One of her cherished girlhood memories is Nottingham Goose Fair when the great market place was packed till there was no room to move. Then, last thing before going home, all brothers and sisters, arms locked together, had a final push through the dense mass of revellers.

Percy Herbert Houghton worked with the firm till ill-health compelled him to leave the lace trade. He is still a director of H. D. Houghton and Sons Ltd. who still own the factory and other properties in Long Eaton and have added the publication and sale of the late Mr H. D. Houghton's religious books to the field of their activities.

170

He married Ada Alice Webster and they have had two children; the daughter, Laura Marjorie, died when about four years of age.

They retired to live near Sidmouth, Devon, in 1940, but have lately returned to Long Eaton to live near their son and his family.

Their son, *Ronald Frederick Fletcher Houghton*, married Mary, the daughter of Mr Stevenson who was the manager of Long Eaton Gas Works. They live in Long Eaton and he is a traveller in tobacco and cigars, etc. for a local firm.

Mabel Nellie Houghton married William C. Rhodes Gregory, partner with Arnold E. Houghton in silk merchanting in Nottingham. They had no children, and my sister, now a widow, lives at Breaston, Derbyshire.

Ernest William Houghton at first worked in the family business, but afterwards for himself as a lace manufacturer. He is now a director of H. D. Houghton and Sons Ltd. and still lives at Long Eaton.

He married Daisy Lilian, daughter of George Smith, lace manufacturer, of Long Eaton. They have two children, *Robert William*, who has a son Robert William and a daughter Elizabeth Ann; and *Josephine Mary*, now *Mrs Ross Stokes* and mother of a son, Adrian.

Pranks of our youth—with belated apologies to the victims.

(1) Arnold and I attended 'Gaffer' Tod's private school, and one morning we were kept in to revise our neglected lesson. Mr Snell, the undermaster, and the Rev. Tod were both in the room when the former asked me 'Where do we get stone from?'

'There are plenty of stones in our garden', I said, 'you can have as many as you want.'

'Ask him another', snapped the 'Gaffer' and 'Where do we get salt from?' came the next question, and my reply was 'From out of the salt pot in the kitchen cupboard'.

Thereupon, old 'Gaffer' Tod looked up from the newspaper he was reading, fixed me with a twinkling eye, and said 'Let them go', and off we rushed home for dinner.

(2) One day, after reading a gardening paper, father got the idea we ought to have some frogs in the garden and offered us twopence each for every one we could get; so we promised to supply him.

We took a sack bag to a spot we knew of in some fields belonging to our friends the Roberts of Toton and brought back about fifty,

171

all sizes from three-quarters-of-an-inch to frogs nearly as big as your fist, and turned them out on to the garden path for father to inspect.

Father was a serious man and rarely laughed, but when he saw the babies, grown-ups and grandfathers all jumping around, he laughed as I never saw him do before.

When he had recovered, he said the tiny ones were not worth two-pence—would we be satisfied with two shillings for the lot? We were, and our pals the Roberts boys got their share on our next visit. The frogs were not very happy with the change as by next day there was not one to be seen in our garden.

(3) When Arnold was about four years old and I three, we lived in a small house in East Street and had a maid named Jane. She had bought a new hat for the school sermons with large red and black cherries on it.

One Monday morning, when she was busy outside the back door ponching the weekly wash, we two boys crept upstairs, found the new hat, pulled off all the bright cherries, put them into a jug of water, opened the bedroom window and poured the lot over her as she worked below. To this day, I blush with shame when I recall the hurt look of dismay she gave us when she recognised the ruined trimmings belonging to the hat she was so proud of.

(4) Arnold and Hiram Fletcher, his cousin, were great friends for many years, and many were the pranks they played together, such as fastening empty walnut shells to the feet of the family cat before letting it loose in the attic. When these young mischief-makers heard Hiram's father coming upstairs, poker in hand, to investigate, they lay low to await the delight of hearing him mutter 'It's them dratted boys again' as the cat flew past him in the dark.

They went too far one day when they shot at the gardener's rear portion with an air-gun as he worked among the shrubs and flowers, so Uncle Robert put them across his knee and added another good strapping to those they had previously well deserved.

Luckily, these spankings failed to curb their tricks, which was as well, since had there been no English dare-devils, history would not have had its Drakes.

(5) And, if I was asked, I could thrill you with stories about some really serious pranks which shocked the wider family circle to the centre of its being fifty years and more ago.

You would then almost see the fights between Fletchers and other surnamed cousins—so fierce were they, that crutches were needed for weeks afterwards to struggle to work upon. You would almost be a part of the feud between 'House' and 'Hall'. You would then know *Why* Uncle Jim removed all his plant from the factory destroyed by fire shortly afterwards. You would, in sympathy, walk in the dead of night with the maiden carrying her best frock over her arm as she crept quietly down the back staircase of her home to join her husband-to-be, who sat waiting for her in a horse-drawn carriage at the crossroads nearby. You would learn much more Fletcher family lore; but since all who took part in these escapades now cannot speak for themselves, I will relate only one short storyette about Uncle Dick Fletcher.

Being thrown from a gig when out for the day with his pals, and having his head deeply cut from forehead to back, he lay very still on the ground covered with blood. One of his pals, believing he was dead, said 'Poor Old Dick, he's gone aloft'. Uncle then opened one eye to look at him and murmured 'Not yet, my lad'. This was a reassuring ending to that adventure.

My niece and I would like to conclude by mentioning our many Houghton family connections, many of whom we have never met.

One of our better known cousins is Douglas Houghton, now Member of Parliament for Sowerby Bridge, Yorkshire. He is the youngest son of John who was Henry Drury Houghton's brother, and many of you will recall his broadcasts in the B.B.C. 'Can I Help You' series.

We hope that our contribution to our Fletcher Story will be enjoyed by you all.

174

PLATE 23
THE HOOTON BRANCH
WALTER and BETSY (née FLETCHER)
and their daughters MARY, ELIZABETH and FLORENCE

CHAPTER XI

THE BETSY-WALTER HOOTON BRANCH
[AUSTRALIAN SECTION]
By Nigel Brock

MARY, the eldest child of Walter and Betsy Hooton, was born at Yarmouth on February 4th, 1869.

In her early childhood the family moved to Long Eaton and built Ireton House when Mr Hooton entered the lace trade, in which he was engaged until his death in 1909, with fluctuating success, according to the economic conditions the lace trade enjoyed or suffered since its inception in Nottingham.

Doubtless, had Walter Hooton been relieved of the cares of industry he would have indulged himself in the arts and sciences, which were nearest to his heart. He was a member of the Archaeological Society, and with a Reverend friend [whose name the writer is unable to recall] enjoyed many a search for treasures of a geological nature.

His artistic temperament was demonstrated in his fondness for old-masters, furniture and gems. On the other hand, he was a natural musician and fond of playing his daughter's accompaniments ever since she could walk.

He engaged Mr Boswell [who later married a Miss Hollingsworth, also of Long Eaton] to give Mary her first music lessons. She sang in her first concert when twelve years of age.

When Madame Fannie Lymn returned to Nottingham following a successful studentship at the Royal Academy of Music, so impressed was she with the beauty of the warm, deep tones of Mary's young untrained voice—nurtured by the effervescent enthusiasm of youth—that she undertook Mary's preparation as a singer.

Under her tuition, the young contralto rapidly progressed and in 1884 Mary made the long journey to London with her father to interview the Principal of the Royal Academy of Music, Sir George Macfaren.

Not yet sixteen, Mary and her father were to receive a very great disappointment when Sir George regretfully told them the rules of the Academy barred students under sixteen years of age!

'However,' he said, 'as they had travelled so far he could see no reason why he should not hear the young lady sing' [*O rest in the Lord*].

Such was the training of Madame Fanny Lymn that Sir George Macfaren was delighted, praised the teacher, and was generous enough to say 'The rules must be broken to allow so promising a young singer to study at this institution'.

Mr Hooton, having placed his daughter under the care of Mrs Hahn—a lady who accepted a very limited number of students [amongst them, one W. H. Squire, of Nottingham district, possibly Long Eaton], later to become famous as a 'cellist—returned home after a touching farewell.

At this juncture it was decided to change her name to Marie because one of Mrs Hahn's daughters was named Mary.

Thus it was that the young vocalist, destined to become one of England's outstanding oratorio singers throughout the British Isles, and, during the many world tours that followed, as a vocalist whose charm of voice and attractive appearance delighted millions—discontinued using the most beautiful name in the English language.

During her six years at the Royal Academy of Music, where she gained excellent tuition under the late Frank R. Cox, Marie Hooton won the coveted Certificate of Merit, the Bronze Medal, the Silver Medal, the Parepa Rosa Gold Medal, and the Westmorland Scholarship as contralto in addition to the Bronze Medal for elocution. [All these awards, except the certificate, were destroyed during the 1940-41 blitz on London.]

Subsequently, she had the honour, during Sir Alexander Mackenzie's regime, on several occasions, of adjudicating at the R.A.M., and Sir William Cumming, Principal of the Guildhall School of Music, also paid her the same compliment.

At the age of twenty-two, Marie Hooton married Edward Branscombe at St Giles-in-the-Fields, London. He was an eminent tenor singer and a lay vicar of Westminster Abbey.

For the next few years they were both engaged, chiefly for oratorio, by all the principal festival and musical societies in the British Isles.

176

Edward Branscombe was considered the greatest authority on English part-singing by no less a master than Sir Frederick Bridge. Until the death of Queen Victoria, the services of these two artistes were in great demand all over the United Kingdom.

When Westminster Abbey was closed in preparation for the Coronation of King Edward the Seventh, Edward Branscombe conceived the idea of forming a party of choristers from the Abbey choir and leading London churches, and of visiting outlying parts of the Empire with the Westminster Glee Party. Three tours were made of Canada and in 1903 the company commenced its first tour of New Zealand and Australia in Auckland—a very big undertaking, the success of which is historic; but it may be mentioned that during the tour the receipts at the Sydney Town Hall amounted to over £1,000 in one week.

This was followed by a tour of the same company in the United States of America.

South Africa and India were visited in 1904, China and Japan in 1905; in the same year a second visit was paid to Australia, the success of this type of work in every part of the English-speaking world being remarkable.

Fresh fields were sought, and embraced the Hawaiian Islands, Fijian Islands, the Bahamas, the West Indies, British Guiana, Java and Sumatra.

It is perhaps needless to say that certain of these places did not show a monetary profit, but immense interest was aroused and in very many places the Westminster Glee Party was the first musical organisation to visit them, notably in Peking, Hankow, the Malay States, Java, Sumatra, Cuba and Newfoundland.

While waiting at Santiago de Cuba for the boat to Jamaica, an amusing—if unremunerative—experiment was tried. The manager of the local theatre, 'Teatro del Oriente', was persuaded to allow some performances to be given. It was an interesting attempt to convey to the people of the Latin race, with its taste for florid and passionate music, an impression of the harmonised lyrical melodies of the Saxon race and the result, though probably not what was hoped for, was, possibly, that which was anticipated—the receipts on the first night were £7, the second £3, and the third night twenty-four shillings! Even the comedy sketches of the man at the piano

failed to evoke the laughter which usually followed them, without the aid of an interpreter. ili · · ... ...
...There were many interesting experiences in these long tours. When the company was travelling by train from Hankow to Tientsin, owing to the staff not being considered reliable, other than in daylight, the train was pulled up each night at six o'clock and was promptly surrounded by the Chinese police to guard against robbery, and the food having given out, members of the company had rather an exciting time going down to the villages to procure more.

To add to the discomfort, all through the night, the police guarding the train—doubtless to keep their courage up—shouted to each other and ejaculated weird noises, making sleep impossible.

On another occasion, when leaving Shanghai after a concert, they had to charter a tug to catch the mail-boat, but the tug struck a sandbank where it remained fast and there the company had to stay in evening clothes all night, to return to Shanghai in the morning. They had of course missed the mail steamer.

During all these tours Madame Marie Hooton was the only lady vocalist. ... ...

It goes without saying that the hearing again of beautiful English singing by vocalists direct from London brought joy to many British exiles living in different countries of the world. ... ...

During rests in England between these tours, Mr. Branscombe formed other concert parties such as 'The Pages of the King', 'The Scarlet Mysteries' which included Mr Ford Waltham, the noted bass, of Nottingham, and Mr Tom Walls. The latter left 'The Scarlet Mysteries' during the Canadian tour to make his name and fortune in London as a great comedian of stage and radio and owner of April the Fifth [his birthday] which won the Derby. ... ...

'The Scarlet Mysteries' gave a lighter type of performance and created a record by touring the world for four years. But Madame Marie Hooton did not accompany them, preferring to continue her work as vocalist with the famous 'Cherniavsky' Trio comprising Leo [violin], Jan [piano] and Mischel ['cello] on their concert tours of Africa, Australia and New Zealand. ... ...
... ...

SOUSA'S BAND

When the tour of South Africa, Australia and New Zealand of Sousa's Band was arranged by Mr Branscombe [through his manager then in London, Mr Nigel Brock], Madame Marie Hooton joined

178

PLATE 24
MARIE HOOTON

him in Australia which, owing to the outbreak of the first World War, rang down the curtain on the innumerable professional appearances of this fair daughter of Nottingham whose name may be rightly added to the long list of notabilities of that city.

Having taken up a career which inevitably involved much travelling, it is only natural that the love of her family—which meant more to her than anything else—took her home to her fond mother and father at Ireton House whenever her musical engagements found her within reasonable distance.

It was her pride and privilege, whenever illness or misfortune or the lace trade was in the doldrums, to come generously to their aid in a very practical manner. In fact, nothing, since that eventful day when a girl of fifteen, Mary became a worthy student of the Royal Academy of Music and left the shelter of the family circle at Ireton House, Long Eaton, to sing her way round the world as Madame Marie Hooton, could lessen the great love and affection she always cherished for her family.

It was probably the saddest moment of her life when, on arrival in England at the termination of a world tour per s.s. *Atrato*, April 29th, 1906. [during which she visited twenty-seven different countries, travelled 72,858 miles, singing at 552 concerts, and thus constituting a record] the news of her dear mother's death a few days before [on April 23rd] was conveyed to her on board the ship.

RELATIONS

Mary had three sisters—Elizabeth, Florence and Gladys—and one brother, Edward Fletcher.

Elizabeth married Frank Wilkinson, son of Frank Wilkinson, head of the firm Wilkinsons Ltd., lace manufacturers, whose outstanding success in the trade was probably due to the exclusive manufacture of silk shawls, stockings and laces. Their union was blessed by the birth of a daughter, Betsy.

Edward was born at Nottingham on March 23rd, 1871, and was educated at Risley Grammar School. He joined his father's business and was considered one of the leading designers in the lace trade. He migrated to Australia in 1912 and died in 1948 at the Royal

179

Melbourne Hospital. It was due to the encouragement from his sister Mary that he took up painting and became well known as a water-colour artist of the Australian bushland.

Florence was born at Long Eaton on June 6th, 1882, and was educated at Stratford Abbey College, Stroud, Gloucestershire. She came to Australia with Edward Branscombe in 1909 when that great impressario, realising the possibilities of the alfresco type of performance in that sunny land, established a small company of artistes known as 'The Jesters' suitably costumed in the Robin Hood style, at St Kilda, a popular seaside resort near Melbourne, Victoria.

The innovation proved popular and during the next few years no less than eight comedy costume companies under the generic title 'The Dandies' enjoyed considerable success throughout Australia and New Zealand.

Florence quickly established her position as soubrette and adopting the stage name of Florence Henderson became a general favourite. In that company she met and married—for the second time—Mr Ben Calvert, the noted English tenor from Halifax, Yorkshire, at Brisbane in 1913.

Later, they took up land in Victoria at Mildura, which is the biggest dried fruit area in the Empire. On the death of her husband, 'Hendy'—as she was popularly known—came to live with her sister Mary and brother in Melbourne until her death in May 1945.

Gladys was born at Long Eaton on January 24th, 1886. She married Reginald Kent, son of Mr Kent of Kent and Cooper of Nottingham, at Nottingham on April 30th, 1908. They had three children—Walter, Stephen and Betsy. During the first World War Gladys did war work at Chilwell munitions factory.

In 1923 the whole family migrated to Australia, and in Melbourne, not long after they settled, her husband died as the result of war wounds. This left Gladys a widow with a young family to fend for under very difficult conditions and it speaks volumes for her courage and resource that they prospered so well.

Walter, born at Long Eaton on January 4th, 1909, was educated at Caulfield Grammar School, Melbourne, and during the second World War employed by the Department of Aircraft Production until he joined the U.S.A. Naval Forces as engineer and visited several theatres of war in the Pacific.

He finished his war service as Commander, and then joined the Commonweal Oil Refinery Ltd. and now holds a lucrative post on the executive.

Stephen, born at Long Eaton December 27th, 1910, also received his education at Caulfield Grammar School, Melbourne, and then entered the soft goods trade. Immediately war broke out he volunteered for service and fought and served on many fronts for ten years until demobilised after service in Japan as Lieutenant. He was mentioned in despatches from Greece. His marriage with Nancy Watson in 1940 was dissolved in 1945 when he returned to manage a copra plantation in New Guinea.

Betsy was born at Long Eaton on December 30th, 1911. She was educated at Shelford C.E. Grammar School and in 1942 married Thomas Stephens only four months before he embarked with the R.A.A.F. Unfortunately, during non-operational flights in Scotland Flying-Officer Stephens' plane collided with another and he was killed. As a war widow Betsy, who lives with her mother, is employed by the Air Board at the Barracks, Melbourne.

MARIE HOOTON'S SECOND MARRIAGE

After she divorced Edward Branscombe in 1915, Mary married Nigel Brock in 1916 in Melbourne, Victoria, who had joined the Westminster Glee Party as manager, in South Africa in 1904 and lived most happily with her to the end of her life in late December 1952.

Having seen so much of the world together, before two great wars brought death and destruction to millions of people and upsetting the peace and tranquillity of those countries which had found life grand and glorious under the gentle sway of the arts, sciences, decency and discipline, Mary and Nigel closed the piano, stored away the music, and with memories which made such a happy anchorage for their thoughts, retired to a quiet backwater of life and allowed the curtain to slowly descend on the career of one of England's most distinguished contralto singers.

181

A Short Poem and Fitting Epitaph

'THE TIME HAS COME'

The time has come for us to fight
For liberty and truth and right.
To stop all war and strife and sin
And turn our hearts again to Him.
To end this war of hate and gain
At others' cost and health and pain,
To work for lasting peace and good
And form a world-wide brotherhood.

[*Marie Hooton Brock, June 23rd*, 1940].

Any comment here would be near sacrilege. The spirit of these moving lines lay bare the rich contents of a great heart for all to see when her soul ascended unto heaven on December 17th, 1952.

[S.B.F.]

MARIE HOOTON: SPECIAL SUPPLEMENT

Appearances in Oratorio

In her chief work—oratorio—throughout the United Kingdom, Marie Hooton appeared with many noted singers including Sir Charles Santley, Andrew Black, Watkin Mills, Ben Davies, Alex Marsh, Ella Russell, Ester Palliser, Mendora Henson, and others.

Conductors

Marie Hooton sang under the baton of England's most famous conductors—Sir Henry Wood [her tutor and friend]; Sir Hamilton Harty, Dr Swinnerton Heap, Dr Mann, Sir Edward Elgar, Sir Alexander MacKenzie, Sir Joseph Barnby, George Risely and Allen Gill.

It is worthy of special mention that she sang no less than seven times in one season at the Birmingham Town Hall for the Birmingham Festival Society. One performance was as the contralto in Swinnerton Heap's *Maid of Astolet*, referring to which 'The Birmingham Post' reported 'Miss Marie Hooton fairly electrified her audiences.'

Halls

Among the halls in which Marie Hooton sang were the Albert Hall, Queen's Hall, St James, Steinway, Aeolian, Crystal Palace,

182

People's Palace, Bechstein in London, and Massey Hall, Toronto, Canada, and leading halls in America and the Dominions.

The last professional appearance in England was conducted by Sir Henry Wood at Queen's Hall, London in 1911, when she retired at the height of her fame.

Needlework

With such good home influence, it is not to be wondered at that all four girls were thoroughly domesticated, and crochet work was a natural gift. Among Mary's treasures was found her 'Celebrity Cloth' containing the names of nearly two hundred famous and well-known musical folk throughout the world who wrote their names in pencil on it and which were then embroidered in silk by Mary herself.

With charming modesty she possessed a simple and generous nature which endeared her to all those who knew her. Endowed with a wonderful constitution, Mary led a very active life until towards the end of her days she became a victim of arthritis. She had little care for the social side of life outside her family and small circle of friends, and wherever possible never allowed her busy fingers to be idle, preferring to take with her some small piece of embroidery when she was invited out. Fond of poetry, she read a good deal and wrote several little poems for her own amusement. From her father she inherited a love for old furniture, pictures, ornaments, etc. and her drawing room at The Elms, Acton Hill, London, was ample evidence of this.

Her many public appearances necessitated maintaining a large wardrobe of gowns made by leading London and Paris dressmakers. Her beautiful figure and excellent deportment completed a picture of loveliness.

The Story of a Nottingham Pie (in her own words)

During the long journey across Canada we gave a concert at Medicine Hat and a Mrs Wilson came round to the artistes' room and we got talking about home.

She was full of excitement at finding I too came from Nottingham. I happened to say 'I'd love to be able to get hold of a good old-fashioned Nottingham pork pie'. We had to travel on early next day, but just as the train was about to leave, lo and behold, up came running Mrs Wilson with a lovely pork pie! The dear soul had sat up all night making it especially for me. Was it not most kind of her?

Outstanding Events and Scenes

When asked for some outstanding events and scenes of her most interesting life, Mary would recall the Sea of Phosphorus at Manila. The ship *Chingtu* which called there with the Westminster Glee Party en route from Hong Kong to Australia aboard, dropped anchor in the bay.

A concert had been arranged in the old city of Manila that night, but transport arrangements went astray and the launch to take the party ashore failed to materialise. Eventually, the captain took us ashore in one of the ship's boats and it was when rowing ashore we ran into a sea of phorphorus. As the lifeboat moved over the water the glow was so strong one could read a newspaper by its light. The fish left a trail of fire as they scurried away and the oars created under-waves of glorious hue.

The Sea Gardens at Nassau, Bahama Islands

These were another unforgettable sight. The gardens are observed through a long glass-bottomed boat while it is being slowly towed over an area of about fifteen acres. At various shallow depths the sea bed is a mass of tinted coral and sponges interspersed with green seaweeds waving in the water as lovely coloured fish glide amongst the undulating sandhills.

The ever-changing beauty of that submarine feature drew forth most excited expressions of amazement from the peering passengers.

Nottinghamians and Long Eatonians Abroad

Mary was always pleased to meet abroad folk from Nottingham and Long Eaton who came to speak to her after the concerts.

One of these meetings happened in Bulawayo, Rhodesia, when a handsome young Scotsman called at her hotel to enquire if she was the Miss Hooton from Long Eaton, as his wife was the daughter of the Rev. Grove, Headmaster of Risley Grammar School. If so, could she possibly visit them at their farm miles out on the veldt. Unfortunately, much as Mary would have loved to see them again, the itinerary allowed no time.

On another occasion she was singing in Mafeking and met a Mr Boswell, a piano teacher, who gave Mary her first music lessons!

184

At Moose Jaw, Canada, Mr Harold Marshall—brother of Zillah—came to see her on the train.

Quite recently, in Melbourne, she met young Guy Bloomer [son of Dr Fred Bloomer of Long Eaton] who, with his wife and family, is farming at Willow Grove in Gippsland, Victoria.

Mary also enjoyed meeting Mr and Mrs Manny Crowe during a business trip connected with the lace trade.

NIGEL BROCK.

A glance at the Hooton backroots shows us that a wealth of intellect and love of adventure characterised this branch of the female line of our family to a very marked degree.

Marie's paternal grandfather and his brothers, particularly Walter, William and Charles, were typical of their stock, and an enthralling story could be woven around their achievements and accomplishments at home and overseas since the early eighteen-hundreds.

Charles Hooton [1810-47], writer and explorer, the most famous of them all, was born at Nottingham in Upper Parliament Street on May 10th, 1810. He was contemporary with Charles Dickens and edited the *Leeds Times* for some time, but came to London where he wielded a prolific pen, producing novels, poetry, ballads illustrating American life and literature, and two skits, 'The True Sun' and 'The Woolsack', one attacking political economy, and the other the Court of Chancery.

Charles Hooton was equally at home with pen, pencil and palette, whilst in politics his views could be described as somewhat radical and rather revolutionary.

He spent nine months in Texas where he led an almost savage life. Newspaper work was afterwards attempted in New Orleans, New York and Montreal, after which he returned to England broken in mind and body.

'The Adventures of Bilberry Thurland', 'Colin Clink', 'Launcelot Widge', 'Peregrine Bunce', 'Woodhouse Lee or The Astrologer', and 'St Louis Isle or Texiana', with additional observations made in the United States and Canada, are his best known novels.

The last-named describes his day-by-day efforts and sufferings in Texas, then a state of unfruitful desolation and attempted colonisation. Copies of this work, presented to the People's Library by

185

Robert William McCallum in 1849, and Martin I. Preston in 1859, are now housed in the City Free Library, Nottingham, where they may be examined.

A Charles Hooton Poem

'REST AND BE THANKFUL'

'Tis pleasant here amid the wilds
 Where all around is still,
A valley deep as ocean's bed
 Shut by a cloudy hill.

For him who weary from afar
 Has travell'd sad and lone
To see such welcome words as these
 Writ on a wayside stone.

The mountain shepherd often stands
 And ponders when he's read
And wonders as he reads again
 To whom these words are said.

Ah! shepherd, turn thine ear
 And list a moment unto me;
Those words are said to all on earth
 That are or e'er shall be.

They say unto us all alike
 When we lie down at night,
Rest and be thankful tho' thy toil
 Comes with returning light.

And so each day and month and year
 When we look on the past,
'Rest and be thankful' echoes Time,
 Ye've reach'd this height at last.

       —Charles Hooton.

These lines, in the form of an inscription on a stone at the top of Glen Coe, Argyllshire, Scotland, were written by Charles Hooton after climbing the heights where it stands. Charles Hooton's stay in Texas completely ruined his health and he died in Nottingham next door but one [Nottingham side] to the

Forest Tavern, Mansfield Road, on February 16th, 1847, following an overdose of morphia taken to deaden continuous pain.

[N.B.—Informative accounts of Charles Hooton can be studied in Godfrey's 'Notes on St Mary's Registers, pages 73-74, and in Wylie's 'Old and New Nottingham', pages 168 and 210, upon which Godfrey based his note.

Before he died Charles Hooton fell on very hard times and had to apply to the Literary Fund for some assistance and was granted £20.—S.B.F.]

William Hooton, shipowner and trader

One of the many references made by Marie about the back-roots of the Hooton sept of our family, concerns her great-uncle William who went over to America about the year 1820 and established a prosperous business in Louisiana.

How long he and his wife lived there is not known, but the owner-ship of several vessels enabled him to do a thriving trade in the Gulf of Mexico.

His sister-in-law, Mrs Pollack, a wealthy slave-owner, made a will leaving all she possessed to her only sister, great-uncle William's wife. She died first, then great-uncle and, as Mrs Pollack had no other next-of-kin, the estate should have come to our family [the Hootons]. Great-uncle William's brother, grandfather Hooton, and their other brothers would not cross the sea to claim this goodly fortune. There was a lot of correspondence on the matter, but there it all ended. It was indeed a very large estate to which we, the rightful descendants, were justly entitled, but received nothing.

This declaration was signed by Mary Brock, née Hooton, on June 19th, 1928, at Perth, Western Australia, and is at present preserved among the collection of Fletcher family papers.

On another occasion Marie mentioned other Hooton interests in the Mechanics Institution and the George Hotel, Nottingham, and in landed property adjoining the River Trent and similar entitlements in and around the town.

To me, this was an echo of the voice of a poor, old, but very valued friend of my wife's mother—a Miss Betsy Hooton, who often spoke of these same local associations and Marie Hooton's wonderful singing over forty years ago.

The 'Who's Who' of it all puzzled me then and it still poses a pretty family identity problem today. So, mindful of the difficulties

187

that may confront a future Hooton delver into history, the 'Seal of Henry de Hoton' is included among the Supplements of our Family Story. This valuable record was handed to me by Nigel Brock after Marie, his wife, died, and it, too, is housed in our family archives. [S.B.F.]

THE LAST WORD ON THIS BRANCH OF THE FLETCHER FAMILY
By Richard Joseph Hooton of Chesterfield

My mother, Ada Moore Eastwood, was the second daughter of Edward Isaac Eastwood, the eldest son of Edward Eastwood who founded the Edward Eastwood Railway Wagon and Wheel Works in 1864.

My grandfather Eastwood died suddenly of pneumonia in his early thirties whilst on a business trip to Russia, where he was buried in the Smolensk Cemetery in St Petersburg, now Leningrad. He was a mining engineer by profession and married Susannah Bush, daughter of a lace manufacturer of Long Eaton.

My mother married my father, Edward Fletcher Hooton, in 1895 and they resided in Long Eaton where my father was a designer of lace in his father's lace works.

There were four children of the marriage, three sons and one daughter, and after my father migrated to Australia in 1912 we stayed in Long Eaton till the end of the 1914-18 War, when we went to live in Chesterfield. There we came under the care of mother's bachelor uncle, Alderman George Albert Eastwood, the second son of the founder of the Eastwood Wagon Works and the owner of the firm.

My eldest brother Walter Edward fought in the first Great War from the early days until he was wounded in the Battle of Passchendaele in 1917, being hit in the left knee which caused him to have a permanently stiff leg.

He married twice, having a son, Michael, by his first wife, and two sons, Martin and Nigel, by his second one.

My elder brother George Eastwood was in the Inns of Court O.T.C. at the end of the Great War and was then transferred to the London Scottish Regiment and served in the Army of Occupation on the Rhine, subsequently joining the Gordon Highlanders.

After his war service he joined the family firm of Edward Eastwood and in 1928 he married Norah Margaret, the daughter of John

188

Henry Green, of the firm of J. H. & F. W. Green, timber merchants, of Chesterfield. They have two children, Anne Elizabeth and Edward George Eastwood.

On the death of Alderman G. A. Eastwood, the Wagon Works passed to his niece, Susan Blanche Eastwood, my mother's elder sister, and my brother George became general manager and later, chairman and managing director when the firm was made into a limited company.

He, George, founded the firm of Hooton & Green, iron and steel merchants of Chesterfield, and is a director of several concerns, including the Renishaw Iron Works at Eckington, Derbyshire. His many personal interests include gardening, fishing and cruising on the Norfolk Broads.

My sister Elizabeth Mary Blanche, the youngest of our family of four, was married at the end of the last war to Ernest, son of the late Herr Strauss of Frankfurt and Amsterdam, and is mother to one little son, Rodney David. Her husband is a district manager for the United Africa Company, a branch of the great concern of Levers, in Nigeria. They spend a very large part of their time in Nigeria, both in the capital, Lagos, and in the various Districts, and during Her Majesty the Queen's visit to Nigeria they attended the Royal Garden Party.

My sister was always a great music lover, and in the nineteen-thirties she and I attended many concerts given by great international artistes. I remember one concert where we heard the great pianist Paderewski snap the strings of his Erard while playing Liszt's Second Hungarian Rhapsody, and we were enthralled by the singing of Chaliapine and Galli-Curci and the violin of Kreisler.

A sideline of my sister's concert-going was the collecting of autographs of the famous, which ultimately spread beyond the confines of the musical world and gathered in literature, politics, sport and the stage, among others.

The third member of our family is myself, Richard Joseph. I was just twelve years old at the end of the first Great War and left school some years later when we went to live in Chesterfield. I received training as a metallurgist at Sheffield University and joined the Staveley Coal and Iron Co. Ltd. of Chesterfield in their laboratories. In 1940 I married Dorothy Margaret, daughter of Albert Whalley of Wood Green, North London.

I was not called into the armed services because of the nature of the work I was doing, but became an area captain in the local fire-guard service where we had the tedious work of organisation but, fortunately, no need for practical use of our labours. The nearest air raid visitations of any severity were the two bad raids on Sheffield and as I was watching the effects from a distance of twelve miles, my thoughts went back twenty-five years to a night in the first Great War when a Zeppelin raid took place near Long Eaton and bombs were dropped close to Stanton Iron Works.

My wife and I made our home with my mother. She is in very good health and over eighty years old. We have no family of our own.

My chief interests have been the study of science, growing cacti, book collecting, and playing chess. I am a past-president of the Derbyshire Chess Association and have acted as county match captain for several years.

Coming to the next generation of our family, my brother Walter's eldest son Michael is married and has a young son, Paul.

My brother George's daughter Anne married Brian, the son of Albert Parsons of A. E. Parsons, electrical contractors Ltd. of Chesterfield. They have no family yet.

Anne's younger brother Edward has done his National Service in the Royal Artillery.

190

PLATE 25

ANNIE MULLIS
(Eldest daughter of RICHARD FLETCHER)

CHAPTER XII

THE RICHARD BRANCH

Compiled from extracts from the 'Fletcher Collection of Family Letters'
supplemented by notes supplied by George Fletcher of Long Eaton
and Leslie Fletcher Townsend

RICHARD Fletcher, the sixteenth child of Edward and Phoebe, born at Heanor March 11th, 1847, was the last of their offspring to see the first light of day there before the whole family moved house to Hyson Green to be nearer the centre of the lace trade in Nottingham.

Richard was some eighteen months old when this change was made, but as the years between boyhood and manhood passed over his head, a love for boxing, angling, cricket and other out-of-doors athletics shaped him into a 'strapping fourteen-stone-five-foot-tenner' whose skills and liking for good company made him a congenial addition to his cronies' divers activities.

Unfortunately, no records exist to measure his achievements in the noble art of self-defence or in handling rod and line, though we do know, without doubt, that he was an exceptionally accomplished cricketer of all round ability.

Richard played for several noted local amateur clubs, including Hyson Green C.C. and Nottingham Forest C.C.

This is what his grandson, Leslie Fletcher Townsend, the famous Derbyshire C.C.C. and England Test cricketer, has to say about him.

'In his young days, grandfather was a very good cricketer indeed and played for Nottingham Forest C.C. for years.

I once saw a photograph of him taken in a check shirt and wearing a top hat—the cricket dress of those serious, yet joyous days.

He was always interested in my cricket ambitions and did much to encourage me in many ways but, to my great regret, did not live to see my dreams and hopes come true.'

Speaking in a similar strain, George Fletcher tells me that his Uncle Dick was indeed a very fine bowler.

Richard was engaged in the trade, either as a manufacturer on his own account, or as foreman in charge of standings of machines in several Long Eaton factories, throughout all his working life. He was an able and trustworthy craftsman.'

By all accounts, these two sections of association with the making of lace occurred approximately between 1875 and 1895, and from about 1896 till he retired from the industry, respectively.

The 1877 issue of Morris & Co.'s Directory and Gazetteer of Nottingham and District contains the first reference to him as a lace manufacturer, with machine holdings in Abbott's Factory, Forest Street, Hyson Green, and a home address at 3 Sheriton's Row, Saville Street, which thoroughfare is beyond Terrace Street, near The Lumley Castle as you travel towards Basford. He had a sleeping partner named Tom Buxton.

How long these two men were in business together cannot be said but most likely the partnership was dissolved when Richard Fletcher made his home in Long Eaton and started in the trade there in the early eighties, or thereabouts.

Ultimately, Tom Buxton left Britain and took a job in Calais, but returned to England later on to work as a levers-draughtsman—his normal occupation.

RICHARD'S LONG EATON ACTIVITIES

Unfortunately, it has not been possible to make any fruitful contacts with Richard Fletcher's local living descendants, so all that can be stated here is that he was a lace manufacturer in Fletcher's Factory, Long Eaton, from 1891 to 1895, and probably had plants of machines in other factories in the district over a longer period.

It is also true to say that in the late 1890's, or early 1900's, Richard served as foreman to Samuel Fletcher of Attenborough, who had standings in Long Eaton, but there is little else of account to add at this stage except that Richard Fletcher passed away on April 10th, 1919, at the age of seventy-two and left a large family to mourn his loss.

RICHARD FLETCHER'S OFFSPRING

These stemmed from his two marriages. The first was to Annie Pearson, by whom he had Annie, Betsy and Arthur, after which Sarah Comery presented him with Richard, Phoebe, George Henry;

Sarah, Ethel. May, Linda. Selina and Percy William, whose names and those of their descendants are set out in the Fletcher family tree.

Though up-to-date, overall news concerning the comings and goings of this particular family group is sparse; there are, nevertheless, personalities among them that will intrigue you.

Probably the most colourful member of them all was *Annie*, the eldest who, immediately after marrying *William Mullis* at Long Eaton in 1891, migrated with him to America where, apart from her half-brother Percy William, she was not to see a kindred face till over half-a-century later.

Annie was supremely active in the service of the church and local social institutions of many kinds till shortly before her death, which occurred at Ravenna, Ohio, on April 17th, 1952.

She loved to linger in her flower garden where, after receiving her copy of the Family Tree, she wrote the first of many joyous and enlightening letters I was privileged to receive.

Before marriage, Annie worked as a winder in her father's factory at Long Eaton, and believed that her grandfather, Edward Fletcher [1797-1871] of Heanor and Hyson Green, made the first pair of Nottingham lace curtains—but she was mistaken.

Mr L. Whitehouse, an authority on these matters, quoting Felkin's 'History of Machine-wrought Lace' awards this honour to Edward Livesy, a draughtsman, of Lenton, near Nottingham, who made the first lace curtains in 1846.

Be this as it may, when Annie Mullis died, our family became another kindly soul the poorer at her passing.

RICHARD FLETCHER JUNIOR

In so far as Young Dick, or Dick's Dick, is concerned, we are, through lack of enough intimate biographical details, unable to pen a picture worthy of this equally colourful personality, and but for George Fletcher's notes, could have said little about him. What there is to retail, however, should be of interest.

HIS LIFE IN THE LACE TRADE

Though Dick, son of Richard, was an exceptionally fine craftsman, he never reached the heights of lace manufacturer, but gave long service instead, as lace-maker, to two master men only—first, Samuel Fletcher, who had standings in various factories, and Arthur

Tunnicliffe, whose machines were accommodated in Stanhope Street Mill, Long Eaton. In these two situations, he worked for Samuel Fletcher all the time he was in business and then served Arthur Tunnicliffe faithfully for many years till he died, rather painfully, in 1949.

As a youth, Richard Junior was definitely fond of mischief, and this is how George Fletcher describes one of his many pranks.

'Uncle Dick paid us a visit at Long Eaton and brought Young Dick with him. You know what lads are. They must be doing something and Master Richard was no exception.

He suggested we clean out the pigsty, so we let the two pigs loose into the garden and got on with the job.

When it came to putting the porkers back, oh, what a game we had. They bolted backwards, forwards and sideways, through the kidney beans and peas, wheeled right and left among the cabbages, and turned the garden into a shambles before we housed them again.'

You can guess what my Dad said—and the rest that followed!

A MASTER OF ROD AND LINE

As the making of lace was the only source of Richard's daily bread, so was angling the one enjoyment in his leisure hours. He lived for it and no other sport. He won many cups and medals in contests promoted by Long Eaton Victoria and Long Eaton Tiger Angling Clubs and the Nottingham Anglers Association.

Dick also fished in national and local championships, and when George Fletcher was once a rod short in the family team for the Midland Counties [*Nottingham Journal*], our subject filled the gap. He had a featherweight catch and the Fletchers finished second to Derby Institute, who beat them by one-and-a-quarter ounces.

When *Sarah Fletcher*, seventh child of Richard, ceased working for him in the New Tythe Street factory, Long Eaton, to wed Frederic William Townsend, and become the mother of four sport-loving sons, she, quite unknowingly, wrote the opening pages of a notable chapter which in years to come was to grace the annals of one of Britain's most popular open-air summer attractions.

Leslie Fletcher Townsend, the firstborn of this quartette, has, at my pressing request, very kindly agreed to the following personal description of how all this happened, being included in our family records, so read on and marvel at what he has to say in his own words.

1 Upland Road,
Christchurch, S.W.2,
New Zealand.
May 4th, 1954.

Dear Cousin,

I received your letter some two weeks ago—many thanks for same. I met our cousin Leslie Fletcher last January and you can imagine much of the good chat we had about the family, during which he showed me the Family Tree you sent him. Naturally, this interested me very much, as did your recent letter about the proposed Fletcher Story, so I will now try to help you in your quest.

Where do the Townsends as a family originate? Well, first of all, my father, Frederic William Townsend, was born at Preston, Lancashire, June 28th, 1872, but was brought up by his grandparents as both his mother and father died when he was a baby. They came to live at Long Eaton when he was thirteen.

My great-grandfather was a wagon builder and coach maker and began working for S. J. Claye of Long Eaton in 1885, but how long he worked there and lived I do not know.

My father, by trade, was a lacemaker and remained so all his life. In his youth he was a good footballer and played for Long Eaton Athletic, but cricket was his game—so much so that he could have been county class had he wished to play professionally.

He was the most stylish batsman in the district and, as a youngster, I saw him make more than one century. I owe father quite a lot for the progress I have made in the game.

He seemed determined to fashion me into an England cricketer if possible, and this I am pleased to say he lived to see when I first played for England in 1929 in the West Indies.

However, what I think gave him most joy was to see me make my record score of 233 against Leicestershire at Loughborough in 1933. Dad died in March 1935 while I was in Auckland, New Zealand, carrying out a coaching engagement there.

Incidentally, his only relative that I have ever heard of was his uncle, Alfred Townsend, who spent most of his life in South Africa but eventually returned to England and lived in retirement at Burton Joyce, Nottinghamshire, where father and I visited him one day. I believe he died there.

195

No other member of our family has emigrated except myself, and my reason for doing so is that I liked New Zealand so much when I visited the country twice some twenty years ago, I always said when I have finished playing first class cricket, this is the land for me, and fortunately, here I am.

My chief interest in New Zealand is, of course, teaching cricket, but by trade I am a joiner, working for the Canterbury Education Board. I have always been fond of woodwork, and apparently take after my great-grandfather Townsend in that respect.

We are definitely settled here and after several years' experience of the conditions, all of us, including our son, Paul Richard, born at Ripley, Derbyshire, November 8th, 1944, like life in New Zealand very much.

GRANDFATHER RICHARD FLETCHER

I not only knew, but can recall him quite well. He was, like most of the Fletchers, in the lace trade, and I can remember many stories mother told me about the days when she and aunt Annie worked for him in the old New Tythe Street factory shop which housed his machines.

As a cricketer, grandfather Fletcher was contemporary with the champion of champions, Dr W. G. Grace insofar that their dates of birth practically coincided.

Two of his sons, George Henry and Percy William, both lace makers by trade, emigrated to America about 1909, but my uncle George came home again in 1914, joined up for World War One, and made the Supreme Sacrifice in 1916.

Uncle Percy went right through this war, too, in the American Army, then after a short stay among his ain folk in England, went back to America to work as a lace maker in Philadelphia till he decided to retire. He died a few years ago in Middletown, Conn., U.S.A. Both these uncles of mine were fine fishermen with rod and line.

I also had an aunt Annie Fletcher who emigrated to America before I was born but never came back and died there recently—April 17th, 1952, to be exact.

The most famous angler in the family was uncle Richard Fletcher who, I believe, died about fifteen years ago.

196

You wish to hear something about myself and my cricket career. Well, one is always diffident concerning talking or writing about oneself, but I will do my best to respond.

To begin with, I was born at 105 College Street, Long Eaton, June 8th, 1903, and must have played cricket before I went to school, in fact, since I can remember.

Even at the age of nine I played for a team in senior company. Long Eaton Town—the club my father played for—were a man short at the last moment and father persuaded the captain to let me make up the side. He eventually agreed, so you can imagine how thrilled I was at the thought of playing with men in a proper match. Father had great faith in me and I did not let him down. They put me in last and I got 2 not out whilst the other end scored quite a number of runs, and the local paper said my fielding was quite fair. I did not get a bowl, of course.

I started playing in senior cricket just before the end of the 1914-18 World War. In those days I often opened the batting with my father—and didn't I hear about it if I got myself out by doing something silly. He literally made me play.

It was in 1919 that I really got going. In one match that year I took seven wickets for one run, including four wickets in four balls, all clean bowled, against one of the strongest teams in Long Eaton. I believe my second cousin, Eric Fletcher [grandson of my great-uncle George of Lime Grove, Long Eaton] played in that game. He, too, was a very good bowler in his day and had a trial with Derbyshire C.C.C.

That season I was recommended to Derbyshire C.C.C. for a trial at the nets by William Locker, who was an old Derbyshire county player.

One morning, early in May 1920, I had an invitation to go to Derby and uncle George Gregg took me there along with my father's cricket bag which contained a bat lent to me by W. A. Wallis, captain of the Long Eaton Town club. After the trial I brought it back to him like matchwood. You should have heard his remarks about 'this so-and-so battered wreck'!

Anyway, I was employed on the ground staff for two months, gained quite a lot of experience and was engaged full-time the following season [1921] during which I played in many second eleven games, my best effort being 102 not out against Warwickshire second eleven at Edgaston.

Season 1922 saw my first game for the County against Northants. at Northampton, my scores being 6 and 8, but I did well in the field and took two good catches. I only played in four matches that season with the first eleven, my best from the bat being 43.

The following season I became a regular member of the County eleven and was awarded my cap just before my twenty-first birthday.

You will see by the Family Tree that I have three brothers, all of whom were exceptionally good cricketers.

Arnold, like myself, played for Derbyshire C.C.C. and gained his county cap also. He played county cricket with Derbyshire for about seven seasons, and his best knock—149 not out—was made against Somerset at Taunton in 1939. Then the war came to rob him of his best years and though he played after the fighting was over, he was never the same again, despite a three-figure innings of 106 not out at Birmingham in 1946.

Incidentally, I made a century the same day for Northumberland, 192 against Durham—the highest single knock ever against them which still stands as a record of its kind.

My other two brothers, Frank and George, did very well in top-grade local cricket, and my cousin, Vera Summers, was a keen participant in the game and played for many years with a Nottingham ladies' club.

HIGHLIGHTS AND THRILLS

You ask me for some highlights and thrills, so I will try and name a few outstanding ones from the many I have enjoyed.

The first—and biggest thrill of all—was bowling George Gunn, the hero of my schooldays [and later ones, too] at Trent Bridge, when I was quite a youngster; bowling Jack Hobbs at Derby in 1925 was an almost equal thriller; by getting Wally Hammond out twice in one day, and 14 Gloucestershire wickets for 60 in the same match —my best bowling performance in a first-class encounter.

An equally big thrill happened when I obtained the wickets of Bradman and Ponsford the same day at Chesterfield in 1934; and I also enjoyed myself very much when, for once, I dictated to Frank Woolley of Kent, on a 'sticky dog' at Ilkeston in 1933 and got him

198

in the end. On this same ground in 1930 I made my first century in first-class cricket, this also being against Kent.

I would like to mention that the 1933 season was the best of my career in which I made my highest score, best bowling performance, most centuries [still a record for Derbyshire C.C.] and being the tenth man in the whole history of cricket to make over 2,000 runs and take 100 wickets during one season.

All in all, I made over 20,000 runs, took just over 1,100 wickets, and did the hat-trick once—against Northants. in season 1931—in first-class cricket.

WAR—AND NORTHUMBERLAND C.C.C.

The second World War marked the end of my first-class cricket career. After hostilities ceased, I was invited to play for Derbyshire again, but being now in my forties and averse to resuming six-days-a-week cricket, I accepted the post of professional-coach to Northumberland County Cricket Club and moved house to Newcastle-on-Tyne.

I had three good seasons with them, making several centuries, but did very little bowling. My best scores included 192, 151 not out, 124, 105 not out, and many knocks in the 70's and 80's.

Some twelve months before my three years' engagement with Northumberland C.C.C. finished we decided to make an effort to come to New Zealand. We eventually arrived at Christchurch to start a new life in a new country, where I was engaged by the Canterbury Cricket Association to coach the youngsters in the district.

They also invited me to take part in the Plunket Shield matches. I asked to be excused this on account of my age and declining powers, but I did undertake to play in the Saturday club games.

So far, I have made a couple of centuries and last season, at nearly fifty years of age, I notched a fighting 86 in helping to win a tight game. I have also achieved honourable mention with the ball a few times, but on the whole I have bowled very little out here.

As is only to be expected, I hope to continue playing in minor cricket a little longer and, to this end, I have fixed up with Nelson Cricket Association as professional for next season, where I shall be coaching at Nelson College also.

Nelson, a small town some 275 miles north of Christchurch, is, we think, the nicest place in the whole of New Zealand. It has a beautiful climate, holds the annual record each year for sunshine, so we are looking forward to moving there to live in September 1954.

My other interests in life as regards games and sports are billiards, ice-skating, shooting, and I hope to include yachting when my son is a little older.

A LAST WORD ABOUT FIRST-CLASS CRICKET

During my county cricket career, besides having the honour of playing in a few Gentlemen versus Players matches—two of them at Lords in 1929 and 1933—I have also taken part in North versus South contests, and played for the Champion County against the Rest of England at the Oval when Derbyshire were head of the table in 1936. I still treasure the lovely gold watch that was presented to me to mark my share in gaining that notable success.

My last word to you recalls, to me, the thrill and pride I felt when selected to represent my country, England, against the West Indies [1929] and India [1933]. These occasions were *Tests* indeed!

This rambling letter about my cricket and myself is what you asked for; so I hope it will help to bring success to our Fletcher Family Story.

Yours sincerely,

LESLIE FLETCHER TOWNSEND.

P.S.—After September next my address will be 61 Torswill Road, Tahuna, Nelson, N.Z., or c/o Nelson Cricket Association.

AN APPRECIATION

An appreciation, published by Northumberland County C.C. for Leslie Townsend's benefit match against Derbyshire at Jesmond, September 4th, 1946, sets out in detail what has only been touched upon in the foregoing letter. The compilers of this 'Northumberland C.C.C. Appreciation' speak of him in these terms:

'*Townsend Joins Northumberland.* The war happily being over, the Committee of the Northumberland C.C.C. at once set afoot a scheme of reorganisation and reconstruction.

The first priority was the search for a sound professional and this search practically started and finished in Derbyshire, the choice falling on Leslie Townsend, at one time spoken of as one of the soundest all-rounders in the country.

Negotiations were opened with him with satisfactory results. Townsend came north and what was Northumberland's gain was Derbyshire's great loss.

Many were the regrets amongst the Derbyshire people that this stalwart player should be leaving them, for, by his prowess in the field as batsman and bowler, by his genial manner at all times, by his kindliness of spirit and high moral character, he had endeared himself to all.

Townsend soon made his influence felt in his new surroundings, for the playing of cricket was his life.'

This official brochure closes its tribute on this delightful note: 'May this form long continue. We wish him the very best of luck and strength to his arm—for his own sake and our own edification.'

PLATE 26

FOUR GENERATIONS

Right to left: GEORGE FLETCHER Senior, GEORGE FLETCHER Junior, ALLEN VINCENT FLETCHER, ALLAN NEWTON FLETCHER

CHAPTER XIII

THE GEORGE BRANCH

Compiled from notes contributed by his son,
George Fletcher of Long Eaton

THE word 'unique' is so often misplaced and so constantly misused that one hesitates to make use of it; but surely no other word is more aptly applicable to George Fletcher, the seventeenth and youngest child of Edward and Phoebe that grew to full manhood.

He was born at Hyson Green, Nottingham, on April 28th, 1849, and died at Long Eaton on July 12th, 1937.

A member of the original lace-manufacturing family of Fletchers —said to be the biggest manufacturers of lace in the British Isles— George Fletcher found time amidst a busy life, to patronise and take part in many forms of sport. Particularly was he interested in angling, billiards, skating, and especially cricket, of which, in his younger days he was a practised exponent, playing for Hyson Green, Burton Joyce and Long Eaton Town.

While with Hyson Green he topped the batting averages nineteen seasons out of twenty and performed a similar feat during the two years he was connected with Alfred Shaw's team at Burton Joyce.

On one occasion he played in the match between the South and the North of Nottingham, and on other occasions played for the Nottingham Castle club against the M.C.C., and was in the representative eleven that opposed Arthur Shrewsbury's first Australian team. He was also included in the Notts. and Derby Colts that met the M.C.C. and figured in many similar matches which claims on space prevents mentioning here.

Prior to coming to Long Eaton, George Fletcher received his education at the National Schools and the People's College, Nottingham.

He was the first member of the original Fletcher family—which is widespread and greatly intermingled—to live to see some of his great-grandchildren, for whom he entertained a great affection, come into being. Much greater would have been his joy if his wife [née Sarah Elizabeth Brewer], who bore him four sons and six daughters, had been spared to share his pride and pleasure.

This 'unique' record of longevity and perpetuity was never equalled by any other member of that generation of the Fletcher family. It has, however, been repeated twice during the present lives of his daughter, Mrs Maude Beatrice Bates, and his son, George, who will now continue with the more private part of his father's story.

When so vast an aggregate of experience and wisdom, coupled with an amazing memory—all so typical of Dad—are involved, it is very difficult for me to choose a point from which to express myself on so intimate a subject for the benefit of younger generations.

Since Dad was the youngest son, he was working for grandfather Edward Fletcher when he died in 1871, and in consequence was not in business on his own account.

He always said that when grandfather retired he ought to have looked after the future of his younger sons more and given them a better start in life, as all the elder ones were already firmly established as lace manufacturers in their own right.

Dad soon learned what earning one's daily bread meant as, at the age of twelve, while attending Nottingham School of Art, he hand punched patterns for grandfather at one shilling per pattern in his off-study time.

He had another revealing experience a little later on when he worked a machine which was not driven by mechanical power. The man in charge faced up to the task of turning it under his own steam, *i.e.* by hand. This necessary rotary operation was made as simple as possible by a zig-zag weighted shafting [see diagram].

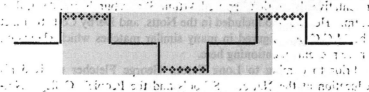

Dad said it was very easy to turn over—so easy, in fact, his brother William dozed as he worked it one nightshift and made a hole in the lace he could walk through. Grandfather made him do so the next morning.

Dad's machine butty was a noted local cricketer of his day named I. Ward who went to America and became a founder member of the Philadelphian C.C. In later years this club crossed the Atlantic to play matches against some of our top-ranking English teams.

About the year 1878 Dad moved our then comparatively small family from Hyson Green to Long Eaton to work for brother Thomas [North House] as manager, and purchased through him the New Inn, spending part of his time at the factory and the hostelry as his presence in each necessitated.

I have already stressed Dad's great love for sport, so it was no cause for surprise when he started a cricket and fishing club at the New Inn and, with Mother's help, made it the rendezvous for many fine concerts and sing-songs and yearly suppers for the distribution of prizes. We had some grand times at club headquarters and as both uncle William and uncle Richard were good singers, there was never any lack of talent or turns to help pass these happy hours away.

Among the most treasured memories of my boyhood are the dozen or more bats Dad gained for topping the averages of the clubs he played for, and seeing him knock up a hundred on many occasions before retiring to give others a chance to bat.

These mementoes of uncanny skill were the theme of much story-telling between sportsmen at the Inn who gathered there for divers refreshment—and how I enjoyed listening to the deeds that gained them, being relived over and over again *ad infinitum.*

As Dad's eldest son, I shall always remember him as a good father to us all and a kindly gentleman who was loved and respected by those who knew him well or met him.

He passed quietly away in his eighty-ninth year, and many close friends and other admirers to this day often speak of him to me about his personal qualities and quote some of his cricket performances they have seen.

FATHER AND MOTHER'S DESCENDANTS

Those kinsmen who possess a copy, will notice that ten additions were made in the second generation to the Tree, and that I, *George Fletcher,* their eldest son, am third in order of seniority by birth of this part of the junior branch of our Fletcher family.

205

As father did, I also saw the first light of day at Hyson Green on December 9th, 1875, and, like him too, I have always taken a great interest in local affairs, particularly sport, since coming to Long Eaton many years ago. My arrival there was a little delayed, as I was left in the care of relations at Hyson Green until my parents were fully settled in their new home.

I received my elementary education at the Church School, and this was followed by a finishing course at a Private Academy. Despite a lack of enthusiasm for close study, achievements there were always satisfactory and rewarding, which prompted one long-experienced headmaster to say that, in my case, 'learning just came naturally'.

As an early teen-aged scholar, I captained Long Eaton National School in the Derbyshire Junior Shield for which I received my first medal. This was an epoch-making event as since then I have taken part in practically every sport as active participator and club official and have won many cups and medals in all of them.

Football, cricket, boxing and angling have been my prime favourites, but the last-named, to my mind, is the best of all.

It was once publicly asserted that 'fewer men in the British Isles are more faithful and persistent devotees of *Isaac Waltonism* than George Fletcher of Long Eaton, and his two sons, Eric and Allen'; but in stating this I am overrunning the story a little—work should be mentioned before pleasure.

On leaving school at the age of sixteen, I started work in the lace trade for cousin Sam Fletcher in the West End Mills, Long Eaton, and learned draughting under Arthur Farnsworth and Tom Buxton Junior. In order to gain a thorough insight into the making of lace, I also learned to work a machine and during the nightshift studied my draft in its relation to the moving parts, thereby gaining a fund of knowledge which in later years enabled me to draft any kind of goods.

I stayed with Sam for about two years and was then apprenticed to George Hardy of Austin's Factory, Long Eaton, where I worked under F. Storer and Percy Rossell. Good progress under these able tutors was rapid, so when Mr. Rossell was leaving to commence business on his own account in the local Regent Street Mills, I was offered, and accepted, his job although still in my apprenticeship.

I continued working for Mr Hardy until trade deteriorated when,

206

as other apprentices were coming along, I accepted a situation with Fletchers of Springfield Mills, Sandiacre, who had taken over the business of Ernest Terah Hooley of Risley Hall, and remained there for quite a time.

My next—and last—post as an apprentice was with J. Davys Ltd. of Long Eaton, for whom I was acting as manager, when about 1909-10 I went into business for myself in the Harrington Mills, and there I remained as a lace manufacturer until my retirement from the trade in 1937.

At this point I would like to describe my first introduction to another sport—cricket. On that great day in 1878 I carried my bat— a toy one—when Dad took me to Trent Bridge County Ground, Nottingham, to see the first Australian team that toured England. What grand players they were, and what stories we could recall about members of both elevens!

Fishermen's Yarns were ever prone to 'tickle' the listener and have raised many a hearty laugh. Nevertheless, with no whit of exaggeration, I offer the reader a limited selection from many true ones with which to conclude the purely personal portion of my contribution to the story.

Individually, I have two English Championship winners' medals; the Nottingham Anglers Association Cup five consecutive years, and many other cups and medals; the Trent [*Nottingham Journal*] Midland Counties Championship; and our local Club and Institute Championship five times winner to my credit.

As a family team we came out top in many contests including the *Nottingham Journal* Midland Counties Championship, fished in the Trent, and the Club and Institute Championship five consecutive years, all held in different waters.

Commenting on these successes and others at the time, the *Journal* opined that 'we were possibly the finest family angling team in the land'. Less kindly critics bluntly said 'What else could you expect— these blighters know every ripple in every reach of every river for miles around'.

Almost invariably, there is an innermost kernel of affection to most hobbies or pursuits which we centre our main interests upon. This applies to my love for angling, and the special attraction is salmon fishing at Christchurch, where my wife and I have spent many delightful holidays 'catching 'em alive-o' in the Hampshire Avon.

The appended press report adequately describes the height of pleasure and the scale of sport we 'Waltonians' enjoyed in these waters.

'*Some fishing.* The friends of mine who found the swan of Wollaton Park lake a nuisance to their pike fishing expedition the other afternoon, no doubt will read of the deeds of Mr George Fletcher of Long Eaton, on the Hampshire Avon, with positive envy. Mr Fletcher, the captain of the family team of that name, has just returned from a month's fishing holiday during which he landed no fewer than 24 salmon—the best, a 24-pounder, gave him an hour-and-a-half's play. Mr Fletcher also had roach up to 2lb. 6oz., barbel up to 9½lb., sea trout up to 6lb., and a number of grayling. Another angler in the same water landed pike aggregating 110lb. in a single day, the heaviest weighing 20lb.'

March 5th, 1898, was the red-letter-day of my life as on that day I married Annie Elizabeth Comery of Nottingham.

We have had three children—Allen Vincent, Edna May and George Eric—who have, up to the time of writing this story increased the size of our Family Tree to the extent of five more 'twigs'—three grandchildren and two great-grandchildren.

Annie and I celebrated our Golden Wedding in 1948 and my only regret is that I was not born early enough to see grandfather Edward Fletcher in the flesh.

Allen Vincent, our eldest child, born at Hyson Green on June 3rd, 1899, entered my lace manufacturing business at Harrington Mills, Long Eaton, straight from school as a salesman.

At the immature age of 16½ years he joined the British Army and saw much heavy fighting in France during 1914-18, being wounded five times and gassed twice. He was last wounded at Bullecourt just before the Armistice was signed, and after receiving his discharge rejoined the business as salesman and manager.

Allen excelled in most sports and many games, his favourites being boxing, golf, tennis, fishing and billiards, in which indoor pastime he was a handicap back marker.

An expert angler, with a wide variety of successes, including the Midland Counties [*Journal*] Individual Championship, to his name, he was also a prominent member of the Fletcher family team of four that used rod and line with outstanding distinction in many waters.

Allen was considered to be a first-class tennis player and but for war wounds would have reached the grade his cousin Helen of Heanor attained. He never fully recovered from the effects of gas and passed away December 2nd, 1953, aged fifty-four, leaving a widow [née Rene Newton of Kegworth, Leicestershire] and a son and daughter to mourn their loss.

Allen Newton, our senior grandson, was born at Kegworth on April 13th, 1924, educated at Long Eaton Council School, and today by profession is a T.V., radar and radio precision engineer. He saw service with the Royal Air Force in Canada, the U.S.A. and Burma where, like many more fighting men, he had a tough time.

There, he successively contracted dysentery, malaria, jaundice and swamp sores before being sent to India to recuperate and then home to England for discharge and the award of a disability pension.

In 1947, Sheila Collingham of Lincoln became his wife and they have one child, Denise Sheila, now in her tenth year.

Yvonne, our only grand-daughter—another Long Eatonian— attended the local Technical School where she studied dental hygiene and was one of fifteen students selected from 250 applicants to attend the first course of training in this subject ever held in this country. At the conclusion of the course, Sir William Kelsey Fry, one of our most famous authorities on dentistry, handed her the Proficiency Cup, which was indeed a rewarding experience.

She married Royston George Manners of Birmingham, a Graduate of the Institute of Mechanical Engineers, now by profession a development and research engineer in connection with aircraft. They have a very young daughter, Carole Anne, and have made their home at Addlestone, Weybridge, Surrey.

George Eric, our younger son, born at Long Eaton on July 14th, 1902, learned his lessons in the local Council School and at the age of fifteen started work at the bottom in my business and became so good a lace mechanic that, eventually, he took over the management of the factory. On November 4th, 1939, he married Florence Essen.

Angling, billiards, bowls, cricket and football were the prime favourites of the many sports and recreations that filled his leisure and he figured prominently in all of them. Not only was he an individual angling champion in contests at or near national level, but when he won the Derby Federation Championship Cup, he was the first angler to take that trophy out of Derby in twenty years. This was typical of the skill he displayed as a member of the Fletcher family angling team.

He was also on Derbyshire C.C.C. ground staff at the same time as his cousin Leslie Fletcher Townsend, the County all-rounder and England Test player. Eric's career as a county cricketer of fast bowler vintage was ended by an accident to his instep—a setback that did not deter him from rendering three-and-a-half years' war service [May 1942-January 1946] with the Royal Artillery in France, Belgium and Germany.

In these days of uneasy peace, relaxation is found on the bowling green, in which sport a cup and other trophies pay tribute to his prowess.

Edna May, our second child, was born at Hyson Green on June 23rd, 1901. She had a technical education which fitted her for the post of cashier and book-keeper in my lace business at Long Eaton.

Like her uncles, brothers and myself, Edna is very fond of open-air sports and, on occasion, has competed with success in angling and tennis contests.

She married Alfred E. Ledger, whose family have been noted basket manufacturers for nearly two hundred years.

He has organised blind welfare work since 1925, first at Notting-ham, then at Warrington, and now he is superintendent and secretary to the Norwich Institution for the Blind where his wife Edna is also the assistant housekeeper and advisor on interior decorating.

This institution [established 1805] houses 134 souls, 85 males and 49 females, and many of them are now valuable members of society by virtue of the efforts of staff experts in the arts of brush making, basket making, mat and rug making, knitwear, and other rewarding crafts.

Norwich Institution for the Blind continues to render its service to the community under Royal Patronage, and today Her Most Gracious Majesty Queen Elizabeth the Second is Patron.

One of the home's most colourful personalities is a seventy-nine-year-old mat-maker named Ellis Lincoln who has tried for a number of years to prove himself a relative of the renowned President of America, Abraham Lincoln, whose family originated from Hingham in Norfolk. Ellis Lincoln's roots are embedded in the soil of

Saxlingham Nethergate and many admirers think that his long span of work is worthy of fame on its own; but all true genealogists hope the seeker will live to see his quest for proof of so illustrious a relationship gratified.

Though official responsibility is very heavy and exacting in an institution of this character, Edna and Alfred did not forget the needs of their own family circle.

Ian Fletcher Ledger, their only son and our junior grandchild, was born at Chilwell, Nottinghamshire, on March 8th, 1933, and studied in the City of Norwich and Lynn Grammar School until he reached the age of nineteen. He then joined the Gloster Aircraft Company and finished a three-years course of apprenticeship with some distinction. Engineering of all kinds has always fascinated him, and he has built, flown and exhibited model aeroplanes with commendable success, as the award of a cup in a competition for this class at Luton testifies. Success and progress has not been confined to the air, as both land and water have been the scene of similar exploits.

He has built and run motor-boats and canoes in their natural habitat and at an early age toured Europe on his motor-cycle, covering nearly 4,000 miles, after which he wrote of his experiences in one of the Norwich newspapers.

Ian began his National Service at 22½ years and studied for a commission at Honiton. This honour has been bestowed with posting to R.E.M.E., Aldershot, and from there a world alive with adventurous spirits beckons him.

I must now finish describing the contribution made by my own family towards our Fletcher family record, but before doing so, I would like to mention with what is, I trust, pardonable pride, the signal honour accorded two of its members.

To mark their appreciation of the services rendered to Norwich Institution for the Blind by my daughter and son-in-law, Royal recognition has been publicly bestowed upon them on several occasions. Edna has been presented to Her Majesty Queen Elizabeth the Queen Mother four times. The last presentation was made in June 1954 when the Lord Bishop of Norwich, the President of the Institution, introduced her. Exactly a fortnight later [July 14th, 1954] both Edna and Alfred attended the Garden Party at Buckingham Palace by Royal Command. The memories these distinctions recall are still our pride and pleasure.

- The contribution made by this, the junior main branch of the family, to our story, is completed by an account of some of the services rendered by a great-grandson of the head of it.

His name and style is *Captain Robert Anthony Flood, M.C.*, the only son of the late Major Robert Reginald Flood [Northampton-shire Regiment] and Mrs Flood, and grandson of the late Mr Harry Bates, lace manufacturer, and Mrs Bates, of West Bridgford, Nottinghamshire.

After finishing at public school, he went through Queen's College, Belfast, and Sandhurst Military Academy; was commissioned, posted to the 11th Hussars, and eventually awarded the Military Cross for acts of outstanding gallantry and devotion to duty displayed in the field of operations that followed 'D' Day landings in Europe.

This decoration was pinned to his breast by Field-Marshal Lord Montgomery before a parade of all ranks, of which ceremony a photographic record has been preserved.

During 1947, Tony and his wife [née Esther Steele-Lincoln] paid a visit to Camworth, New Hampshire, U.S.A., to meet members of her family, and when they returned home to Britain, our young kinsman decided to study medicine at St Andrew's University, Fife. Today he is 'walking the hospitals' in final preparation for establishing a practice of his own.

With the recording of the birth of *Frederick Allen Fletcher*, the youngest son of Edward and Phoebe, August 26th, 1850, at Hyson Green; his death there on August 18th, 1853, and burial in St Paul's Churchyard, we close the domestic part of this story.

PART II

DOCUMENTARY SUPPLEMENTALS

216

The Family Tree of Joseph Fletcher and Elizabeth (née Fletcher) of Pentrich, married at Pentrich, Derbyshire, 24th. June, 1778.

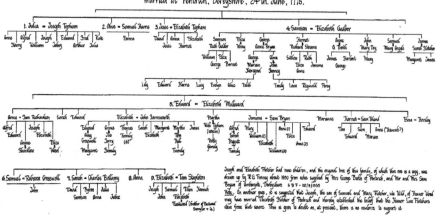

6. Samuel = Rebecca Cresswell
John

7. Sarah = Charles Bellamy
David | Byron | Julia
Samson | Anna | Jabez

8. Anna

9. Elizabeth = Tom Stapleton
Joseph | Samuel | Ellen | Hannah
John | | Elizabeth
Eastland (brother of Eastland Stapleton + Co.)

Joseph and Elizabeth Fletcher had nine children, and the original tree of this family, of which this one is a copy, was drawn up by R.G. Fenney about 1890 from notes supplied by Mrs George Booth of Pentrich, and Mr and Mrs Sam Bryan of Ambergate, Derbyshire. S.B.F – 22/3/1955

Note. On another page, it is suggested that Joseph, the son of Samuel and Mary Fletcher, née Wild, of Heanor Wood may have married Elizabeth Fletcher of Pentrich and thereby established the belief that the Heanor Line Fletchers stem from that source. This is open to doubt as, at present, there is no evidence to support it.

213

Pedigree of Robert Fletcher of Heanor and formerly of Denby, Kilborne and Smalley, and second son of Robert Fletcher of Kilbourne.

(A) See the Grants of Arms.

From Reynolds collections jones A.N. Juniorum.

Robert Fletcher of Kilbourne Co. Derby == Goodere of Heanor erroneous Co. Derby. (A.)

Catharine one of the coheirs. and heirs of Will. Richardson of Smalley Esqr.

2.1
Robert Fletcher of Heanor. raised a fortune from coal winning

John Fletcher of Stainsby House C. Derby Esqr. Sheriff of Derbyshire 1752. increased his patrimony by Coal Mining.

Sarah Askin of Highedge Co. Derby.

1.

Goodere Fletcher Esqr. of Heanor Sheriff of Derbyshire 1755 - also a Justice of the Peace for Derbyshire. ob. v.p. 19 Mar. 1770.

Sam Fletcher of Heanor living 1772

Will. ob obbits.

Eliz. wife of John Wood

Cath. wife of John Buckwant of Langley

Richard, eldest son John Fletcher of Stainsby Hall Esqr. ob. v.p. married to Miss Josbrook in 1752 Grant May.

Francis Barber of Greasley Castle Com: Nott. Yeom.

== Sarah

John Barbor Esqr. of Stainsby House C. Derby and of Waddington Com. War. == dau. of Geo. Goodwin of Manyash. C. Dorb.

Note: The original Pedigree, of which the above is a copy, is part of the Bloro Collection housed in the University Library, Cambridge. We bring it to your notice as a likely source of our descent through some member of the family to which this Robert Fletcher of Heanor belongs.

217.

Note for the Pedigree of Fletcher of Langley, p. Heanor, Co. of Derby.

† Do not confuse this Goodere Fletcher with the one mentioned in the note below, who was already dead.

John Fletcher of Langley, p. Heanor. bapt. m. 6/4/1779 at Heanor when † Goodere Fletcher was witness. † Goodere Fletcher buried.

married

Elizabeth, daughter of Fletcher of p. Heanor

Children:

Mary bapt. 27/12/1779 at Heanor	
Ann bapt. 11/8/1782 at Heanor	
Jenine bapt. 28/5/1784 at Heanor buried 22/3/1795 at Heanor	
William Fletcher bapt. 25/12/1785 at Heanor	
Elizabeth bapt. 15/8/1787 at Heanor buried 15/12/1794 at Heanor	
Sarah bapt. 11/1/1789 at Heanor	
※ **Jane** bapt. at Heanor; buried 22/10/1790	
Britain error bapt. 21/5/1792 at Heanor probably Britannia	

218

Note: This marriage between John Fletcher and Elizabeth Fletcher is of some importance as it might represent a marriage of a brother (bapt. 12/11/1753) or a sister (bapt. 9/4/1749) of Samuel Fletcher of Heanor, the eventual heir of Goodere Fletcher of Heanor, deceased 19/3/1770.

※ This entry was found in the registers of Burials but no entry in respect of her Baptism.

Note for the Pedigree of Fletcher of Heanor, Co. Derby.

Edward Green Fletcher sojourner in p. Heanor, bapt. m. 8/8/1775 at Heanor where the witnesses were Fletcher and John Bullivant of Heanor; and was a Churchwarden buried in 1782.

Elizabeth, dau. of Fletcher of p. Heanor, bapt. buried

William Bennet = Catherine
bapt. 27/5/1776 at Heanor, m. 30/9/1799 at Heanor.

Edward Fletcher
bapt. 10/8/1779 at Heanor.

Edward Green Fletcher
bapt. 25/12/1760 at Heanor

Elizabeth
bapt. 15/7/1781 at Heanor.

John Fletcher
bapt. 18/3/1783 at Heanor.

Sarah
bapt. 15/7/1786 at Heanor.

Note for the Pedigree of Fletcher of Shipley, p. Heanor, Co. of Derby.

* William Fletcher
of Shipley, p. Heanor, Co. Derby.
bapt.
m. by licence at Heanor 24/5/1788
buried.

═ Elizabeth, daughter of
Glover of

Richard Glover Fletcher
bapt. 15/12/1788 at
Heanor.

Betty
bapt. 20/4/1790
at Heanor.

Robert Fletcher
bapt. 18/11/1792 at
Heanor.

Lucy
bapt. 21/2/1793
at Heanor.

※ Marriage licence dated 22/5/1788 describes him as a widower aged 40 ; she is described as a spinster aged 30. Marriage to take place at Ilkeston p. Church. I believe his first wife to have been Elizabeth Woodward whom he married at Heanor in 1785 and by whom he had one son, Goodwin Fletcher, born 8/11/1785 : one cannot eliminate yet the possibility of his first wife having been either Susannah Skerrit, married at Heanor in 1772, or Mary Bingin married at Stanley in 1768, who had one daughter Mary, baptised at Heanor 5/1/1775.

Note for the Pedigree of Fletcher of p. Heanor, County Derby.

Samuel Fletcher = Mary, daughter of

of Jay Hill, p. Heanor, Co. Derby; buried at Heanor 14/10/1788. Will dated 6/5/1787 proved 15/10/1788 at Lichfield.

Authority: The Will of Samuel Fletcher.

- **John Fletcher** b. 12/11/1753 at Heanor. m. 19/5/1777
- **Mary** = Thomas Allen b. 31/5/1755. m. 13/2/1772 at Heanor.
- **Ann** = Robert Aldred b. 6/5/1756. m. 28/6/1774 at Heanor.
- **Hannah** = Hodgkins b. 4/5/1760 at Heanor.
- **Joseph** b. 18/7/1762 at Heanor.
- **William** b. 4/5/1764 at Heanor.
- **Joseph** = Lydia, Wife of Alfreton. m. 23/3/1780 at Heanor.

Eleanor = Joseph Clay
"my Grand Daughter" m. 2/10/1791 at Heanor.

221

This is undoubtedly the Pedigree of Samuel Fletcher, the father of John and Grandfather of Edward Fletcher. This view is strongly supported by the Parish Awards of 1791 for the Parish of Heanor and Codnor made by H.M. Commissioners John Nuttall of Matlock, Benjamin Chambers of Tibsholf and Thomas Fletcher of Whitwell, who allotted plot 42 to Thomas Allen; plot 43 to John Fletcher; and plot 44 to John Elay on Jay Hill. These families occupied the original dwelling-places, two houses adjoining either side of a small shop, that stood thereon, now numbered 78, 78A and 80 Derby Road, Heanor. They are still inhabited today, and if Phoebe Allen emerged as a bride (as is very probable) from the home then standing on plot 42, to wed Edward Fletcher, who lived next door, they would be first cousins.

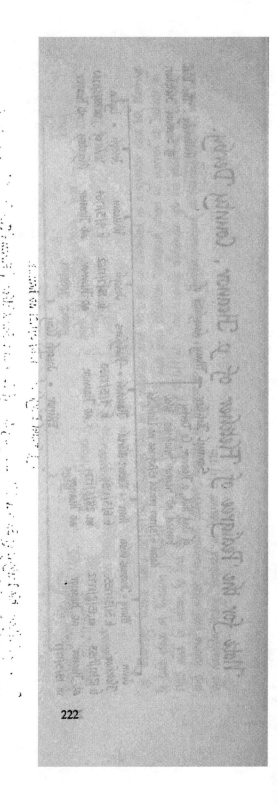

222

A Note concerning the family of Samuel Fletcher of Loscoe Lane, Heanor, extracted from the Pedigree of Fletchers of Kilbourne.

Andrew Fletcher = **Alice**, daughter of
of Kilbourne, p. Horsley, Co. Derby, Husbandman. Will dated 1588 proved at Lichfield.

Children:

- **William Fletcher**
- **Robert Fletcher** = **?**
  - **Robert Fletcher** = **Anne**, daughter of Hunter, of Kilbourne; married at Horsley 1/7/1651, and buried there.
- **Francis Fletcher**
- **John Fletcher**
- **Elizabeth**
- **Jane** = **Thomas Johnson** of Kilbourne

Next generation:

- **Anne**
- **Robert Fletcher** = **Anne Cooke** of Kilbourne, married 25/11/1669 at Horsley and buried there.
- **Sarah** = **Robert Burton**
- **Mary** = **Francis Cooke**
- **John Fletcher** of Holbrook, p. Duffield = **Sarah Willimett**

Next generation:

- **Robert Fletcher** = **Catherine**, daughter of Samuel Richardson, Cordwainer, of Smalley Hall, Co. Derby.
  of Kilbourne; Smalley Hall, Heanor Hall; Cordwainer. Died 1755.
- **John Fletcher** of Stainsby House, p. Smalley, Cordwainer and one of the richest men of his day; had Grant of Arms. Arms displayed in Horsley Church.
- **Sarah** = **Edward Holden**
- **Mary**

Next generation:

- **Goodere** the eldest son died unmarried. High Sheriff of Co. Derby 1753.
- **Samuel Fletcher** of Heanor, Gentleman = **Mary**, dau. of Richardson of Spondon.
- **William**
- **Elizabeth** = **John Wood** of Swanwick
- **Catherine** = **John Bullivant** of Langley Common p. Heanor.

Bottom generation:

- **Samuel** died 1770 a bachelor
- **Robert** died in 1777
- **William** of Owlgreaves
- **Goodere** of Heanor or Shipley died 1777
- **Thomas** died in 1777
- **Samuel** died 1795 the last of the family
- **Mary** died unmarried
- **Ann** = **Thomas Hall**
- **Sarah** = **George Radford**
- **Elizabeth** widow of Edward Grew Fletcher of Heanor.

223

226

Extract from the Pedigree of the Wylds of Codnor, County Derby.

John Wyld = **Rebecca Wyld**

of Codnor, Co. Derby, yeoman. Will dated 6/6/1757, witnessed by Isaac Wright, John Luther and Samuel Burgin. proved at Lichfield 22/4/1760 by John Wyld, the sole executor: directed his burial at Heanor.

"my loving wife". made her Will 15/1/1767 proved at Lichfield 19/10/1770 by John Wyld, the sole executor named: witnesses James Woolley, Ann Hickson and Samuel Peake.

John Wyld = ?

my son of Codnor, Co. Derby, sole executor, clockmaker to whom his father devised three closes in Codnor called Marshfield, Upper Field and Codnor Birks being ten acres or thereabouts and in the occupation of the testator, Isaac Wright and John Beecham: together with a chief rent of 3/6 p.a. issuing out of the two Cank Fields and Codnor Meadows formerly part of my estate: and a workshop in Nottingham, held of Mr. Lupton: He had joint possession, with Samuel Burgin, of a freehold estate at Codnor, which he conveyed to his cousins, Joseph Woolley of Ripley and Samuel Woolley of Codnor on trust for sale by his Will dated 13/4/1773, proved at Lichfield 5/11/1773 by the said cousins the executors named.

Joseph Wyld = ?

had a legacy of £30 from his father and £10 from his mother.

Benjamin Wyld

"my grandson" a legacy of £20 at his majority and a further £10.

Mary   Rebecca

£5 apiece, and at their majorities had also their grandmother's feather bed.

(John) Fletcher = **Hannah**

married at West Hallam 1745

"my daughter" 9 pence per week for life and her quarters

Daniel Fletcher called "my grandson" by Rebecca Wyld who left him £10 when of age.

John Wyld my grandson my silver cup and £5 from his grandmother

Philip Wyld

Sarah Barker "my daughter"

Ann Brighton "my daughter" mentioned also in her mother's will.

Mary Wyld Wood "my daughter" had an annuity of 40 shillings p.a. for life issuing out of two freeholds on the heath of her mother.

Joseph Wyld "my son" had the chief rent and £120.

Samuel Fletcher = **Mary Wyld**

married at Heanor 1742.

"my daughter" £100

Ann unmarried £100.

Taylor = **Sarah** "my daughter" £100.

This extract is a note for Wylde of Codnor Castle, Co. Derby.

The items in brackets are additions supplied from a pedigree in Ince's collection in the Cavendish Bemrose Library, Derby. Losco is of course Codnor, alias Heanor.

225

Extract from the Pedigree & the Wills of Kirk Ireton, Co. Derby.

(John Wild
of Loscoe
Wild 19/4/1764)

Daniel Wild = Edith Wild

Daniel Wild of Kirk Ireton, Co. Derby, Blacksmith, died intestate. Administration granted to his relict at Lichfield 8/4/1788. Buried at Kirk Ireton 3/5/1788.

Edith Wild of Kirk Ireton, widow. Having administered her husbands goods, made her Will 1/5/1795: proved at Lichfield 14/10/1796 by John Wilcockson, gentleman, the sole executor named.

Samuel Harrison = (Hannah)

* my son in law, farmer of the parish of Wirksworth had one sh.

(Hannah)
(bapt. at Kirk Ireton 1/8/1745: married there 3/11/1762: buried there 28/9/1763)

Arthur Spencer = Daughter ----?

Daniel Harrison — Had £25 apiece at their majorities →

John Harrison

Hannah

Edith

Sarah
— all unmarried: had a legacy of £50 apiece. →

Elizabeth
unmarried: also had a legacy of £50

The items in brackets are additions supplied from a pedigree in Ince's collection in the Cavendish Benrose Library, Derby. Loscoe is of course Cashnor, alias Cashnor, alias Hannor.

227

PLATE 27

WILLIAM FLETCHER'S RUSSIAN PASSPORT

It is not uninteresting to see the revival of a clan interest in Russia, since it was in the sixteenth century (1588) that *Giles*, a *Fletcher*, son of *Richard*, of Cranbrook, Co. Kent, and Bishops Stortford, Co. Herts., the first British Ambassador to Russia, went to that country and concluded a Treaty of Trade and Navigation

[P.T.O.

on behalf of the Russia Company of London and, thereafter, wrote one of the earliest travel books entitled *The Russe Commonwealth*. He was born 1548-9; educated Eton and King's College, Cambridge; M.P. for Winchelsea 1585; Master of Requests and Remembrancer City of London 1596. He had two sons, *Phineas* and *Giles*, by his wife *Joan*, née *Sheafe*, and died in 1611.

THE LAST WILL AND TESTAMENT OF

ROBERT FLETCHER OF HEANOR

GENTLEMAN

In the Name of God Amen the twenty Seventh Day of Aprill in
the Year of Our Lord God One thousand seven hundred and
fifty one I Robert Fletcher of Heanor in the County of Derby
Gentleman being of sound and perfect mind and memory God
be praised Do make and ordain this my last will and testament
in manner following (that is to say) First I commend my Soul
into the hands of Almighty god my merciful Creator hoping
1 and stedfastly believing to obtain everlasting life through the
precious and meritorious Death & Suffering of my Lord and
Saviour Jesus Christ and my body to the earth to be Decently
buried at the discretion of my executor herein after named Also
I do hereby constitute and appoint my Son Goodere Fletcher
to be sole executor of this my last Will and Testament Also I
give and bequeath unto my loving wife the sum of one Hundred
pounds of Lawfull money of Great Britain and also such of my
household goods and quick stock as she shall please to accept
2 and make choice of Also I give and bequeath unto my son
Samuel Fletcher the sum of ten pounds of like lawfull money a
Year to be paid to him his Executors or Administrators Yearly
and every year for the term of ten years next after my Decease
out of my personal estate Also I give and bequeath unto my
Daughter Elizabeth Fletcher the sum of twenty pounds of like
lawfull money Also I give to my said wife for her life the use of
all my plate Except a Silver Salt Stand which was my grandmothers And also of all my linnen and after her decease or as
soon as my wife shall please to part therewith I give and bequeath
all my said plate Except the Salt Stand And also my said linnen
unto my two Daughters Elizabeth & Catherine equally betwixt
them Also I give and devise unto my said Daughter Elizabeth

Fletcher and to her heirs and assigns for Ever all that my Messuage or tenement and farm with all and Singular the Lands tenements and hereditaments therewith now let or thereto belonging Situate lying and being in Kilbourn in ye parish of
4 Horsley in the said County of Derby now or late in the tenure or occupation of William Aldred And also all those my three Closes in Kilbourn aforesd called the Coat ? Closes now or late in ye tenure or Occupation of William Shaw And also all that my messuage or tenement in Kilbourn aforesd wherein my Sister Mary Fletcher did and William Hulland doth now inhabit together with ye Close & pingle now laid together lying on ye
5 backside the sd house And Also all those my four Cottages or tenements in Kilbourn aforesd now or late in the respective tenures or occupations of Thomas Stafford John Sanders Joab Bateman & Thomas Radford and also all that my Close or parcell of land in Heanor aforesd called the Searsow Meadow now or late in the tenure or occupation of John Mitchell together with all barns stables buildings Yards Gardens Orchards backsides Ways Waters Easments Commons profits priveledges emoluments hereditaments and appurtenances whatsoever to ye sd premises or any part thereof belonging And also all & all manner of tithes wtsoever yearly or otherwise coming growing or renewing in and out of the sd premises or any part thereof Also I give
6 and devise unto my said Daughter Catherine and to her heirs & assigns for ever All those my two Closes in Heanor aforesd Called the two Langley Meadows now or late in the tenture or occupation of Jonathan Moore and also all that my Close in Heanor aforesd Called the Hallows now or late in the tenture or
7 occupation of Samuel Coleclough And also all that my Close in Heanor aforesd Called Hunters Pingle now or late in ye tenure or occupation of Robert Saxton and all and all manner of tithes whatsoever Yearly or otherwise coming growing or renewing in & out of ye sd four Closes last mentioned with all hereditaments & appurtenances to ye said Closes or any of them belonging Also all and Singular my Coal mines & Coal works & Parts and Shares of Coal Mines & Coleworks Leases of Coal mines & Coal works The Coals in the Lands hereby given to my Daughters only excepted And all ye rest & residue of my goods Chattels Debts owing unto me and personal Estate whatsoever and

wheresoever not hereby otherwise disposed of after payment of my Debts Legacys and Funeral expences I give and bequeath unto my said Son Goodere And Lastly I do hereby revoke all former wills by me made In Witness whereof to this Duplicate of this my last will and Testament I have set my hand and Seal the Day and Year first above written

ROBt FLETCHER

Signed Sealed published and Declared ⎫
by the before named Testator Robert ⎪
Fletcher for and as his last will and ⎪
testament in the presence of us who all ⎬
Subscribed our Names as Witnesses ⎪
hereto in ye presence of the said Testator ⎭

      John Platts
      Frans Tantum junr
      John Taylor

                 At Lichfield 15th August 1754

Let a probate be made to Goodere Fletcher Esqr sole Executor named in the above written will

Jno Fletcher   Being sworn before me
                                 Thos White Sur.

THE LAST WILL AND TESTAMENT OF

GOODERE FLETCHER

ONE-TIME SQUIRE OF HEANOR
HIGH SHERIFF CO. DERBY 1753 AND A JUSTICE
OF THE PEACE

In the Name of God Amen This is the Last Will and Testament of
Goodere Fletcher of Heanor in the County of Derby Esquire First I
commit my Soul into the Hands of Almighty God hoping through
his Mercies and the Merits and Mediation of my Blessed Saviour
Jesus Christ to obtain Eternal Salvation and my Body I commit to
the Earth to be privately interred at the direction of my Executors
hereinafter named And I do hereby order and direct that all my just
Debts be Immediately paid after my Decease and I do by this my
Will Give and Devise all my Real and Personal Estate in manner
following I Give and bequeath unto my Niece Catherine Bullivant
my Desk and Glass over it in my little Parlour and my Spring Clock
I Give and bequeath unto my two Nephews John Bullivant and
Fletcher Bullivant One Hundred Pounds apiece to be paid to them
respectively at the end of Two years after my Decease I also Give
and bequeath unto my said Nephew John Bullivant my old large
Silver Tankard and my very old pair of Peramidical Plate upon
Express Condition that he never parts with or disposes of the same
out of my family it being my Desire that they may always be kept
therein And it is my Desire and I Do hereby Give full power and
authority to my Brother-in-law John Bullivant my Sister his wife and
all their Children family and friends with his and their consent to
fish or angle in any of my Ponds or Waters in the flats in Heanor
aforesaid and in all my Ponds Stews and Basons at my Summer
House near Loscoe Laund and to enter and permit into and upon
the Lands adjoining thereto for that purpose and I Give and bequeath
unto my Brother John Bullivant (in-law) the one half of the fish that

232

shall be at any time during his life in all or any (my) Ponds and I do hereby Order and Direct that no fish whatever shall at any time During his lifetime unless with his Consent be taken out of any of my Ponds with Nets or by Letting off the water I Give and Devise unto my Servant Anne Mapples and her assigns for and During the Term of her natural life ALL THAT Tenement or Dwellinghouse with the Orchard Garden Croft or Appurtances thereto adjoining or belonging Situate and being upon Langley Common in the Parish of Heanor aforesaid now in the Tenure or Occupation of Thomas Osborn and I Also Give and bequeath unto the said Anne Mapples for and during the term of her natural life One annuity or yearly sum of Ten Pounds to be paid to her free of all Deductions and abatements whatsoever yearly and every year by four equal Quarterly Payments the first Payment thereof to begin and be made at the End of three Calendar Months after my Decease and I do hereby Subject and Charge all and every my Messuages Farms Closes Lands Tenements Coal-mines and Hereditaments whatsoever in Heanor aforesaid or elsewhere in the said County of Derby with the Payment of such Annuity with full Power and Authority to and for the said Anne Mapples from time to time and at all times during her life to enter into and upon all or any part of the said Premises and to Distrain for the same or any part thereof and to take all lawful Methods whatever for recovering and obtaining the same or any part thereof I Give and bequeath unto the said Anne Mapples Five Pounds to be paid to her Immediately after my Decease to buy her Mourning I also Give to the said Anne Mapples my Cuckoo Clock and my little Trundle Bedstead with the feather Bed two pair of flaxen sheets (two good pair of Blankets) and a Coverlid all which I do Give to the said Anne Mapples over and besides what I shall happen to Owe her at my Decease for Wages or otherwise in part and towards a recompense for her long and faithful services to me and my family And I Give and bequeath unto Eleanor Mapples the Daughter of the said Anne Mapples now of the Age of Six years or thereabouts for and during the term of her natural life One Annuity or yearly sum of Twenty Pounds to be paid to her the said Eleanor Mapples clear of all Deductions and abatements whatever yearly and in every year by two equal half yearly payments the first payment thereof to begin and to be made at the end of Six Calendar Months next after my Decease and I do hereby Subject and Charge all and

233

every my Messuages Farms Closes Lands Tenements Coal-mines and Hereditaments whatsoever in Heanor aforesaid or elsewhere in the said County of Derby with the payment to such annuity with full Power and Authority to and for the said Eleanor Mapples from time to time and at all times during her life to enter into and upon all or any part of the said Premises and to Distrain for the same or any part thereof and to take all lawful Methods whatsoever for recovering and obtaining the same or any part thereof I Also Give and bequeath unto the said Eleanor Mapples Five Pounds to buy her Mourning I Give and bequeath unto Sarah Mapples Sister of the said Anne Mapples Five Pounds to be paid to her at my Decease I Give and bequeath unto my Servant Anne Smith Five Pounds over and besides what I shall happen to owe her at my Decease for Wages or otherwise to buy her Mourning if in my Service at my Decease and not otherwise I Give and bequeath unto Samuel Seal and Hannah his Wife during their lives and the longer liver of them during his or her life All That my House Gardens and Orchard near my fish ponds in Heanor aforesaid and now in Possession of Richard Upton Provided always and upon this Condition none the less that if the said Hannah shall happen to survive the said Samuel Seal her husband and shall after his Death shall Intermarry with any Person whatsoever then and in such case and from and Immediately after such her Inter marriage I Do Give and Devise my said House Gardens and Orchard near my said fish ponds unto such person or persons and in such manner as in this my Will is hereinafter mentioned and Subject to the Estate and Interest of the said Anne Mapples and Samuel Seal and Hannah his Wife in the said Messuages Lands Tenements and Hereditaments so Given and Devised to them respectively by this my Will as aforesaid and Chargeable with the Payment of the said two Annuities of ten pound and twenty pounds and to the payment of all my Just Debts and the Legacies by this my Will Given or bequeathed I do Give and Devise all and every my Messuages Farms Closes Tenements Tithes Coal Mines and Hereditaments whatsoever in Heanor aforesaid and in Langley in the said Parish of Heanor in Kilborne in the said County of Derby or elsewhere in the said County of Derby as well freehold as Customary or Copyhold with their and every of their rights Members and Appurtenances unto and to the use of my brother Samuel Fletcher and his Assigns for and during the Term of his natural life without

234

Impeachment of or for any manner of waste and from and Immediately after his Decease I do Give and devise all and every my said Messuages Farms Closes Lands Tenements Tithes Coal Mines and Hereditaments whatsoever with their and every of their rights Members and Appurtenances unto and to the use of Samuel Fletcher the first and Eldest Son of the said Samuel Fletcher my Brother by Mary his now Wife and all of and every other the issue Child and Children Son and Sons Daughter and Daughters of the Body of my said Brother Samuel Fletcher already born or begotten or to be born or begotten and of their several and respective Heirs and Assigns forever as Tenants in Common and not as Joint Tenants provided always and I do hereby Declare it to be my Mind and Will that in case the said Samuel Fletcher the Eldest Son of my said Brother Samuel Fletcher shall happen to Die without Issue of his Body lawfully begotten that then and any such case the part or share of and in my said Messuages Farms Closes Lands Tenements Tithes and Coal Mines Hereditaments and Premises so Given and Devised to him in and by this my Will as aforesaid shall Go and I do hereby Give and Devise the same unto and among all and every other the Issue Child and Children of the Body of the said Samuel Fletcher my Brother and of their several and respective Heirs and Assigns forever as Tenants in Common and not as Joint Tenants anything in this my Will contained to the Contrary thereof in any wise notwithstanding I Give and bequeath unto my said Brother Samuel Fletcher his Executors Administrators and Assigns all my ready Money and Securities for money Household Goods and Furniture Goods Chattels Personal Estate and Effects whatsoever and of what nature or kind soever not by this my Will otherwise Given or Disposed of Subject nevertheless to the payment there out of all my Just Debts Legacies and Funeral Expenses And Lastly I do hereby Nominate Constitute and Appoint the said Samuel Fletcher my Brother and the said John Bullivant my Brother-in-law Joint Executors of this my last Will and Testament hereby revoking and making void all former or other Wills by me heretofore made

In Witness whereof I the said Goodere Fletcher have this to my last Will and Testament set my hand and seal this Third Day of July in

the Seventh year of the Reign of King George the Third and in the
year of Our Lord One Thousand Seven Hundred and Sixty Seven

G. FLETCHER

Signed Sealed Published and
Declared by the said Goodere
Fletcher the Testator as and for
his last Will and Testament in
the presence of us who in his
presence and of each other have
subscribed our names as Witnesses thereto

Robert Evans
Edward Kenyon
I. Wills
D. J. Crofts

This Will was proved at London on the Eighteenth Day of July in the
Year of Our Lord One Thousand Seven Hundred and Seventy One
before the Worshipful George Harris Doctor of Laws Surrogate of
the Right Worshipful George Hay also Doctor of Laws Master
Keeper or Commissary of the Prerogative Court of Canterbury
Lawfully constituted by the Oath of John Bullivant one of the
Executors named in the said Will to whom Administration was
Granted of all and singular the Goods Chattels and Credits of the
deceased he having been first Sworn duly to Administer Power
reserved for making the like Grant to Samuel Fletcher the other
Executor when he shall apply for the same

THE LAST WILL AND TESTAMENT OF

SAMUEL FLETCHER OF TAG HILL HEANOR

IN THE CO. OF DERBY

In the Name of God Amen I Samuel Fletcher of Heanor in the
County of Derby Being in Perfect Health and of Sound Mind
Memory and Understanding do Make Publish and Declare this my
last Will and Testament in Manner and forme Following—First of
all I give and Bequeath unto my Daughter Ann Alldred the sum of
Ten pounds Also I give and Bequeath unto my Son John Fletcher
the sum of Ten pounds Also I give and Bequeath unto my Daughter
Liddy (Lydia) Wild the sum of Ten pounds Also I give and Bequeath
unto my Daughter Hannah Hodgkins the sum of Ten pounds Also
I give and Bequeath unto my Son Joseph Fletcher the sum of Ten
pounds Also I give and Bequeath unto my Son William the sum of
Ten pounds all this I give to them in Hand paid of good and Lawfull
Money Twelve months after my Decease by My Executrix hereafter
Mentioned—Item I Also give and Bequeath unto my Grand Daugh-
ter Ellinor Fletcher Five pounds of good and Lawfull Money—Item
I give and Bequeath unto my Daughter Mary Allen and Thomas
Allen her Husband the Possession of the House I now Live in with
Brewhouse Stable and all Appurtnants—thereunto Belonging with
all my Household Furniture quick and Dead stock goods and
Chattels and Effects whatsoever and of what kind soever with all
my Ready Money and Securitys for Money and it is my Will that
my said Daughter Mary Allen doth quietly Enjoy and Possess all
of what is by me to her given as aforesaid Paying all my Funeral
Expenses and Legacies Afore mentioned And I hereby Nominate
and Appoint my said Daughter Mary Allen my Sole Executrix of
this my last Will and Testament hereby revoking all Former Wills
by me heretofore made In Witness whereof I have hereunto set my

237

hand and seal this Twenty Sixth Day of May and in the Year of our Lord one Thousand Seven Hundred and Eighty Seven

Signed Sealed Published and Declared by the above named Samuel Fletcher as and for his last Will and Testament in the Presence of us who have hereunto Subscribed our Names as Witnesses thereto in the presence of the said Testator and in the presence of Each Other

his
Samuel   ×   Fletcher
mark

Wittnefs Richd Redfearn
Thos Colclough

At Ufton Hall 15th October 1788
Let a Probate be made to Mary Allen wife of Thomas Allen the sole Executrix

Jno. Fletcher

She being sworn and that the personal estate is not 100L before T. Buckeridge Sur.

The Pedigree, derived from the above written will, only mentions those children of the Testator that were still living at the time of its making. It may well be the will of the Samuel Fletcher that married Mary Wild on 2nd December 1742 and since especial mention is made therein to the name of Allen, the whole of its contents could represent the Last Testamentary Wishes of the Grandfather of Edward Fletcher, the founder of the Fletcher family lace business. This is a distinct possibility that cannot be ignored.

238

THE LAST WILL AND TESTAMENT OF

JOHN FLETCHER OF LOSCOE

This is the last Will and Testament of me John Fletcher of Loscoe in the Parish of Heanor in the County of Derby, Carrier, made published and declared the nineteenth day of August one thousand eight hundred and nine.—In the first place I Will and direct that all my just debts and funeral expences shall be paid and discharged by my Executrix hereinafter named as soon as conveniently may be after the time of my decease, and in that behalf I charge and make subject all my Personal Estate and

1 effects whatsoever which I shall be possessed of at the time of my decease.—I give and bequeath unto my Son Joseph Fletcher of Loscoe aforesaid in the County aforesaid the sum of one shilling current Money of Great Britain to be paid to him or his lawful representative immediately after my decease.—I give and bequeath unto my Daughter Hannah Hogg (Widow of Christopher Hogg) of Loscoe aforesaid in the County aforesaid the sum of one shilling of current Money of Great Britain to be paid to

2 her or her lawful representative immediately after my decease. All the rest residue and remainder of Household Goods, Chattels, quick and dead Stock, Money and Securities for Money, and other my Personal Estate and effects whatsoever and wheresoever appertaining to me at my decease, I give devise and bequeath the same and every part and parcel thereof (subject as aforesaid) unto my Wife Hannah Fletcher her Executors Administrators and Assigns.—And lastly I do hereby nominate constitute and appoint my said Wife Hannah Fletcher sole Executrix of this my said Will, revoking all former Will and Wills by me heretofore

239

made.—In Witness whereof I have hereunto set my hand and
Seal the day and year first above written.

Signed, Sealed, published, and declared ⎫
by the said John Fletcher the Testator, as ⎪
and for his last Will and Testament in the ⎬ John Fletcher.
presence of us, who in his presence and the ⎪
presence of each other have subscribed ⎪
our names as Witnesses to the same. ⎭

    Humphrey Smith
    William White.

At Alfreton 11th October 1826
Let probate of this Will be made
to Hannah Fletcher the sole
Executrix named therein.

She being first duly sworn
also that the personal estate
will not amount to 200£.
Before me John Pepper

             Surrogate.

240

THE LAST WILL AND TESTAMENT OF

JOHN FLETCHER OF LANGLEY

IN THE PARISH OF HEANOR

This is the last Will and Testament of me John Fletcher of Langley in the Parish of Heanor in the County of Derby Framework Knitter, made published and declared the thirteenth day of January in the year or Our Lord one thousand eight hundred and thirty one. In the first place I Will and direct that all my just debts, funeral and Testamentary expenses shall be fully paid and satisfied, so soon as conveniently may be after the time of my decease, and in that case I do hereby charge and make chargeable as well my Real as my Personal Estate with payment thereof and subject and chargeable as aforesaid. All the rest residue and remainder of my Real and Personal Estates whatsoever and wheresoever and of what nature or kind soever I give devise and bequeath the same and every part and parcel thereof (subject as herein before and hereinafter declared) unto my Friend William Millington of Langley aforesaid in the said County of Derby Farmer his Heirs Executors and Administrators In trust, for the sole use benefit and Behoof of my Wife Elizabeth Fletcher and her Assigns for and during the term of her natural life. And from and after the decease of my said Wife Elizabeth Fletcher, I give devise and bequeath all the aforesaid rest residue and remainder of my Real and Personal Estates in manner following (that is to say) I give and bequeath all that my thirty four Gauge plain Stocking Frame marked number three, unto my Son Daniel Fletcher his Executors or Administrators.—Also I Will and ordain that my said Trustee and Executor hereinafter named of this my last Will and Testament, or his Executor or Administrator, shall and do with all convenient speed after the decease of my said Wife, bargain sell and convey all my aforesaid rest residue and remainder of my Real and Personal Estates (saving and excepting that Stocking Frame marked number three already bequeathed) for the doing executing and perfect finishing whereof I do by these presents give, grant, Will and transfer to my said Trustee and Executor herein after named, and

241

to his Executor or Administrator, full power to grant, alion, bargain, sell, convey and assure all those my Messuages, Cottages, Lands, Tenements and Hereditaments situate in Langley aforesaid, to any Person or Persons and their Heirs for ever in Fee-simple, and for the most Money that can be obtained for the same, and I hereby give to my Son Daniel Fletcher the first preference to purchase my said Real Estate if he shall think proper, and that my said Trustee and Executor hereinafter named Receipt shall be a good and sufficient discharge. And the Money arising from such sale as aforesaid, after payment of my just debts, funeral and Testamentary expenses, I give and bequeath the same, unto my Sons Daniel Fletcher, Thomas Fletcher, and John Fletcher, and my Daughters Mary Brough and Sarah Holden equally share and share alike. And lastly I do hereby nominate constitute and appoint the said William Millington sole Executor of this my said Will contained in one sheet of Paper, revoking and making void all former Will and Wills by me at any time heretofore made. In Witness whereof I have hereunto set my hand and Seal the day and year first above written.

Signed, Sealed, published and declared
by the said John Fletcher the Testator,
as and for his last Will and Testament,   John
in the presence of us, who in his presence   Fletcher
and the presence of each other have
subscribed our names as Witnesses.——

    John Moore
    John Spray
    Wm White

   At Alfreton 19th October 1831.

Let a Probate of this Will be made to William Millington the sole Executor named therein.

Testator died on   ⎫   He being first duly Sworn and
12 May last   ⎬   also that the personal estate will
             ⎭   not amount to 20£ Before me
                                             John Pepper
                                               Surrogate

THE LAST WILL AND TESTAMENT OF

EDWARD FLETCHER LACEMAKER

OF HYSON GREEN

This is the Last Will and Testament of me, Edward Fletcher of Hyson Green in the County of Nottingham Lacemaker as follows. First I direct the payment of my just debts funeral and testamentary expenses by my Executors as soon as convenient after my decease - Next as concerning all those my two Freehold Messuages Shops Garden and premises situate at Tagg Hill in the Parish of Heanor in the County of Derby. And Also all those my two other Freehold Messuages Shops Gardens and premises situate at Hyson Green aforesaid. And All Other my Real Estate whatsoever and wheresoever I Give and devise the same unto my two sons Joseph Fletcher and Samuel Fletcher their heirs and assigns Upon Trust to receive the rents and profits thereof from time to time and after paying thereout the necessary expenses of keeping the same premises in tenantable repair and insured from fire and other necessary expenses. Upon further trust to pay the residue of such rents and profits unto my Wife Phoebe Fletcher and her assigns during her life And after her decease Upon trust to sell and dispose of my said Real Estate either by public Auction or private contract for the best price or prices in money and at such times and upon such terms and stipulations as to my said Trustees may seem advisable with liberty to buy in the same or any part thereof and to resell the same at any future time without being liable for any loss occasioned thereby And as to the monies arising from such sale or sales after paying and discharging thereout the expenses attending any such sale or sales and of

243

making out the Title to the property sold Upon trust to pay and divide the same amongst my Thirteen children, namely, John Fletcher the said Joseph Fletcher and Samuel Fletcher Thomas Fletcher James Fletcher Catherine the Wife of Joseph Farnsworth Robert Fletcher Henry Fletcher William Fletcher Mary Fletcher Betsy Fletcher Richard Fletcher and George Fletcher as shall be living at the decease of my said wife or the issue then living of any who may be then dead leaving lawful issue him or her surviving in equal shares and proportions to and for their own respective use and benefit absolutely such issue to take equally the share or shares only which his her or their parent or parents would have been entitled to if then living. Next as concerning all those my Six Twist Nett Lace Machines Warping Mill Winding Wheels Household Furniture Linen and pictures I Give the usufruct and enjoyment thereof to my said wife during her life And after her decease I direct my said Trustees to convert the whole thereof into money and after paying thereout all necessary expenses attending the sale thereof Upon trust as to the residue of such proceeds And all other my personal Estate and Effects whatsoever to pay and divide the same unto and equally between and amongst such of my said above named children or their issue as shall be living at my said Wife's decease in manner as above directed with reference to the proceeds of my said Real Estate. Provided and I do hereby direct that in case of the death of my said Wife during the minority of any of my said children my said Trustees shall put out at interest his or, her presumptive share in the above residuary trust monies on Real or personal security and apply the income thereof from time to time in and towards his her or their, maintenance education and bringing up—Provided and I do hereby, further direct that the receipt and receipts in writing of my said Trustees for any purchase or other money payable to them under or, by virtue of this my Will shall be an effectual discharge for the money therein acknowledged to be received and the person or persons paying the same shall not afterwards be liable for any loss misapplication or nonapplication thereof. And lastly I hereby nominate and appoint my said Wife Phoebe Fletcher and my said two sons. Joseph Fletcher and Samuel Fletcher joint Executrix and Executors of this my Will and Guardians of such of my children as may be under age at my decease and hereby revoking all former and other Wills by me heretofore made I declare this to be my last. In Witness

244

whereof I have hereunto subscribed my name this twenty-sixth day of June one thousand eight hundred and sixty one.

Edward Fletcher

Signed published and declared by the above named Edward Fletcher the Testator as and for his last Will and Testament in the presence of us present at the same time who in his presence at his request and in the presence of each other have hereunto subscribed our names as witnesses————————

Jno. Johnson Solr. Nottm.

J. N. Martin his Clerk
Joseph Fletcher
Samuel Fletcher

THIS IS THE LAST WILL AND TESTAMENT OF ME JOHN FLETCHER OF HEANOR IN THE COUNTY OF DERBY

LACE MANUFACTURER

I Hereby revoke all former Wills and Testamentary Dispositions made by me and I appoint my four sons William Fletcher Thomas Fletcher John Keyworth Fletcher and Joseph Edward Fletcher (hereinafter called "my trustees") to be the Executors and Trustees of this my Will I Bequeath my Gold Watch and chain and also the Crayon Portrait of myself to my said Son William Fletcher I bequeath the Crayon Portrait of my late Wife Mary Fletcher to my Daughter Elizabeth Handford I give all the residue of my estate and effects both real and personal unto my trustees upon the trusts and with and subject to the Powers and provisions hereinafter declared concerning the same (that is to say) Upon trust that my trustees shall continue to carry on the business of a Lace Manufacturer now carried on by me at Heanor and Nottingham until my son George Henry Fletcher shall attain the age of twenty one years with liberty for my trustees to use and employ in the said business such part of my residuary estate or the proceeds thereof as they may think fit and shall employ my said sons John Keyworth Fletcher and Joseph Edward Fletcher to be the managers of the said business and with liberty to employ such assistants and servants in the said business and to pay and allow such managers assistants and servants such salaries and wages and generally to conduct and carry on the said business in such manner as my trustees in their discretion think fit and subject to the direction hereinbefore contained in relation to the carrying on of the said business I direct and declare that my trustees shall sell and convert into money my real estate and residuary personal estate (including in such residuary personal estate the whole of the stock of manufactured lace and other goods which shall be in my possession at the time of my death) or such part thereof as shall not consist of money and shall out of the moneys to arise from such sale and conversion and out of the ready money pay my funeral and testamentary expenses and debts and the legacies hereby bequeathed and shall invest the residue of the said moneys with power for my trustees from time to time at their own discretion to vary such investments And I Further Declare that when and so soon as my said son George Henry Fletcher shall have attained the age of twenty one years my said trustees William Fletcher and Thomas Fletcher shall offer the said business And also all the lace machines machinery and plant used therein other than engines boilers shafting and fixtures for sale to my said three sons John Keyworth Fletcher Joseph Edward Fletcher and George Henry Fletcher to be carried on by them in Co-partnership and if they shall refuse such offer my said trustees William Fletcher and Thomas Fletcher shall offer the said business for sale to my said three sons John Keyworth Fletcher Joseph Edward Fletcher and George Henry Fletcher as may then be living in order one after the other according to the seniority of age and if each of my said sons shall decline to accept such offer my trustees shall sell the said business to any person or persons in such manner as they may think fit And I Declare that my said three sons John Keyworth Fletcher Joseph Edward Fletcher and George Henry Fletcher and that each of my sons to whom an offer of sale shall be made as aforesaid shall be allowed ten days within which they or he must either accept or decline such offer and if they or he shall not accept the same within such ten days they or he shall be deemed to have declined it And I further declare that if my said three sons John Keyworth Fletcher Joseph Edward Fletcher and George Henry Fletcher of if any of them shall accept the said offer the price to be paid for the said business shall be ascertained by the valuation of two indifferent persons one to be named by the said William Fletcher and Thomas Fletcher and the other by the purchasers or purchaser or in the case of their disagreement by an umpire to be chosen by such valuers and if either party shall fail to name a valuer or to notify it in writing to the other party for the space of ten days after the day on which the offer shall be accepted or if the valuer named by either party shall refuse or neglect to act then the valuation shall be made by the valuer of the other party alone Provided Always that no purchasers under this my Will shall be obliged or concerned to see or enquire whether the business has been duly offered for sale to my said sons as hereby directed nor whether any such offer shall have been accepted or declined nor shall the title of such purchaser be afterwards impeached on the ground that the said business had not previously been duly offered for sale as aforesaid or that any such offer (if made) had not been duly declined And I Further Declare that if my said sons John Keyworth Fletcher Joseph Edward Fletcher and George Henry Fletcher or any of them shall purchase the business as aforesaid my trustees shall grant to them or him a lease of the premises at West Valley Heanor at which the business is carried on consisting of a lace factory and of all the boilers engines shafting and fixtures in and about the same for any term not exceeding ten years in possession from the granting of such lease at a rent the amount whereof shall be determined by valuation in the same manner as in hereinbefore directed with regard to the purchase money of the said business And the said lease shall contain covenants by the Lessees or Lessee for keeping in repair the said premises and the said boilers engines shafting and fixtures therein for substituting plant and machinery of equal value in the place of any that may be removed by the lessees or lessee during the term and for delivering up the said premises plant and machinery at the end of the term in as good repair and condition as at the commencement of such term and such other covenants and conditions as are usual in leases of the like nature And I further declare that if my said three sons John Keyworth Fletcher Joseph Edward Fletcher and George Henry Fletcher or if any of them shall purchase the business as aforesaid they or he shall pay such purchase money by ten equal annual instalments the first of such instalments to be paid at the expiration of one year after the date of the said Valuation or as much sooner as they may think well it being my intention that my said sons shall have a space of ten years and no more in which to pay the said purchase money but shall be at liberty to pay such purchase money sooner if they shall think well and the purchase money for the time being unpaid may remain a debt from them or him to my estate from the time of completion and shall be secured in the meantime with interest thereon after the rate of Four pounds ten shillings per centum per annum by a mortgage of all the interests of the purchasers or purchaser under this my Will in my residuary estate or the proceeds thereof And I further declare that in ascertaining the sum of money to be paid for the purchase of my

248

said business by my said sons or any of them as aforesaid nothing shall be allowed for the goodwill of the business And I further declare that my three said sons John Keyworth Fletcher Joseph Edward Fletcher and George Henry Fletcher shall have the option of purchasing my said business as aforesaid notwithstanding the fact that two of them namely John Keyworth Fletcher and Joseph Edward Fletcher have been appointed by me and shall act as Executors and Trustees of this my Will And I further declare that at the expiration of the said period of ten years or upon their having paid the full amount of the said Valuation for such purchase my said three sons John Keyworth Fletcher Joseph Edward Fletcher and George Henry Fletcher or the survivors or survivor of them shall have the option of purchasing from my trustees the said Freehold premises at West Valley Heanor aforesaid at which part of the said business is now carried on and also the said boilers engines shafting and fixtures thereon And if the said price to be paid for such freehold premises cannot be agreed upon between the said William Fletcher and Thomas Fletcher and the purchasers such price shall be determined by valuation in the same manner as hereintobefore directed with regard to the purchase money of the business And I further declare that when and so soon as my said Son George Henry Fletcher shall have attained the age of twenty one years my trustees shall stand possessed of my residuary estate including the proceeds of the aforesaid business In Trust for my children to be divided between them in equal shares Provided Always and I declare that my trustees shall retain the share of each of my daughters of and in my residuary estate Upon the trust following (that is to say) upon trust to pay the income thereof to my same daughter during her life and so that if and while she shall be under coverture the same shall be for her separate use and she shall have no power to dispose of the same in the way of anticipation and from and after the decease of such daughter Upon trust to pay the income thereof to any husband of such daughter who may survive her during his life and from and after the decease of such daughter and any husband who may survive her in Trust for the children of my same daughter who being male shall attain the age of twenty one years or being female shall attain that age or marry in equal shares and if there be only one such child the whole to be in trust for that one child and in case there shall be no child of my same daughter

249

who being male shall attain the age of twenty one years or being female shall attain that age or marry then in trust for my other children in equal shares and so that the share or shares accruing to each or any daughter of mine under this trust shall be subject to the Trusts hereby declared concerning the original share of the same daughter under this my Will Provided Always and I hereby declare that if any child of mine shall die in my lifetime leaving a child or children who being male shall attain the age of twenty one years or being female shall attain that age or marry then and in every such case the last mentioned child or children shall take (and if more than one equally between them) the share which his her or their parent would have been entitled of and in my residuary estate if such parent had survived me and attained the age of twenty one years including any share or shares which would have accrued to such parent under the trust and provision in that behalf hereintobefore contained And I declare that my trustees shall have power to raise any part or parts not exceeding together one moiety of the vested or expectant share of any grandchild of mine under the trusts of this my Will and apply the same for his or her advancement preferment or benefit as my Trustees shall think fit but so that no such moneys shall be raised and applied as aforesaid during the existence of any prior interest or interests therein under this my Will without the consent in writing of the person or persons having such prior interest or interests And I Declare that if any Grand daughter of mine shall marry while an infant the income of the share (if any) of my residuary estate to which she shall for the time being be entitled in possession under this my Will may be paid to her during her infancy and her receipt shall be sufficient discharge for the same And I also declare that my trustees may postpone the sale and conversion of my real and personal estate or any part thereof for so long as they shall think fit and that the rents profits and income to accrue from and after my decease of and from such part of my estate as shall for the time being remain unsold and unconverted shall after payment thereout of all incidental expenses and outgoings be paid and applied to the persons and in the manner to whom and in which the income of the moneys produced by such sale and conversion would for the time being be payable or applicable under this my Will if such sale and conversion had been actually made And I also declare that all moneys liable to be invested under this my Will may be invested in or upon any stocks funds or securities of or guaranteed by the Government of the United Kingdom or of any British Colony or dependency or in stock of the Bank of England or the debentures or debenture stock or guaranteed or preference Stock or shares of any railway or other Company in Great Britain or India incorporated by Act of Parliament or Royal Charter and paying a dividend on its Ordinary Stock or Shares or upon real or leasehold securities in England or Wales but not elsewhere such leasehold securities being held for a term whereof sixty years at least shall be unexpired at the time of such investment And in lending money on any mortgage security my trustees may accept whatever title or evidence of title shall appear to them sufficient and in particular may in the case of leasehold securities waive the production of the lessors title without being answerable for any loss arising thereby and my trustees may release any part of the property comprised in any mortgage security if satisfied that the remaining property is a sufficient security for the money owing thereon And I also declare that my trustees may at their discretion make any sale subject to any conditions (whether actually required by the state of the title or other circumstances or not) which may be deemed expedient and on loan of money may at their discretion fix the amount to be advanced not exceeding two thirds of the value at the time of making such loan ascertained by a valuation obtained in the usual course of business of the property to be comprised in the security without regard to any rule limiting the powers of trustees in those respects and may also at discretion dispense wholly or partially with the production or investigation of the Lessors title in case of a loan on leasehold securities and may otherwise lend on any security or purchase or acquire any hereditaments with less than the title which a purchaser is in the absence of a special contract entitled to require and my trustees shall not be liable for any loss incurred through any act done or omitted to be done or the exercise of any discretion in reference to the matters aforesaid and I empower my trustees that upon any such sale or sales as are authorised by this my Will or in contemplation thereof to expend any money in the completion of any buildings in course of erection by me at my decease or to lay out any part of or parts of my said trust estates as or for streets or roads and to form and make any such streets or roads and also main sewers for the accommodation of houses or other buildings to be erected on land sold or

251

proposed to be sold in building plots and also on any such sale or sales as aforesaid shall be thought expedient the ownership of the soil in any such streets or roads and in the case of the exception or reservation to give easements only over such soil as shall from time to time be thought expedient and generally to deal with my said trust estates as my said trustees might do if absolutely and beneficially entitled thereto and on any such sale or sales to enter into such covenants and to require such covenants to be entered into of a mutual character restrictive or otherwise for the better enjoyment of the land sold and retained or of lands sold to different persons only as my trustees shall think proper and for the purposes aforesaid to pull down any buildings standing on my said estates and to sell or use the materials thereof the moneys arising therefrom when received to be held upon and for the trusts and purposes herein expressed and declared and concerning the moneys to arise from the sale of my said trust estates and for all or any of the purposes aforesaid to enter into and make execute and concur in all such contracts conveyances and assurances as my said trustees shall think proper and to alter vary or modify on terms or gratuitously any such contracts conveyances and assurances and to concur with any co-owner in doing any of the acts hereintobefore authorised with respect to any lands belonging to me at my decease jointly with any other person or persons In Witness whereof I the said John Fletcher the Testator have to this my last Will and testament contained in this and the five preceding sheets of paper set my hand this sixth day of November one thousand eight hundred and eighty eight.

Signed and declared by the said John Fletcher the Testator as and for his last Will and Testament in the presence of us who being both present at the same time have at his request in his presence and in the presence of each other hereunto subscribed our names as witnesses—

John Fletcher

Frederick Cattle, Solicitor, Clerk to Messrs Thurman & Slack, Solicitors, Ilkeston

Joseph B. Sheldon, Grocer, West Hill, Heanor

This is a Codicil to the last Will and Testament of me John Fletcher of Heanor in the County of Derby Lace Manufacturer which Will bears date the sixth day of November one thousand eight hundred and eighty eight Whereas my said Will contains a Declaration that when and so soon as my son George Henry Fletcher shall have attained the age of twenty one years my trustees William Fletcher and Thomas Fletcher therein named shall offer my business of a Lace Manufacturer now carried on by me at Heanor and Nottingham and the machinery and plant used therein to my three sons John Keyworth Fletcher Joseph Edward Fletcher and George Henry Fletcher to be carried on by them in co-partnership and if they should refuse such offer my said trustees William Fletcher and Thomas Fletcher should offer the said business for sale to each of my said three sons John Keyworth Fletcher Joseph Edward Fletcher and George Henry Fletcher as might be then living in order and if each of my said sons should decline to accept such offer my (trustees) should sell the said business to any person or persons in such manner as they may think fit And Whereas my said Son George Henry Fletcher has now attained the age of twenty one years Now I hereby revoke my said Will as far as hereintofore recited And I declare that my said trustees William Fletcher and Thomas Fletcher shall as soon as conveniently may be after my decease offer my said business machinery and plant for sale to my said three sons John Keyworth Fletcher Joseph Edward Fletcher and George Henry Fletcher to be carried on by them in co-partnership and that if they shall refuse such offer my trustees shall sell the said business to any person or persons in such a manner as they may think fit it being my intention that if the said John Keyworth Fletcher Joseph Edward Fletcher and George Henry Fletcher shall not purchase the said business as a partnership concern the same shall not be offered to them separately on the terms contained in my said Will And in all other respects I confirm my said Will In Witness whereof I the said John Fletcher the Testator have to this a Codicil to my last Will and testament contained in this and the preceding sheet of paper set my hand this fourteenth day of April one thousand eight hundred and ninety one —John Fletcher—Signed and declared by the said John Fletcher the Testator as and for a Codicil to his last Will and testament in the presence of us who being both present at the same time have at his request in his presence and in the presence of each other hereunto subscribed our names as witnesses

> Frederick Cattle, Solicitor, Heanor and Ilkeston
> Joseph B. Sheldon, Grocer, West Hill, Heanor.

This is a Codicil to the last Will and Testament of me John Fletcher of Heanor in the County of Derby Lace Manufacturer which Will bears date the sixth day of November one thousand eight hundred and eighty eight Whereas my said Will contains a Declaration that my trustees therein named shall retain the shares of each of my daughters of and in my residuary estate Upon the trusts therein declared concerning the same Now I Will and declare that notwithstanding the said declaration and the trusts contained in my said Will my trustees shall at such time or times after my decease as they may in their own absolute and uncontrolled discretion think fit pay to each of my said daughters who may survive me the sum of three hundred pounds on account of their respective shares of and in my residuary trust fund And for such sums the receipts of my said daughters shall be an absolute discharge to my trustees And in all other respects I confirm my said Will and the Codicil thereto bearing date the fourteenth day of April 1891 in witness whereof I the said John Fletcher the testator have to this Codicil to my last Will and testament set my hand this seventh day of July one thousand eight hundred and ninety two——John Fletcher——Signed and declared by the said John Fletcher the Testator as and for a Codicil to his last Will and testament in the presence of us who being both present at the same time have at his request in his presence and in the presence of each other hereunto subscribed our names as witnesses ——Frederick Cattle——Joseph B. Sheldon.

Testator died 4th January 1893

Will proved in the Principal Registry by the within named William Fletcher John Keyworth Fletcher and Joseph Edward Fletcher the Executors on 20th day of February 1893

Estate sworn at £7803 „ 14 „ 1

254

LETTERS OF ADMINISTRATION OF THE

PERSONAL ESTATE OF SAMUEL FLETCHER

OF HEANOR IN THE COUNTY OF DERBY

GENTLEMAN

(L.S.)

By Decree
of Court.

Richard Smalbroke Doctor of Law Vicar General of the Honorable and Right Reverend Father in God James by Divine permission Lord Bishop of Lichfield and Coventry To George Buckstone, William Webb and William Langley Clerks jointly and severally Sendeth Greeting:—Whereas We have Decreed Letters of Administration of the Personal Estate of Samuel Fletcher of Heanor in the County of Derby Gentleman who died Intestate (limited only as far as concern certain Terms of Six Hundred years Ninety nine years and Six Hundred years of and in a certain Messuage or Tenement in a certain Street called St Johns Street in Ashborne in the County of Derby vested in the said Samuel Fletcher as is alledged in and by a certain Indenture bearing the date of fifth day of April 1771) to be granted to John Beresford of Ashborne in the County of Derby Gentleman for the purpose of assigning the same or the Residue thereof as the Nominee of Erasmus Darwin Doctor of Physic the person entitled to the said premises We Therefore empower you jointly and severally to administer the Oath underwritten to the said John Beresford and we require you to Certify us what you shall do in the premises together with these presents

Dated at Lichfield this Twenty first day of April in the year of our Lord 1794

Hand, Proctor   Wm. Mott D: Regr.

THE OATH

Your Oath is that you believe that Samuel Fletcher late of Heanor deceased died without a Will that you will faithfully administer his Personal Estate as far as concerns certain terms of years vested in him and by a certain Indenture bearing date the 5th. day of April 1771 that you will exhibit an Inventory of such Personal Estate with an Account of your Administration thereof unto the Bishops Court at Lichfield when lawfully required and that you believe such Personal Estate will not amount in value to Five Pounds

So help you God

John Beresford

On the eighth day of May 1794 This Commission was duly executed and the said John Beresford Sworn before me

George Buckston

Commissioner.

256

LETTERS OF ADMINISTRATION OF THE

ESTATE OF LYDIA WILD OF ALFRETON

IN THE COUNTY OF DERBY

WIDOW

Administrations — In the Bishops Court of Lichfield
In the Goods of Lydia Wild, Deceased

Appeared Personally Elizabeth Briddon heretofore Elizabeth Wild now the wife Abraham Briddon the party applying for Letters of Administration of the Estate and Effects of the said Lydia Wild late of the parish of Alfreton in the County of Derby Widow - Deceased, and made Oath, that the Estate and Effects of the said Deceased, for, or in respect of which, the said Letters of Administration are to be granted, exclusive of what the said deceased may have been possessed of, or entitled to, as a Trustee for any other person or persons, and not beneficially, but including the Leasehold Estate or Estates for Years of the deceased, if any, whether absolute or determinable on Lives, and without deducting anything on account of the Debts, due and owing from the said deceased, are under the value of Four hundred and fifty Pounds, to the best of his Deponent's knowledge, information and belief.

Sworn on the 13th
Day of October 1824 } Elizabeth Briddon
before me,
John Papper Surrogate

FLETCHER, AND ITS VARIANTS, FLECCHER, FLECHER AND FLEACHER

LIST OF WILLS AND ADMINISTRATIONS
PROVED AND GRANTED IN
THE LICHFIELD CONSISTORY COURT
1550—1838

These are now housed in The Birmingham Probate Registry and photostat copies can be obtained from The Registrar at a reasonable cost. The compiler of The Story found in them a source of valuable help in his research into the past.

Date of proving		Fletcher Christian Name	Place of Origin	
1550	— Sept. 15	Thomas Fleccher	Aston-on-Trent	
1551	— July 8	Thomas Fleccher	Shenstone, Staffs.	
	— July 26	Robert Fleccher	Wirksworth	
	— July 26	William Fleccher	Wirksworth	
	— Sept. 16	John Fleccher	Staveley	
	— Sept. 19	Humphrey Fleccher	Alstonfield, Staffs.	
1552	— May 30	John Fleccher	Penkridge (Pentridge?)	
	— Aug. 1	Oliver Fleccher	Horsley	
	— Aug. 28	Agnes Fleccher	Coventry	ADM.
	— Oct. 6	Richard Fleccher	Edgmond, Salop.	
1553	— May 17	Roger Fleccher	Alstonfield, Staffs.	
	— July 8	Roger Fleccher	Tissington	
	— July 12	Henry Fleccher	Tatenhill, Staffs.	
1554	— Sept. 12	Roger Fleccher	Chesterfield	
	— Oct. 4	John Fleccher	Drayton-in-Hales, Salop.	
1555	— May 16	John Flecher	Penkridge	
1556	— June 17	Humphrey Fleccher	Penkridge	ADM.
	— June 27	Richard Fleccher	Yoxall, Staffs.	
	— Sept. 17	Christopher Fleccher	Ashover	
1557	— Apr. 26	Christopher Fleccher	Duffield	

259

Date of proving	Fletcher Christian Name	Place of Origin	
1557 — Aug. 31	Geoffrey Fleacher	Withybrook, Warwicksh.	ADM.
— Sep. 13	William Fleccher	Derby	
— Sep. 15	Elizabeth Fleccher	Chesterfield	
1558 — Apr. 19	Thomas	Chesterfield	
1561 — Sep. 17	John	Staveley	
1562 — Apr. 6	Nicholas	Duffield	
1563 — Apr. 20	Agnes Flecher	Staveley	
1564 — Apr. 10	Robert	Duffield	
1566 — Apr. 25	Oliver Flecher	Ashborne	
1567 — June 4	Henry	Chesterfield	
1569 — May 11	John Fleccher	Penkridge	
1572 — May 7	Thomas	Duffield	
1573 — Apr. 20	Richard	Horsley	
1574 — Oct. 6	John	Penkridge	
1576 — May 21	Richard Fleccher	Derby	ADM.
1579 — May 5	Isabel	Horsley	
1583 — Nov. 26	Peter	Chesterfield	
1585/6 — Jan. 25	William	Tissington	
1587 — June 6	Christopher	Duffield	
— June 7	Thomas	Derby	ADM.
— Oct. 12	Thomas	Chesterfield	ADM.
1588 — Apr. 16	Andrew	Horsley	
— May 27	Henry	Duffield	ADM.
1590 — Dec. 12	Thomas	Staveley	
1591 — Sep. 10	Anthony	Duffield	
1591/2 — Jan. 10	James	South Normanton	
1598 — Aug. 2	Henry	Repton	
1598/9 — Feb. 1	John	Chesterfield	
1600/1 — Jan. 22	Richard	Duffield	ADM.
1601/2 — Jan. 16	Alice	Chesterfield	ADM.
1602 — Apr. 19	Roger	Carsington	
— Apr. 23	Margery	Derby	ADM.
1604 — July 3	Margery	Chesterfield	ADM.
— July 23	Margery	Brimington	
1606 — Nov. 28	Ralph	Duffield	ADM.
1607/8 — Jan. 19	William	Derby	ADM.
1609/10 — Mar. 24	Godfrey	South Normanton	
1611 — Sept. 24	William	Allestrey	

Date of proving	Fletcher Christian Name	Place of Origin	
1615/6 — Mar. 1	Oliver	Duffield	
1619 — May 20	George	Marston Montgomery	
1620 — Nov. 15	William	North Wingfield	
1621/2 — Jan. 22	Robert	Duffield	
1623 — Aug. 28	Nicholas	Allestrey	
1624 — Nov. 25	William	Duffield	
1626 — June 6	John	North Wingfield	
1631 — June 6	Thomas	Ashbourne	
1631/2 — Mar. 15	Margery	North Wingfield	
1632/3 — Mar. 19	Francis	Ashbourne	
1634 — May 6	Robert	Allestrey	
1635/6 — Feb. 19	Exuperius	Duffield	
1637 — Aug. 26	William, the elder	Ashbourne	
1638 — Oct. 19	Richard	Duffield	
1639 — Nov. 27	Henry	Tissington	ADM.
1640 — May 30	Thomas	Wingerworth	
— July 24	Amy	Tissington	
— Sept. 21	John	Horsley	
1642 — June 17	Richard	Ashbourne	
— June 17	William	Crich	
1646 — Dec. 16	Thomas	Wingerworth	ADM.
— Dec. 16	William	Chesterfield	
1647 — Oct. 4	Robert	Tissington	
— Oct. 6	Richard	Chesterfield	
1648 — June 7	Francis	Wingerworth	
1650 — July 30	Roger	Doveridge	
1660 — Aug. 22	Ellen	Ashbourne	ADM.
1661 — Aug. 29	Thomas	Darley	
1661 — Oct. 4	Thomas	Derby	
1662 — May 12	Thomas	Doveridge	ADM.
— July 18	Nicholas	Derby	
1663 — Oct. 7	Richard	Duffield	
1668 — Oct. 24	John	Wirksworth	
1669 — July 26	Mary	Doveridge	
1670 — May 5	Robert	Derby	ADM.
1671 — Mar. 27	Thomas	Derby	
— Oct. 4	Richard	Chesterfield	
— Oct. 17	Richard	Tissington	
1671/2 — Feb. 21	Joseph	Derby	ADM.

S

Date of proving	Fletcher Christian Name	Place of Origin	
1674 — Nov. 16	Anthony	Derby	ADM.
1678/9 — Feb. 21	Joseph	Rolleston, Notts. or Staffs.	
1679 — May 7	Paul	Stone Gravels	ADM.
— May 7	Robert	Tissington	
— Nov. 26	William	Calow	
1680/1 — Mar. 3	Roger	Doveridge	
1681 — Apr. 23	Thomas	Heage	ADM.
1682 — May 15	Elizabeth	Wilne	
1683/4 — Jan. 13	Samuel	Stockton	ADM.
1684 — May 20	Patrick	Denby	
— Oct. 16	Thomas	Ashbourne	
— Oct. 17	Robert	Derby	
— Dec. 27	George	Sudbury	
1685 — Oct. 29	Ann	Derby	ADM.
— Oct. 29	Ruth	Derby	ADM.
1686 — Apr. 28	Elizabeth	Duffield	ADM.
— Sept. 24	Catherine	Derby	ADM.
1687 — June 4	John	Derby	
1689 — Oct. 15	William	Moreton	
1690 — July 1	Thomas	Donnington	
1691/2 — Feb. 18	John	North Wingfield	
1693 — Apr. 26	George	Chesterfield	ADM.
1694 — Apr. 13	William	Derby	ADM.
1695 — Apr. 26	William	Somershall Herbert	ADM.
— Oct. 4	John	Duffield	
— Oct. 4	William	Tissington	
1696 — Apr. 15	William	Chesterfield	
— Apr. 17	Samuel	Derby	
1697 — Oct. 8	John	Derby	
1698 — May 11	Mary	Chesterfield	
1699 — Apr. 14	John	Horsley	
— Oct. 17	Godfrey	Brampton	ADM.
— Oct. 17	Ralph	Chesterfield	ADM.
1700 — Apr. 2	William	South Wingfield	
— Oct. 4	Helen	Derby	
— Oct. 4	Henry	Derby	
1702 — Apr. 21	Charles	Chesterfield	ADM.

262

Date of proving			Fletcher Christian Name	Place of Origin	
1702	— May	7	Elizabeth	Donnington	
1703	— Oct.	6	William	Chesterfield	ADM.
1704	— Aug.	2	James	Derby	
1705	— Apr.	13	Robert	Tissington	
1706	— Apr.	12	Thomas	Tissington	ADM.
	— Oct.	2	Edward	Chesterfield	ADM.
1711	— Oct.	5	William	Denby	ADM.
1712	— Apr.	9	Thomas	Alfreton	
	— Apr.	11	Lucy	Horsley	
	— Apr.	11·	Robert	Horsley	
	— Aug.	1	John	Comberford	
1714	— Oct.	6	Vincent	Denbigh	
1715	— Oct.	4	Joseph	Pentrich	
	— Oct.	4	Mary	Derby	
1716	— Apr.	6	William	Wirksworth	
	— Oct.	19	Francis	Kirkhallam	
	— Nov.	9	William	Lullington	
1717	— Apr.	24	Robert	Dawley	
1719	— Apr.	7	Robert	Wirksworth	
	— Apr.	8	Joseph	Alfreton	
1719	— Sept.	30	Thomas	Darley	
	— Oct.	2	Susannah	Denbigh	
1720	— Oct.	1	William	Dronfield	ADM.
1721	— Apr.	19	Jonathan	Heage	ADM.
	— Apr.	20	James	Tupton	
	— Oct.	3	Sarah	Wirksworth	ADM.
1722	— July	9	Robert	Derby	
1723	— July	22	Henry	Lullington	
	— Sept.	30	Mary	Clifton	
1724	— Apr.	14	Joseph	Wirksworth	ADM.
1725	— May	7	Samuel	Spondon	ADM.
1726	— Apr.	26	Elizabeth	Ashborne	ADM.
1727	— May	31	Emma	Derby	ADM.
1728	— Apr.	9	Oliver	Horsley	ADM.
	— Oct.	3	Paul	Brampton	
	— Oct.	4	Alice	Duffield	ADM.
1728/9	— Mar.	18	John	Dronfield	ADM.
1729	— Apr.	22	Robert	Denby	
	— Apr.	22	William	Ashborne	ADM.

Date of proving	Fletcher Christian Name	Place of Origin	
1729 — Oct. 14	James	Derby	
1730 — Apr. 14	Jonathan	Pentrich	
— Oct. 13	Francis	Ashborne	ADM.
1733 — Oct. 31	Matthew	Brampton	
1735 — Apr. 22	John	Horsley	
1739 — Apr. 19	Simon	Horsley	ADM.
— Aug. 28	John	Ashborne	ADM.
1740 — Oct. 16	Barbara	Chesterfield	ADM.
1740/1 — Mar. 10	Henry	Derby —	
1742 — Apr. 21	Joseph	Heanor	ADM.
— Oct. 6	Thomas	Denby	ADM.
1744 — Oct. 17	Mary	Hathersage	
1745 — Apr. 17	Mary	Horsley	
— Apr. 17	Richard	Ashborne	
— Apr. 17	Robert	Heanor	
1747 — Oct. 29	William	Chesterfield	
1749 — Apr. 11	George	Ashborne	
1751 — Sept. 26	Mary	Darley	
1752 — Apr. 14	Rev. George	Cubley	
— Apr. 15	Henry	Wirksworth	
— Nov. 21	William	Derby	ADM.
1753 — Jan. 20	Rebecca	Denby	ADM.
— May 17	Mary	Chesterfield	
1754 — May 14	John	Denby	ADM.
— Aug. 15	Robert	Heanor	
1755 — Aug. 15	Richard	Derby	ADM.
1757 — Apr. 28	John	Wensley	
— Oct. 21	Jane	Derby	ADM.
— Oct. 21	Sarah	Greasley, Co. Notts.	
1758 — Mar. 29	Godfrey	Stapenhill	
1759 — May 4	Susanna	Derby	ADM.
— Oct. 19	Joseph	Stanton	
1761 — June 18	Henry	Spondon	ADM.
— Aug. 29	John	Denby	
1762 — Jan. 6	John	Glossop	
— Aug. 17	William	South Wingfield	
1763 — Oct. 27	Edward	Walton, Stone	
1766 — Feb. 24	John, Esq.	Stainsby	
1770 — Oct. 18	Robert	Morton	ADM.

Date of proving			Fletcher Christian Name	Place of Origin	
1772	—	May 19	Hugo	Ashborne	
1773	—	Apr. 27	Joseph	Ripley	
1775	—	Oct. 19	Martha	Staveley	ADM.
1778	—	Oct. 15	Thomas	Darley	
1779	—	Feb. 17	Daniel	Newhall	
1781	—	Mar. 11	Elizabeth	Denby	
	—	Mar. 11	Sarah	Denby	
1782	—	Mar. 25	Francis	Ashborne	
	—	Apr. 18	William	Chesterfield	
1784	—	July 6	Selene Maria	Cubley	
1785	—	Aug. 3	Vincent	Pentrich	
1787	—	Oct. 18	Patrick	Denby	
	—	Oct. 29	Elizabeth	Bonsall	
1788	—	Oct. 15	Samuel	Heanor	
	—	Nov. 18	William	Pentrich	ADM.
1789	—	July 16	John	Heanor	
1793	—	May 13	Benjamin	Mappleton	
1794	—	May 12	Samuel	Heanor	ADM.
	—	Aug. 22	Vincent	Horsley	
1795	—	Apr. 21	Walter	Breadsall	ADM.
1796	—	Apr. 13	Thomas	Alfreton	
1797	—	July 1	Thomas	Whitwell	
	—	Oct. 12	Godfrey	Brampton	
1798	—	Apr. 26	William	Chesterfield	
	—	Oct. 18	Benjamin	Chesterfield	
1799	—	Oct. 16	Robert	Pentrich	
1800	—	Apr. 12	Thomas	Chesterfield	
1801	—.		George	Cubley	
			(copy Will proved D.C.)		
	—	Jan. 10	Mary	Ashborne	
	—	Apr. 22	George	Pentrich	
1802	—	Oct. 12	John	Derby	
	—	Nov. 8	Thomas	Duffield	ADM.
1803	—	Apr. 23	Robert	Whitwell	ADM.
1804	—	Feb. 7	Elizabeth	Derby	
	—	Feb. 10	John	Derby	
1805	—	Apr. 18	George	Staveley	
1806	—	Jan. 14	John	Stapenhill	
	—	Apr. 22	Ann	Kilburn	

1806	— Apr. 24	Elizabeth	Chesterfield	
	— Oct. 16	William	Youlgreave	ADM.
1807	— Feb. 17	Dorothy	West Hallam	ADM.
	— Apr. 14	Robert	Denby	
1808	— Oct. 11	Carter	Boylstone	
	— Oct. 24	Thomas	Whitwell	ADM.
1809	— Apr. 19	Jonathan	Pentrich	
	— Oct. 12	Ann	Wirksworth	
1810	— Apr. 10	Thomas	Tissington	
	— Apr. 30	Joseph	Matlock	
	— Dec. 19	Samuel	Derby	ADM.
1811	— Aug. 9	Elizabeth	Bonsall	
1812	— Apr. 27	William	Newhall	
1813	— June 2	Elizabeth	Mappleton	
1814	— Feb. 23	John	Church Gresley	
	— Apr. 26	Henry Viccars	Derby	
	— Oct. 13	Joseph	Matlock	
1815	— Apr. 13	Robert	Darley	
1816	— Mar. 20	William	Denby	
	— Mar. or			
	May 20	Ellen	Denby	
1818	— Dec. 29	Joseph	quoda bona	ADM.
1819	— Apr. 27	Mary	Derby	
	— Apr. 27	Robert	Derby	
	— Apr. 28	Samuel	Heanor	
	— May 12	William	Church Gresley	
1820	— Oct. 12	William	Matlock	
1822	— Sept. 28	Luke	Church Gresley	
1823	— Feb. 5	Mary	Heanor	
	— Apr. 17	George	Eckington	
	— May 27	John	Denby	
	— July 16	Henry	Spondon	
	— Oct. 15	Daniel	Denby	
	— Oct. 16	John	Whitwell	
1824	— May 6	William	Chesterfield	
	— Aug. 16	William	Shirland	
	— Oct. 13	John	Pentrich	
1825	— Apr. 20	William	Morton	
	— Apr. 21	Francis	Chesterfield	

1826 — Oct. 11	John	Heanor
— Nov. 24	Daniel	Stapenhill
1827 — Jan. 3	Robert	Hartshorne
— Oct. 9	Hannah	Wirksworth
1828 — June 25	Godfrey	Church Gresley
1829 — Apr. 22	Elizabeth	Shirland
— July 27	Charles	Sutton-on-the-Hill
1831 — Apr. 20	William	Alfreton
— Oct. 19	John	Heanor
1832 — May 3	William	Staveley
1833 — May 24	Thomas	Stapenhill
1834 — Apr. 9	George	Ripley
1836 — Apr. 11	William	Heanor
— Apr. 25	Thomas	*quoad bona*
— Apr. 27	Thomas	*quoad bona*
— Oct. 12	William	Pentrich

NOTE—The foregoing were, with a few exceptions, all domiciled in Derbyshire at the time of death. Those that follow on from here claimed Shropshire, Staffordshire or Warwickshire as their County of Origin.

1562 — May 8	Fletcher, Nicholas	Yoxall
1564 — Apr. 12	John	Burton-on-Trent
		ADM.
1580 — Mar. 26	Joyce	Aston, Birmingham
		ADM.
1582/3 — Jan. 7	Thomas	Walsall
1585 — Aug. 4	Richard	Lilleshall
1586/7 — Mar. 23	John	Alstonfield
1588/9 — Mar. 1	Thomas	Patshull
1591 — June 7	Roland	Shenstone
1597 — July 3	Alice	Albrighton
1601/2 — Jan. 7	Francis	Footherley, Shenstone
1602 — Aug. 28	John	Shenstone
1604/5 — Feb. 25	Elizabeth	Alstonfield
1607 — May 8	Robert	Sutton Coldfield
1617 — Apr. 16	Richard	Tamworth
— Dec. 18	John	Shenstone
1618 — May 26	John	Albrighton

Date of proving	Fletcher Christian Name.	Place of Origin	
1618 — Sep. 22	Catherine	Shavington	
1619/20— Feb. 11	Clement	Monks Kirby	
1620 — Nov. 15	Jane	Wellington	
1621 —	Richard	Tamworth	
1622/3 — Feb. 7	William	Walsall	ADM.
1624 — Dec. 17	Thomas	Tamworth	
1628 — Apr. 8	Ann	Lilleshall.	
1631 — Sep. 30	John	Ashley	
— Oct. 31	Thomas	Drayton-in-Hales	
1632 — Sep. 4	James	Footherley	
1633/4 — Feb. 21	Nicholas	Bitterscote	
1634 — Oct. 9	John	Betley	
1637/8 — Jan. 19	William	Tatenhill	
1639 — May 21	William	Yoxall	
1642 — Aug. 5	Elizabeth	Snowdon Heath	
1647 — May 22	Mary	Lilleshall	
— Aug. 20	Samuel	Uttoxeter	
1648/9 — Jan. 23	Thomas	Ryton upon Wildmoor	
			ADM.
1649 — Nov. 22	William	London (apprentice)	
			ADM.
1661 — Sep. 20	Henry	Stockton	
1664 — Nov. 26	Thomas	Aston, Birmingham	
			ADM.
1665 — May 10	John	Sutton Coldfield	
— July 13	Elizabeth	Aston, Birmingham	
— Oct. 6	Thomas	Aston, Birmingham	
1665/6 — Feb. 3	William	Burslem	
1666 — Apr. 7	Ralph	Burslem	
1669 — Sep. 27	Richard	Tatenhill	
— Dec. 16	Jane	Sutton Coldfield	
1670 — July 25	Mary, *alais* Mort	Sheen	
1672 — Aug. 3	William	Donnington	
1675 — Apr. 27	Thomas	Ashley	
1675/6 — Mar. 6	Alice	Coventry	
1678/9 — Feb. 21	Joseph	Rolleston, Notts. or	
		Staffs..	
1680 — May 19	John	Great Packington	
— July 13	Mary	Burslem	

Date of proving		Fletcher Christian Name	Place of Origin	
1681	— Apr. 19	Thomas	Wellington	
1683	— June 11	William	Tamworth	
1683/4	— Jan. 13	Samuel	Stockton	ADM.
1685/6	— Jan. 1	Thomas	Haughton	ADM.
1687	— June 14	Thomas	Tamworth	ADM.
1688	— Apr. 6	William	Coventry	ADM.
	— Nov. 16	James	Footherley	
1689	— May 31	Samuel	Walsall	ADM.
	— Oct. 15	William	Moreton, Salop. or Notts.	
1689/90	— Mar. 6	John	Blymhill	ADM.
1690	— Nov. 21	Ellen	Dunstall	ADM.
1691	— June 17	Mary	Hopwas	
1692	— Nov. 16	Thomas	Norton	
1695/6	— Feb. 21	Edward	Hamstall Ridware	
1695	— Apr. 19	John	Keele	
1696	— Nov. 17	Thomas	Ryton	
1696/7	— Mar. 16	Elizabeth	Tamworth	
1700	— Mar. 4	Richard	Tamworth	ADM.
1702	— May 15	Robert	Southam	
1706	— Apr. 26	Richard	Newport	
1707/8	— Jan. 6	Nicholas	Bitterscoat	
1711	— June 1	Joseph	Stoke	
	— Oct. 11	Richard	Grindon	
1713-4	— Feb. 16	Samuel	Walsall	
1714	— Oct. 22	John	Ryton	
	— Oct. 22	Thomas	Blymill	
	— Nov. 5	Samuel	Rushall	
1717	— Mar. 29	Mary	Wyken	
1718	— Dec. 30	John	Yoxall	
1720	— Apr. 22	Mary	Whitchurch	
1722	— Apr. 13	Richard	Newport	
	— Oct. 27	Griselda	Whitchurch	
1724	— Apr. 25	William	Wolstanton	
1727/8	— Jan. 17	John	Hopwas	
1728	— May 31	James	Shenstone	
	— Oct. 7	Daniel	Anslow	
1729	— Oct. 31	Thomas	Brinston	

Date of proving	Fletcher Christian Name	Place of Origin	
1730 — Oct. 29	Thomas	Wellington	
1733 — June. 8	William	Tamworth	
1734 — Dec. 17	Samuel	Shifnall	ADM.
1735 — May 2	Richard	Shenstone	
1740 — Sep. 16	William	Bushbury	
1745 — Apr. 19	Samuel	Worfield	
1751 — Dec. 19	Samuel	Worfield	
1752 — Feb. 10	Ann	Whitchurch	
1753 — May 12	Joseph	Leek	
1755 — May 12	Edward	Aldridge	
1757 — Nov. 2	Samuel	Worfield	
1759 — Oct. 19	Joseph	Stanton	
1763 — Apr. 13	Ann	Newport	
— May 6	Hannah	Tatenhill	ADM.
1767 — May 5	John	Tutbury	
1771 — June 10	Samuel	Patteshall, Northants.	
1775 — July 3	Joseph	Leek	
1778 — May 29	Thomas	Weston-under-Lizard	
— Oct. 22	Theophilus	High Ercall	
1782 — Dec. 5	Nicholas	Birmingham	
1784 — Apr. 14	John	Birmingham	
— Nov. 3	John	Stafford	
1791 — Dec. 21	William	Handsworth	ADM.
1792 — Sep. 13	William	Walsall	
1793 — June 28	John	Fillongly	
1797 — Oct. 7	Job	Coleshill	
1799 — Aug. 6	Mary	Kinver	
1800 — Feb. 27	Thomas	Abbots Bromley	
— Apr. 16	John	Birmingham	
1800 — Apr. 30	John	Uttoxeter	
— Oct. 11	John	Minworth	
1802 — July 16	Joseph	Sedgley	
1803 — Jan. 19	Thomas	Darlaston	ADM.
1805 — Apr. 10	William	Darlaston	
1806 — May 1	Thomas	Checkley	
1808 — Apr. 30	Richard	Burslem	
— June 29	Sarah	Birmingham	
— Aug. 23	Frances	Pattingham	
1809 — Apr. 12	Richard	Cherrington	

270

Date of proving	Fletcher Christian Name	Place of Origin
1809 — Oct. 31	John	Birmingham
1811 — June 21	William	Yoxall
— Sep. 6	John	Yoxall
1812 — Apr. 25	Lawrence	Drayton-in-Hales
1813 — Oct. 21	William	Lilleshall
1814 — Apr. 20	Joseph	Shiffnall
— July 6	Ann	Sutton Coldfield
1815 — Oct. 19	Edward	Lilleshall
1817 — Jan. 18	William	Whittington
— Feb. 5	Sarah	Aston, Birmingham
		ADM.
— Oct. 10	Thomas	Walsall
— Oct. 23	Thomas	Coalbrook Dale
1818 — Mar. 7	Thomas	Woolstanton
1819 — May 7	Peter	Sedgley
— Nov. 24	Mary	Baddesley Clinton
1820 — Oct. 14	Thomas	Chetwynd
— Dec. 19	James	Wednesbury
1821 — Apr. 13	James	Rugby
— Apr. 30	Thomas	Birmingham
— May 9	John	Uttoxeter
1822 — June 4	Margaret	Tutbury
— June 17	Elizabeth	Donnington
1823 — Nov. 6	William	Birmingham
1824 — Apr. 26	Elizabeth	Sutton Coldfield
1824 — Aug. 6	Edward	Hamstall Ridware
1826 — June 28	John	Measham, Leicester-shire
1827 — Jan. 12	Edward	Hamstall
— May 10	Joseph	Leek
1828 — Jan. 26	Elizabeth	Yoxall
— Aug. 11	William	Barton-under-Needwood
1829 — Nov. 5	John	Hockley, Birmingham
1830 — Feb. 26	Thomas	Hamstall Ridware
— Mar. 17	Susanna	Birmingham
— Mar. 19	John	Hamstall Ridware
— Mar. 26	Ann	Handsworth
1832 — Mar. 2	Samuel	Walsall

Date of proving	Fletcher Christian Name	Place of Origin
1832 — Nov. 13	William	Solihull
— Nov. 14	Joseph	Rowley Regis
1833 — July 31	Amos	Birmingham
— Sep. 14	Sophia	Walsall
1836 — Apr. 25	Thomas	*quoad bona*
— Apr. 27	Thomas	*quoad bona*
— Oct. 19	William	Tibberton
1837 — Jan. 10	William	Churcheaton
— Apr. 26	William	Uttoxeter
— Apr. 27	John	Stoke-on-Trent
— June 10	Amos	Birmingham
1838 — Jan. 29	John	Enville
— Oct. 9	James	Birmingham

WILD, AND ITS VARIANTS WYLD, WYLDE AND WILDE

LIST OF WILLS PROVED AND ADMINISTRATIONS

GRANTED IN

THE LICHFIELD CONSISTORY COURT

1601—1838

These are now housed in The Birmingham Probate Registry and copies may be obtained from there.

Date of proving	Wild etc.—full names	Place of Origin	
1601 — Aug. 10	Wylde, John	Doveridge	ADM.
1602 — Aug. 26	Wilde, Agnes	Sudbury	
1605 — July 1	Wilde, George	Crich	ADM.
1609/10— Mar. 22	Wilde, John	Radborne	ADM.
1610 — Oct. 9	Wylde, William	Crich	
1613 — Aug. 3	Wyld, Godfrey		
	alias Hoult	Morton	
— Dec. 8	Wilde, Roger	Doveridge	
1616 — Dec. 17	Wilde, Elizabeth	Doveridge	ADM.
1618 — May 11	Wilde, Francis	Doveridge	
1621 — Aug. 2	Wilde, James	Heanor	ADM.
1622/3 — Mar. 14	Wilde, Eleanor	Heanor	
1626 — May 23	Wylde, Richard	Darleigh (Darley)	
1627 — May 29	Wilde, Robert	Codnor	
1628 — Dec. 19	Wylde, Thomas	Doveridge	
1631 — Oct. 24	Wild, Nicholas	Butterley	
1633 — Sep. 19	Wilde, Richard	Ashover	
1634 — May 23	Wild, Thomas	Doveridge	ADM.
1635 — May 26	Wilde, Anthony	Crich	
1638/9 — Mar. 4	Wild, Duke	Crich	ADM.
1639 — Apr. 18	Wylde, James	Darley	
1639/40— Jan. 24	Wilde, Anne	Doveridge	

273

Date of proving			Wild etc.—full names	Place of Origin	
1641/2	— Mar.	23	Wyld, Thomas	Duffield	
1648	— June	7	Wylde, Edward	Dronfield	
1648/9	— Feb.	2	Wilde, Thomas	Tansley	
1660	— Sep.	6	Wilde, John	Derby	
1665	— Apr.	17	Wyld, Thomas	Doveridge	
1672	— Sep.	11	Wyld, William	Ashover	ADM.
1673	— May	2	Wylde, Thomas	Pentrich	
	— Oct.	25	Wyld, Zouch	Codnor Castle	
1677	— May	16	Wyld, Ellen	Glossop	
1676	— Feb.	5	Wylde, Jane	Doveridge	ADM.
1679	— May	7	Wyld, John	Glossop	
1680	— July	29	Wylde, John	Glossop	ADM.
1681/2	— Mar.	22	Wylde, Elizabeth	Glossop	
1683/4	— Jan.	1	Wylde, Stephen	Eyam	ADM.
1686	— Aug.	11	Wilde, Zouch	Heanor	ADM.
1689	— Oct.	14	Wild, John	Glossop	
1690	— Oct.	1	Wild, Philip	Heanor	
1695	— Apr.	26	Wyld, Henry	Heanor	ADM.
1698	— Oct.	19	Wild, Francis	Eyam	
1701	— Nov.	12	Wild, Sarah	Ashover	
1705	— Apr.	13	Wild, Thomas	Wirksworth	
1711	— Mar.	27	Wild, Thomas	Eyam	
	— Mar.	28	Wyld, Eleanor	Pentrich	
1717	— Apr.	24	Wilde, John	Darley	
1719	— Apr.	7	Wild, John	Great Appleby	
1720	— Sept.	23	Wylde, Thomas	Heage	
1721	— Apr.	18	Wilde, Vincent	Heanor	ADM.
	— Apr.	20	Wild, Martha	Chesterfield	ADM.
1724	— July	8	Wild, William	Glossop	
1726	— Apr.	29	Wild, Mary	Horsley	ADM.
1729	— Apr.	22	Wild, John	Aston-on-Trent	
	— Oct.	16	Wyld, Hugh	Glossop	
1731	— Apr.	21	Wild, Thomas	Eyam	
	— Apr.	23	Wild, Mary	Duffield	ADM.
	— Oct.	21	Wyld, Thomas	Chesterfield	- ADM.
1734	— Nov.	8	Wild, Samuel	Chesterfield	ADM.
1735	— Apr.	24	Wild, Gervase	Glossop	
1739	— Apr.	13	Wild, Mary	Derby	ADM.
1741	— Apr.	16	Wild, Peter	Eyam	

274

Date of proving			Wild etc.—full names	Place of Origin	
1741	— Apr.	16	Wyld, Mary	Glossop	
1746	— Apr.	15	Wylde, James	Belper	
	— Oct.	16	Wyld, James	Glossop	
1748	— Oct.	21	Wyld, Elizabeth	Glossop	
1747	— Oct.	27	Wild, Elizabeth	Heanor	
1751	— Apr.	23	Wild, William	Glossop	
1756	— Nov.	23	Wylde, Margaret	Glossop	ADM.
1760	— Apr.	22	Wyld, John	Codnor	
1763	— July	8	Wild, Samuel	Ashborne	
1764	— May	4	Wilde, Mary	Derby	ADM.
1768	— Apr.	19	Wyld, John	Heanor	
1769	— Apr.	26	Wild, John	Norton, Co. Derby	
					ADM.
	— Oct.	10	Wild, John	Derby	
1770	— Oct.	19	Wyld, Rebecca	Codnor	
1773	— Apr.	27	Wild, William	Aston-on-Trent	
	— Nov.	3	Wyld, John	Codnor	
1774	— Apr.	20	Wild, John	Glossop	
	— May	5	Wyld, Thomas	Norton, Co. Derby	
1775	— Apr.	28	Wild, Grace	Derby	
1778	— June	3	Wylde, James	Glossop	
1781	— May	2	Wild, Mary	Norton, Co. Derby	
1782	— Apr.	16	Wild, John	Derby	
1785	— Apr.	12	Wyld, Joseph	Belper	
1786	— Apr.	27	Wild, Mary	Alfreton	
1788	— Apr.	8	Wild, Daniel	Kirk Ireton	ADM.
	— Apr.	10	Wild, Peter	Glossop	
	— June	9	Wild, Anthony	Derby	
	— Aug.	12	Wyld, Thomas	Hadfield	
	— Nov.	22	Wild, Ellen	Dronfield	
1791	— Oct.	11	Wild, Richard	Brassington	
1792	— Apr.	26	Wild, John	Brampton	
1793	— Jan.	7	Wild, John	Brampton	
1796	— Jan.	2	Wild, William	Ilkeston	ADM.
	— Apr.	14	Wild, William	Matlock	
	— Oct.	11	Wild, Edith	Kirk Ireton	
1802	— Sept.	30	Wild, George	Stony Middleton	
1803	— Apr.	28	Wild, Job	Scarcliffe	
	— Oct.	13	Wild, Luke	Youlgreave	

275

Date of proving	Wild etc.—full names	Place of Origin
1804 — Oct. 18	Wilde, Elizabeth	Brampton
1805 — Apr. 18	Wild, John	Chesterfield
1806 — Apr. 24	Wild, Mary	Eckington
— Oct. 16	Wilde, John	Darley
1807 — Aug. 12	Wild, John	Alsop-le-Dale
1813 — Apr. 20	Wylde, Thomas	Ockbrooke
1814 — Apr. 28	Wild, George	Bolsover
1815 — Oct. 2	Wild, Richard	Wirksworth
1816 — Sep. 23	Wild, Benjamin	Glossop
1817 — Mar. 31	Wild, Peter	Glossop
— Apr. 23	Wylde, John	North Wingfield
1818 — Oct. 15	Wild, Elizabeth	Chesterfield
1819 — May 29	Wyld, Phoebe	Darley
— Aug. 14	Wyld, Thomas	Dronfield
— Oct. 14	Wild, Samuel	Glossop
1820 — Apr. 19	Wild, Joseph	Alfreton
1821 — Dec. 12	Wild, Elizabeth	Kelinworth
1824 — Jan. 17	Wild, Anne	Chesterfield
— May 11	Wild, Ann	Wirksworth
— Oct. 18	Wild, Lydia	Alfreton
1825 — Apr. 21	Wilde, George	Scarcliffe
— June 24	Wild, Thomas	Alsop in the Dale
1827 — Apr. 10	Wylde, Nathan	Nottingham
1830 — Oct. 15	Wild, James	Glossop
1832 — Jan. 9	Wild, Immanuel	Mellor
— July 27	Wild, Jonathan	Winster
1833 — Apr. 18	Wild, John	Crich
1835 — Apr. 23	Wild, Samuel	Chesterfield
1838 — Apr. 28	Wild, William	Stony Middleton
— Aug. 2	Wylde, Joseph	Derby
— Dec. 22	Wild, Thomas	Great Dawley

NOTE—The foregoing were all domiciled in Derbyshire at the time of death, whilst those that follow on from here claimed Shropshire, Staffordshire or Warwickshire as their County of Origin.

1624 — Dec. 2	Wilde, John	Stoneleigh
1635 — Oct. 16	Wilde, John	Uttoxeter
1660 — Sep. 21	Wylde, John	Bromshall

Date of proving	Wild etc.—full names	Place of Origin	
1661 — Sep. 20	Wyld, Ralph	Longslow	
1663 — June 31			
(sic)	Wyld, Barnabas	Pitchford	ADM.
1687 — Apr. 21	Wild, John	Uttoxeter	
1702 — Oct. 15	Wilde, Samuel	Drayton	
1703 — Apr. 29	Wild, Ralph	Drayton	
1715 — Apr. 20	Wild, William	Cound	
1717 — Apr. 5	Wilde, Ralph	Drayton	ADM.
1720 — Apr. 22	Wilde, Catharine	Drayton	
1721 — May 28	Wilde, John	Checkley	
1724 — Oct. 9	Wild, Charles	Calton	
1724 — Apr. 10	Wild, George	Chetwynd	
1730 — Apr. 28	Wild, George	Woodseaves	
1732 — Nov. 2	Wild, Margaret	Cound	
1734 — May 22	Wild, Jane	Chetwynd	ADM.
1736 — Apr. 28	Wild, John	Drayton	ADM.
1740 — July 11	Wyld, William	Rocester	ADM.
1742 — Apr. 28	Wild, Mary	Edgmond	ADM.
1751 — Jan. 29	Wyld, James	Stafford	ADM.
1775 — Apr. 21	Wild, John	Bubbenhall	ADM.
1802 — Apr. 29	Wild, Thomas	Hodnet	
— Oct. 27	Wild, William	Rocester	
1803 — Apr. 20	Wild, Thomas	Newport	
1807 — Nov. 3	Wild, Nathan	Castle Bromwich	
1810 — May 2	Wild, John	Leigh	
1812 — Feb. 20	Wild, Mary	Hodnet	
1813 — Apr. 26	Wild, George	Hodnet	
1814 — May 4	Wild, Ann	Rocester	
1826 — Feb. 4	Wild, Thomas	Hodnet	
— July 24	Wild, Robert	Stone	
1827 — Feb. 26	Wild, Elizabeth	Stone	
— May 10	Wild, William	Stoke-on-Trent	
1832 — Jan. 9	Wild, Immanuel	Mellor, Cheshire	
1835 — Aug. 1	Wild, Joseph *alias* Whilde		
		Birmingham	

HOW, AND WHERE, THE FIRST FLETCHER LACE FACTORY SITUATE ON TAG HILL, HEANOR, ORIGINATED

This indenture made the 26th December, 1838 between Joseph Gronow of Charlton Kings, near Cheltenham, Gloucester, of the one part and EDWARD FLETCHER of Heanor, Derby, lace manufacturer of the other part Whereas by indenture dated the 7th March, 1835 made between Henry Eley and John Bestwick, lace manufacturers, both of Heanor, of the first part and Matthew Wood of the second part, Henry Frearson of the third part and Joseph Gronow of the fourth part reciting that by a certain indenture dated the 19th April in the twelfth year of the reign of King James I made between John Cross and S. Holland a lease of 1,000 years was thereby created in the hereditaments hereinafter described and that the residue of the said lease was invested in Joseph Harrison, Derby, by virtue of indenture of assignment dated the 13th August, 1824, made between Thomas Woodhead and Henry Wood and said Joseph Harrison for securing to him the repayment of the sum of £250 and interest the same property therein and hereinafter described and intended to be assigned were granted and transferred to the said Joseph Gronow for the remainder of the said term of 1,000 years subject to the payment of said mortgage, etc............and whereas EDWARD FLETCHER has contracted with the said Joseph Gronow for the purchase of the land and buildings subject to the said mortgage in the sum of £150, now this indenture witnesses that in pursuance of the said contract and in consideration of the sum of £150 to the said Joseph Gronow now paid by EDWARD FLETCHER for the purchase of the said hereditaments hereinafter described subject to the said mortgage Joseph Gronow has granted to EDWARD FLETCHER all that leasehold plot of land situate and being in Heanor aforesaid and was staked and marked out containing by survey 877 sq. yds. or thereabouts bounded on the East by land belonging to Mr. Ramsey, on the West land belonging to John Jackson, on the North by land belonging to Samuel Colclough and on the South by turnpike road leading from Heanor to Derby and those two dwelling houses and shop.

278

A REVEALING FLASH-BACK INTO JARDINE
FAMILY HISTORY

THIS INDENTURE WITNESSETH THAT John Jardine (aged fourteen years on the fourteenth day of January last) son of Thomas Jardine of the Town of Nottingham, Jeweller, doth put himself APPRENTICE to Charles Lees of the said Town of Nottingham, clock and watch maker to learn his art and with him after the manner of an apprentice to serve from the date hereof until the full end and Term of seven years, from thence next following, to be fully complete and ended; during which term the said apprentice his said Master faithfully shall serve, his secrets keep, his lawful commands everywhere gladly do: he shall do no Damage to his said Master nor see it done by others, but to his power shall let or forthwith give notice to his said Master of the same: the goods of his Master he shall not waste, nor give or lend them unlawfully to any: he shall neither buy nor sell without his Master's leave: Taverns, Inns or Alehouses he shall not haunt: at cards, Dice Tables or other unlawful games he shall not play: matrimony he shall not contract nor from the Service of his said Master Day or Night absent himself: but in all things, as a faithful apprentice, he shall behave himself towards his said Master and all his family during the said TERM AND the said Charles Lees for and in consideration of the sum of ten pounds of lawful British money the said apprentice in the art of a Clock and Watch maker which he now useth, shall and will teach and instruct, or cause to be taught and instructed in the best way and manner that he can, and shall and will pay unto the said apprentice three shillings a week during the second and third years, five shillings a week during the fourth year, six shillings a week during the fifth year, seven shillings a week during the sixth year, and eight shillings a week during the seventh and last year of the said Term and the said Thomas Jardine hereby agrees to provide and find his son with sufficient meat, drink, apparel, washing, lodging and all other necessaries during the whole of the said Term and it is hereby agreed between and by the said parties that the said John Jardine shall not be required by the said Charles Lees to work or employ himself at his said Trade for more than ten hours a day during the said Term—Sundays excepted. AND for the Performance of all and every the said Covenants and Agreements, each of the said Parties bindeth himself unto the other firmly by these Presents. IN WITNESS whereof, the Parties abovesaid to these indentures have interchangeably set their Hands and Seals the eighteenth day of June in the second Year of the Reign of our Sovereign Lady Victoria by the Grace of God, of the United Kingdom of Great Britain and Ireland Queen Defender of the Faith, and in the Year of our Lord one Thousand Eight Hundred and Thirty Nine.

Sealed and delivered (being   John Jardine.
first duty stamped in the   Thomas Jardine.
presence of.   Charles Lees.

Seal of Henry de Hoton

tempus Edward III

Richard de Vernon, the Norman Baron of Shipbrook was grantee at the conquest of the lands of Hooton. "isdem Ricardus tenet Hotone" etc.. In the reign of John, or Richard I, Hooton was obtained in marriage by Randle Walensis as appears by a charter whereby Thomas, son of Randle Walensis, releases to Richard, his brother, all the lands of his father in Cheshire, and his right in Hooton, also, which was the inheritance of his Mother.

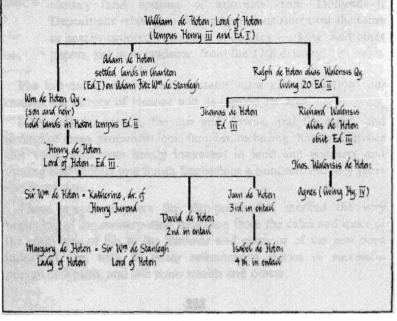

William de Hoton, Lord of Hoton
(tempus Henry III and Ed. I)

Adam de Hoton
settled lands in Charleton
(Ed. I) on Adam Fitz Wm de Stanlegh.

Ralph de Hoton alias Walensis Qy.
living 20 Ed. II

Wm de Hoton Qy •
(son and heir)
hold lands in Hoton tempus Ed. II

Thomas de Hoton
Ed. III

Richard Walensis
alias de Hoton
obiit Ed. III

Henry de Hoton
Lord of Hoton . Ed. III.

Thos. Walensis de Hoton

Sir Wm de Hoton • Katherine, dr. of
Henry Jurond

Joan de Hoton
3rd. in entail

Agnes (living Hy. IV)

David de Hoton
2nd in entail

Margary de Hoton • Sir Wm de Stanlegh
Lady of Hoton   Lord of Hoton

Isabel de Hoton
4 th. in entail

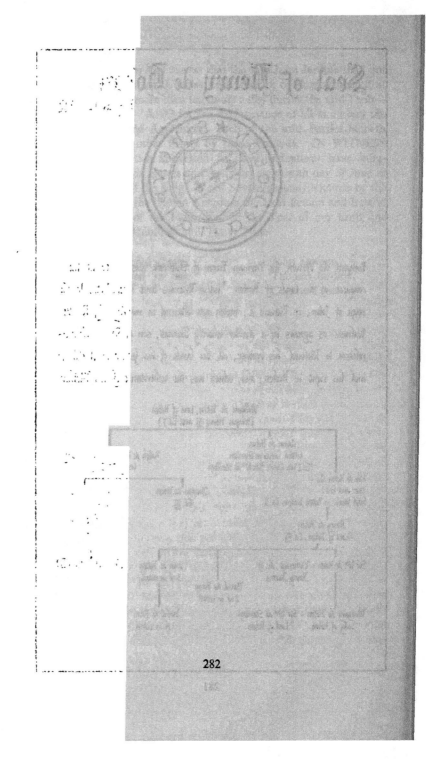

CHARLTON PAPERS

The Charlton Papers were deposited at the County Record Office through Messrs. Freeth, Cartwright and Sketchley, Solicitors of Nottingham. They represent part of the very large collection of the family and can be divided as follows:—

1. A few deeds of land purchased before 1800.

2. Deeds of land at Chilwell, Beeston, purchased after that date (many of the deeds are earlier than this).

3. Papers of Charlton property at Rearsby and Gaddesby in Leicestershire, 18th-19th century.

4. Deeds of the Sherwin family in Leicestershire, mostly at Great Peatling and Arnesby, apparently of land acquired from about 1675.

5. Many papers of colliery dispute at Heanor in the 19th century, which includes abstracts of title from the 16th century (and epitome of abstracts from Domesday); Depositions relating to this and previous suits over the same or nearby property; accounts of colliery working; and other papers, put in as evidence, from the 17th century.

The last-named section is a veritable mine of information concerning the history of Heanor and its immediate area.

It records, in writing, the ups and downs, and the rights and wrongs of many prominent local families, including those of Fletcher and Wild, who were keenly interested in land and property and turning coal in East and South Derbyshire a hundred and fifty years and more ago.

Those operations were the sign-posts that marked the very beginning of the country-wide transition from the calm and quiet of the rural way of life to the hammer and clamour of the new-born industrial age, with its many adventurous stories in successful pursuit of wealth, and still more wealth and power.

If you would like to dwell in the atmosphere of those days of old awhile, join me in browsing through The Charlton Papers. You may discover therein something thrilling about your family, as I did, when I came across the following

LETTER. [copy of] written by SAMUEL FLETCHER OF HEANOR to his solicitor in 1779.

Loscoe Lane,
Heanor.

Sir

If you please to inform Mr. Bullivant that I have greatly importuned you to use your endeavours to get an amicable reference and inspection into our affairs that hath been transacted between us and to inform him that I have gave it you under my hand, that I will abide by yr determination of such Persons disinterested herein, as you and him, should fix upon to amicably inspect all accounts etc. that hath been transacted between us. And as you are always willing to promote friendship, and particularly among your friends and acquaintances. Therefore you hope these lines will meet with his approbation as you know he is capable of explaining his affairs in a proper manner. If you Please to write something to yr above purpose will oblige I, Yrs etc Saml Fletcher

P.S.

I can get no sleep, am as unhappy a man as can be, I doubt me and family shall suffer the greatest distress, upon all accounts nothing can comfort me.

[Between Thomas Charlton Senr and Sam Fletcher Papers '79]

Who exactly was the writer of this poignant appeal? Was he a kinsman of ours—or not? The solution to this puzzle and many other similar problems may well be among the triumphs of an enthusiastic searcher of the future.

284

A FLETCHER ECHO OF THE YOUNG
PRETENDER

To:— Castle-Donnington Jan. 21 Anno Salut. 1745.
Mr. Goodere Fletcher.
To be left with Mr. Richard
Redfern at The White Hart
in Haynor.

When I review your kindness and great civility to me at Haynor,
tho' entirely a stranger to you, I must think myself highly culpable,
if I do not endeavour to manifest my gratitude and thankfulness in
the best manner I am able. As you were pleased to express a
satisfaction on sight of a few lines composed upon the present and
unnatural Rebellion, I have reason to hope these few occasion'd be
the precipitate Retreat of the Rebels into Scotland, and the dis-
apointment the French have hitherto met with in their intended
embarkation may be agreeable to you. I never much credited the
report of the French carrying any great number of the Troops here,
notwithstanding all the bustle they have made about it, it being
natural to them to talk of one thing, and at the same time to act
quite the contrary; and at this juncture especially an invasion from
them must, one would think, be impracticable, the Treaty of Dresden
having cut out other work for them, and it is now to be hop'd a few
campaigns will make it appear to the world, that the French are
neither such able Warriors, nor such profound Politicians, as they
would be thought to be. But lest it should be deemed trifling to
enlarge on a subject so palpable and self-evident as this is, with my
Sincere Wishes, for your Happiness and Prosperity, I shall conclude
only beging leave e'er I do so, to subscribe my self, Sir, your obliged
most humble, and most obedient Servant

Tho. Fletcher

285

No clouds are now on our Horison seen,
All fair the North, and all the South serene,
The Holy East, the ruddy West's the same,
And thankfull numbers bless great William's name:
Affrighted Rebels to their holes retreat,
And hostile faction flies the crowded street;
Heav'n smiles upon his Agent here below
Infernal Aid's constrained to leave the Foe;
Blest be the Pow'r, that guards the British Land,
Still may his Arm protect illustrious Cumberland.
    [Meaning the North of England only]

NOTE FOR A HISTORY OF THE FLETCHERS
OF HORSLEY AND HEANOR

Contributed by a Clansman

It is a great misfortune that Glover's "History of Derbyshire", despite its occasional inaccuracies, came to an end at the letter "D". For as his collections for the subsequent letters, now preserved in the Cavendish-Bemrose Library, Derby, show, there were many pedigrees and church notes, of interest to the historian and the genealogist in Derbyshire, which would have been published. Mr. Samuel B. Fletcher's work is a pious continuation of the interest in the history of the County, to which he has asked me to contribute this note. For some general observations from someone who has been interested independently of himself, in research into the history of families settled in much the same area as his own may, he believes, help to induce others to follow the like course on which he is embarked.

Mr. Fletcher's researches have been cut short for the moment by his decision to publish the results of his work so far. It is the certainty that once publication is past he will renew his research, which leads me to offer the following observations, which I have recorded at his request, as nearly as I can recall them as they arose between us in discussion.

Genealogical research, being as it is, concerned with family and blood lines, can all too easily become so specialised as to militate against its own success. It is most important to remember that the persons with whom the research is concerned were human beings, with much the same passions and preoccupations as ourselves; who lived real lives within the framework of the economic, social and political circumstances of their day. If these considerations are applied to the study of the Fletchers of Heanor, some very interesting pointers to their earlier history emerge; and it is against this background that I suggest that further research should be undertaken.

A short inspection of parish registers shows that the greatest density of Fletchers in Derbyshire during the period from which parish registers existed, that is to say about 1558, is in the parishes of Horsley and Chesterfield. They are also found in the parishes of Duffield, Heanor and Alfreton and, of course, in the chapelry of Denby which has since become an independent parish. Yet later they are to be found at West Hallam in Derbyshire and as early as the 16th century, across the border in Nottinghamshire. Their wills, therefore, are to be found registered in the two provinces. Side by side with this there is a continuing record of them in the churches of the borough of Derby and, perhaps because of the greater concentration of talent in the cities than in the country side, the very earliest records of them, long prior to the general existence of parish registers, are to be found there. In All Saints we find John Fletcher held a messuage abutting on the river, and yet another John Fletcher was buried at St. Alkmund, where as is recorded in the latin of the day, he "fell into the river and was drowned when drunk".

It seems, therefore, as if the Fletchers in East Derbyshire were a clan, but that within that clan there were a number of septs; and that although perhaps they all had the same patriarchal origins, a great deal of research work has to be done before we come to consideration of the patriarch. When and if that day arrives, it may well be found that the Fletchers of East Derbyshire and of Nottinghamshire were part of a larger family with important branches in Staffordshire, Leicestershire, Lancashire and Cheshire, to say nothing of London and Kent. Travel was arduous; but travel there was, so that the genealogist must not operate in blinkers.

Indeed it is established beyond doubt by examination of Wills that Robert Fletcher of Stoke Bardolf, in the parish of Gedling, Nottinghamshire, and of Chesterfield, to whom a grant of arms was made by Cooke Clarenceux, dated 10 November 1553, was the elder brother of Thomas Fletcher of Morey Hall, Staffordshire, whose descendants appear as Fletcher of Wyrley Magna and Lawnswood, Staffordshire, in the "Landed Gentry", 1952. Robert and Thomas Fletcher were two of the sons of Richard Fletcher of Morey Hall, near Lichfield, whose wife was Ellen Marbury, of Marbury in Cheshire, a family now extinct in the male line. His Will was proved at Lichfield on 27th June 1556. While Robert Fletcher bore the arms granted to him by Cooke, which there is some reason to think were traditional arms of Fletcher, or a variation thereof, Thomas Fletcher, his younger brother, bore the arms of Marbury of Cheshire countercharged, after his mother. Nothing could be clearer, however, than the evidence as to the common origin of these two families, generally supposed to be distinct.

The original grant of Arms to Robert Fletcher of Stoke Bardolf dated 10 November, 1553, is described in the Stowe MS. 670, fo. 28, and in Harleian MS. Cod. 1116, fo. 61b, thus:

"Robert ffletcher of Stoke Bardolphe in Nottingham beryth sa a crosse flory arr voyded of the fyld between i i i i escallops, of the second, on a wreth ar/sa a demy talbot b (i.e. azure) a crowne aboute the necke and eres or, 1552". These Arms are recorded in the College of Arms under Bedn 28., F 13-28, 24. 103.

If one turns now to Burke's "General Armory" we find Arms described as follows:

"Fletcher (Staffordshire): Sable a cross flory between four escallops argent."

"Fletcher (Gloucestershire): Sable a cross flory between four escallops ar. Crest: a demi bloodhound (i.e., a talbot) azure langed gules ducally gorged or."

"Fletcher (Staffordshire: descended from Thomas Fletcher of Water Eyton, esq. living temp. Elizabeth, and Margaret his wife daughter and heiress of Ralph Alport of Cannock, esq., and now represented (1844) by Thomas William Fletcher, esq., F.R.S.): Ar. a cross engr. Sable betw. four pellets each charged with a pheon or on a canton azure a ducal crown gold. Crest: A horse's head erased ar. gorged with a ducal crown azure."

"Marbury (Marbury, Co. Chester, temp. Edward II): Sable a cross engrailed ar. betw. four piles (or pheons) of the second."

It will be noted that the armorial bearings described for Fletcher of Staffordshire, in the first Staffordshire entry above, and for Fletcher of Gloucestershire, are identical; while the Crest for Fletcher of Gloucestershire is identical with the Crest described in the grant by Cooke Clarenceux to Robert Fletcher of Stoke Bardolf above.

Similarly, if we turn to Fox-Davies' "Armorial Families", 1902, we find the following entry:

"John Fletcher, Esquire, Justice of the Peace for the counties of

289

Haddington and Edinburgh and Deputy Lieutenant . . . eldest son of the late Andrew Fletcher, Esquire, of Saltoun Hall . . .

Armorial bearings: Sable a cross flory between four escallops argent and impaling the arms of Talbot, namely gules a lion rampant within a bordure engrailed or. Crest: A demi bloodhound azure, ducally gorged or."

Burke's "Landed Gentry", 1952, gives the same arms and crest and says that they were matriculated at the Lyon Office by Sir Robert Fletcher of Saltoun, 1672-1677 and again in 1825.

It will be noted that the Arms born by Fletcher of Saltoun are the same as the Arms of Fletcher of Staffordshire and Gloucestershire but are not the same as the Arms granted by Cooke to Fletcher of Stoke Bardolf.

On the other hand Fletcher of Saltoun bears the same Crest as Fletcher of Stoke Bardolf, and as Fletcher of Gloucestershire which by implication is presumably the same as that borne by Fletcher of Staffordshire, the branch of the family named first by Burke, as shown above.

The same Arms and Crest were also borne at an early date by Fletcher, Mayor of Plymouth.

Rider "A"

There is also a pedigree of Flesher, alias Fletcher, descended from William Flesher of Knaresborough, Co. Yorks. draper, recorded in the pedigree of Vincent to be found in the Genealogical Office, the Castle, Dublin, which was formerly the Ulster Office of the College of Arms. This pedigree, which I have verified, appears over the signature of William Segar, Garter Principal King of Arms dated 28th March, 1700, the reference being G.O. Reg. Ped. Vol. 161. The Arms, which are tricked in G.O. MS. 72, Funeral Entries, 1640-1663, Volume 9, are the Arms of Fletcher of Stoke Bardolf as described above. The Crest, however, is as follows: On a wreath an arm in armour embowed holding an arrow all proper point or. The motto: "Per Angustam."

It will be noted that in the second entry relating to Fletcher of Staffordshire shown in Burke's "General Armory", Fletcher of Water Eyton's Arms are the same Arms as Marbury of Chester but counter-charged in their tinctures and with the canton gules charged with a ducal crown.

The Will of Robert Fletcher of Stoke Bardolf is to be found in P.C.C. where it was proved, registered under 31 Bakon, in 1579. In this he refers both to his mother living at Morey Hall, near Lichfield, and to his brother, Thomas Fletcher of Morey.

The following entries in the Supplementary Patent Roll No. 68, being the Pardon Roll of Queen Elizabeth I, preserved in the Public Record Office, carry the evidence further:

"Robert Fletcher of Stoke Bardolf, Co. Nottingham, alias of Grayes Inn, Co. Middlesex, alias of Morrey, Co. Stafford."

"Thomas Fletcher of Clements Inn, Co. Middlesex, gentleman, alias a minister of Chancery, alias late of Stoke Bardolph, yoman."

Robert Fletcher's Inquisition post mortem was taken at Nottingham where he was buried on 25 August 24 Elizabeth I, which describes his lands. Francis Fletcher was found to be his son and heir. P.R.O. c142, Series II, Volume 196, No. 39.

Robert Fletcher's first wife, whom he married by licence of the Faculty Office, dated 20 April 1547, was Margaret daughter of Sir Edmond, or Edward Molyneux, of Teversal, Co. Notts, Knight Commander of the Bath, Judge of the Court of Common Pleas. By her was born his eldest son, Francis Fletcher, Esquire: who, having married Frances, daughter of Francis Molyneux of Haughton, Esquire, at Teversal, by licence on 6 February, 1580, appears with some of his children in the pedigree of Molyneux, or Molineux, in the Visitation of Nottinghamshire taken in 1614. Through them the Fletchers contributed to the blood of the Fletchers of Chesterfield and probably, the Fletchers of Yorkshire. Indeed there are reasons for thinking, which in a short article of this type it is impossible to particularise, that the Fletchers of Beverley, and possibly the Fletchers of Campsall in Yorkshire, were cousins of some degree. Robert Fletcher himself, however, apart from his son Francis, Keeper of the Castle of York, who himself had five sons, was also the father of George Fletcher of London, a goldsmith, the pedigree of whose descendants was entered at the Visitation of London in 1633/4 and who bore the Arms granted by Cooke to Robert Fletcher, differenced by the crescent appropriate to a second son.

We come now to a very curious circumstance. Fletcher of Saltoun is, of course, the family of that great Fletcher who played so large a part in the negotiations for the Act of Union of the Crown of Scotland and England. His family had been settled in Dundee since the 16th century apparently, or' as was alleged. "Certainly, David Fletcher purchased the lands at Innerpeffer; so that by that time it might be right to describe the family as Scots, particularly having regard to some of its marriages.

The family claimed, however, and the pedigree entered at the matriculation at the Lyon Office, which I have not seen, presumably shows their descent from Cumberland, where there were Fletchers established at Hutton and Moresby.

These last named Fletchers however, bore the Arms of Fletcher of Water Eyton and are represented today by the families of Aubrey-Fletcher and Fletcher-Vane.

More curious still, in the Scottish family, Andrew as a christian name appears in several generations. It appears nowhere, so far as I have been able to discover, either in the Cumberland branch, or in the Water Eyton branch, or in the known Stoke Bardolf branch.

There is, however, a very interesting Will of Andrew Fletcher of Horsley, proved at Lichfield, made in 1588, in which he describes himself as "Husbandman", and refers to his "four eldest sons", Robert, William, Francis and John.

The name Andrew appears once thereafter in Horsley Parish Registry, being the birth of the first named Andrew's grandson.

The use of the description "Husbandman" indicates that Andrew Fletcher had not become either a freeholder, or a copyholder, but was in fact a tenant farmer.

Robert Fletcher, however, perhaps his son, appears as "Yeoman", indicating that he was at least a copyholder.

There is no record of this Robert Fletcher's marriage in the parish register. But at the head of the pedigree in the possession of Messrs. Robert Barber & Sons, of Stanford House, Castlegate, Nottingham, Solicitors, there appears Robert Fletcher married to Frances Byron.

This allegation, although not substantiated by any proof which I have seen, is of great interest. For some of the lands of Horsley had been in the occupation of the Byrons of Newstead since Domesday, in which Ralph de Burun is shown as holding the castle of Horestan in Horsley, which was the seat of barony. The Byrons certainly still held lands in Horsley down to the 16th century, as charters in the Public Records Office attest, so that it seems probable, though final proof is still wanting, that the Fletchers first became seized of lands in Horsley by a marriage with one of the daughters of New-stead.

The above may seem rather discursive: but these observations are made to emphasise the necessity of reading the evidences regarding the Fletchers of East Derbyshire in relation to the evidences of Fletchers in other parts of the country, with some at least of whom there were close ties of blood. If research based on this principle, of getting outside the area and looking in, is followed, much evidence will be found to be available; evidence which the most patient examination of local records will fail to provide, because of the inevitable destruction and the fading of records occasioned in the making of history.

If we turn now to consideration of the world in which such Fletchers lived, we must remember that Derbyshire and Nottingham-shire, lying as they do mainly across the Trent, represented in those days, the end of the area in which the King's writ ran easily. To the south of them lay the gentle, rich lands of Leicestershire, while around Nottingham lay the great Shire wood. To the north of Derby the land begins to rise immediately, gently at first and then steeply, to the then nearly impenetrable district of the High Peak. It was this mere inaccessibility that accounted for the fact that the Sheriffs of Derbyshire and Nottinghamshire were frequently a joint appointment. Both Nottingham and Derby moreover, were them-selves towns of the greatest importance, an importance strategically emphasised by the control of communications with the North which the possession of Nottingham Castle made possible; and indeed which contributed greatly to their growth. It was recognition of these hard facts of geography which led William the Conqueror to bestow 179 lordships, of which the High Peak was the strong point, on his reputed bastard, William Peveral of Nottingham, a fief as large as those granted to William's two cousins Richard FitzGilbert de Clare and Baldwin FitzGilbert de Okehampton.

Between lay the Erewash which divides the two counties geo-graphically. The land on both banks is hilly, so that the valley through which the river runs is accordingly fairly deep, falling from the crest on the Derbyshire side gently to the town of Derby itself. The lands on either side of the river Erewash have proved to be of the greatest economic significance to this country. Indeed it may well be the case that it is to this area that we must look for the origins of industrial civilisation as we know it today. For it was from this area that the shallow pits first of all in East Derbyshire and later in

Nottinghamshire, have contributed a growing output of coal; which, easily won, could be made available to supply not only nearby markets, such as Derby, but later by shipment down the Derwent and Trent as sea coals for yet more distant places., This development of the East Derbyshire coal field at a time when the opening of the New World gave England, by her piratical raids, the first considerable supplies of gold and silver to make possible the transformation of society, removed from a basis of barter by the development of the bill of exchange during the Middle Ages, to a society freely using coinage.

No family contributed earlier, or more, to this development than the Fletchers of Horsley and of Heanor, the operation of whose Company "Robert and John Fletcher and Partners" was one of the earliest examples of large scale joint stock enterprise in this country. It was this development by "Robert and John Fletcher and Partners" and their eventual successors the Drury-Lowes at Denby; the Suttons at Heanor and the Miller-Mundays at Shipley, which provided that steady stream of wealth bringing coin and bills to the area, to which the rise of the banking house of Smith, Payne and Smith of Nottingham, now part of the National Provincial Bank, owed so much.

Robert and John Fletcher were the sons of another Robert Fletcher, Yeoman of Horsley, probably the grandson of Andrew Fletcher. Their Mother was Anne Hunter from Heanor and from the time of that marriage the inter-relationship of those two families and their cousins is the background for much further work. The elder brother, Robert, having made a substantial fortune through the opening of what is today called Denby Colliery, inherited further coal lands through his wife, Katherine, from her father, Samuel Richardson of Smalley Hall. He moved to Smalley Hall on the death of his father-in-law without male surviving issue, and there his children were born. Shortly thereafter, however, he moved to Heanor, perhaps to be closer to his newer and deeper pits; and Heanor Hall and Owlgraves, or as the site nowadays appears on the Ordnance Survey map, Aldgrave Hall, remained Fletcher properties until the first was purchased in the late 18th century by Robert Sutton, and the latter passed to a younger branch of the Lowes of Denby.

John Fletcher, the younger brother, appears to have been even more successful financially and possibly of a more thrusting character. He left two sons, neither of whom, however, had legitimate issue, and two daughters, one of whom married John Barber of Castle Greasley in Nottinghamshire and thus laid the foundation of the great enterprise of Barber, Walker and Sons.

John Fletcher's second son, John Fletcher of Stainsby House, had a grant of Arms in 1731 which are an allusion to the Arms of Thomas Fletcher of Morey, which in turn were, as shown above, an allusion to the Arms of Marbury of Cheshire. The Arms are described in the original grant thus: "Argent on a cross ingrailed Sable a compass dial in the centre and four pheons Or. A Chief Gules charged with a Level Staff between two Coal Picks of the third. And for the Crest on a Wreath of the colours an Horse's Head gorged argent Gutte de Sang".

This John Fletcher was Sheriff of the County of Derbyshire in 1732 and at his death in 1734 left a fortune of over £20,000 in gold, securities and coal lands unsettled, an enormous fortune in those days.

Reverting now to Robert Fletcher of Denby, Smalley and Heanor, he had three sons and two daughters, namely Goodere Fletcher, who after being Sheriff of Derbyshire and having subscribed with his father to the loyal Association of Defence against the Pretender in 1745, died unmarried in 1770. Goodere Fletcher left his estate for life to his younger brother Samuel, with remainder to his nephew Samuel, eldest son of Samuel Fletcher.

William Fletcher the third son of Robert and youngest brother of Goodere, died unmarried at the age of 20.

The two daughters of Robert Fletcher, the sisters of Goodere Fletcher, married John Bullivant of Langley in the parish of Heanor; and John Wood, eventually vicar of Chesterfield, respectively. Katherine Wood had no children and at her death her estate passed to her nephew Fletcher Bullivant, whose kinsmen are still living.

The Will of Goodere Fletcher, proved in P.C.C. on 18 July, 1771, provided that in the event of the death without issue of Samuel Fletcher, the nephew of Goodere who was to have the remainder of Goodere's estate, after the death of Samuel Fletcher, his father, the estate of Goodere should be divided between the other (Kerry says ten) children of Samuel Fletcher, the younger brother of Goodere, when the youngest of them became of age. In fact, Samuel, the eldest of these children, did die in 1770 without issue and apparently unmarried; or so it is said in the pedigree in possession of Messrs. Robert Barber and Sons, referred to above, and also in the manuscript notes of the Rev. Charles Kerry. So that the estate of Goodere Fletcher was divided. It was from the purchase of the estate from the heirs, several of whom died childless, that the Sutton family and that of Miller-Munday acquired their interests in the coal pits, formerly developed by Robert and John Fletcher and Partners of Denby, Heanor and Kimberley.

That sale brought to an end the principal Fletcher connection with the coal trade. But by the time it had happened at the end of the 18th century, the firm associated with the name had laid the foundations of a financial and industrial interest which could be developed by other energetic men.

It is probably no exaggeration to say that that contribution had a great bearing on the provision of the capital resources from which the earlier stages of the industrial revolution of the late 18th and early 19th century were financed.

With the sale of the coal interests, the family of Samuel Fletcher, the younger brother of Goodere, became dispersed; but some blood lines undoubtedly continued at Heanor where they continue to this day. While further proof is necessary to establish the exact relationship, I have no doubt in my own mind that Mr. Samuel B. Fletcher, the author of the work to which I am contributing this note, is a descendant of the Fletchers of Denby. For Elizabeth, one of the daughters of Samuel Fletcher, the younger brother of Goodere, married Edward Green Fletcher, who apparently came from outside Heanor but was, in all probability, a cousin drafted in to maintain a name and blood line. Unfortunately, the parish register of Heanor has at times been very badly kept and mutilated, with the result that the proofs still required are unlikely to be forthcoming from that source; and it is elsewhere that we must look for materials, including perhaps to London records.

Among such materials, there is a valuable collection of papers once in the hands of a partnership of family solicitors, named elsewhere in this book, called the Charlton Papers, now deposited at the Nottingham County Record Office. These papers are the counterpart of another collection of manuscript paper now lodged among the Additional Manuscripts at the British Museum. They were papers collected by the respective parties to a law suit in the parish of Heanor, an action on which was fought in the early 19th century. I have no doubt that a careful examination of this body of papers will yield genealogical information of the greatest possible interest, not only to the family of Fletchers but to others in the area as well.

For the land which was the subject of dispute, as indeed much of the land in that district, was towards the end of the 15th century, the property of the Lords de Codnor of Codnor Castle. The last Lord Grey died in 1496 leaving his three aunts as his co-heiresses; since his three sons were all illegitimate, though indeed each seized of important properties by settlements made on them during their father's life.

The three co-heiresses married Newport of High Ercall, County Salop, now represented by the Earl of Bradford; Lenthall, represented by Lenthall of Burford and Bessels Leigh; and Sir John Zouche of Codnor, Knight, who inherited the castle in right of his wife, by agreement with the other heiresses.

The Zouches continued at Codnor with various vicissitudes until 1634 when the then Sir John Zouche, Knight, and his son, John, having suffered heavy losses in the iron trade which they had fostered in an undertaking which was the origin of the Butterley Company, joined in selling their lands to Archbishop Neale and his nephew Sir Paul Neale. With the capital thus realised they emigrated to Virginia where they had a plantation by grant from the Virginia Company of London. This venture, however, was little more successful than had been the venture in iron making, and when he died in 1636 Sir John Zouche had little to bequeath to his son, save the plantation and the contents of the house there. His Will was proved at York in 1639.

It has always been alleged, on the basis of a manuscript pedigree in the archives of the College of Arms, London, prepared by Dale, that both Sir John and his son John, were killed in an Indian rising in 1636. So far as I know this view has never been challenged until I began my own researches into the family, arising out of the examination of the ancestry of William Hunter of Kilburn Hall in the parish of Horsley, my own ancestor.

My own researches have established beyond doubt the incorrectness of Dale's allegation, which in any case seems to depend solely upon the testimony of Sir John's grand-daughter, who could not possibly have known him, nor in all probability, known her uncle John Zouche, Esquire. Moreover it seems clear that the Civil War divided the Zouche family and left Sir John's daughter, the wife of Colonel Devereux Wolsley, a widow in impoverished circumstances. What is certain is that John Zouche, Esquire, had a fresh grant of probate of his father's Will, in P.C.C. in 1639, the executors having renounced; was a Burgess to the Assembly for Virginia for Henrico County in which his plantation lay in 1643; and was living, apparently in poor circumstances in 1652 in London, when his kinsman, John Babington of London, left him an annuity.

. Since this is a note upon the family of Fletcher, I shall not attempt to go deeper into the question of whether the Zouches in fact left male descendants: but whether indeed they did, or not, it is clear that the Fletchers of Horsley and Heanor and their descendants, are at least one representative of the family of Zouche of Codnor, though in fact, I think a junior branch.

We have now to turn back to the origins of Katherine Richardson, wife of Robert Fletcher, father of Goodere, Samuel, William, Katherine and Elizabeth Fletcher. Katherine Richardson's mother was the daughter of Henry Goodere of Codnor, Esquire, Inspector of Highways for the district. He was descended from an ancient armigerous family, whose pedigree is to be found in the Visitation of Warwickshire, 1619. His wife was a Roper of Farningham in Kent and Codnor in Derbyshire and her mother was Mary Zouche of Codnor. It was thus that some parts of the lands of Grey passed into the hands of the family of Fletcher in the first instance, though indeed they evidently purchased other lands in the parish of Horsley, originally the property of the Keyes, the Sacheverells and the Johnsons whose pedigrees appear in the Visitation of Derbyshire, 1611.

. The lands of the last named passed by the re-marriage of my own ancestor Dorothy Sacheverell of Stanton, widow of William Johnson, of Horsley, to Jasper Lowe. Jasper Lowe thus became seized of the Manor of Park Hall, Denby, not as is alleged erroneously by Lysons' "Derbyshire", p. 188, by purchase of the Frechevilles. To complete this aspect of the question, I may mention briefly that the Lowes of Denby failed in their male issue; and a daughter having married Drury, Alderman of Nottingham, he took the name of Drury-Lowe. That family failed again in its male issue in the 19th century; and a daughter having married Gilbert of Locko Park, County Derby, the name Drury-Lowe was reassumed by Mr. Gilbert, a name which is borne by Mrs. Drury-Lowe of Locko Park in 1956. The so-called Drury-Lowe pit in Denby, today one of the more efficient properties of the National Coal Board is the original colliery from which the Fletcher fortune was raised.

This was no accident, save the accident of inheritance of that particular area of coal bearing lands. Undoubtedly Robert and John Fletcher and their Partners were men of energy and vision; but it must be said that they were greatly favoured by the fact that their first coal bearing lands lay in a gentle valley, whose declivity, in the times before metalled roads were the rule, was a matter of importance, since it enabled the transport of coal to Derby and to the water side, to be maintained in all but the severest weathers. This geographical location was the reason for Denby Colliery and its environs being developed much earlier than the deeper pits, such as Shipley. For coal from such pits which could not be "drifted", apart from the greater problems of mining, had to be taken over the not inconsiderable hills and in particular had to traverse Kidsley Park, the right of way across which was a continuing dispute with the Sacheverells of Morley, and on occasion of outright prohibition. For those who are interested in this question, a convenient starting point for study are two books published by Bemrose & Co. of Derby in 1906, by the Rev. Charles Kerry, the rector of Smalley. Kerry was a painstaking genealogist and local historian, who in addition to his printed contribution, left, as mentioned above, an important collection of papers, how housed in the Cavendish-Bemrose Library in the Wardwick in Derby, where the collection awaits the services of an annotator to make a proper study and an index.

I have said above that I have no doubt in my own mind that Mr. Samuel B. Fletcher is a descendant of Robert Fletcher and his second son Samuel, of Horsley and later of Heanor, though this awaits further proof. In his present work Mr. Samuel B. Fletcher alleges his descent from Mary Wild who is said to have been the wife of Mr. Fletcher's earliest known ancestor, another Samuel. This marriage with Mary Wild is the marriage that occurred at Heanor on 2 December, 1742.

Undoubtedly there was a son born to Samuel Fletcher, another Samuel, baptised at Heanor shortly thereafter on 18 January 1747.

But whether that child was the son of Mary Wild seems very doubtful. Certainly we find a Samuel Fletcher of Losco in the parish of Heanor, where Goodere Fletcher undoubtedly had lands, marrying Rebecca Barker at West Hallam in December 1762, by whom he had a son, baptised John Wyld Fletcher at Heanor on 7 January 1768, the Wyld being tantalisingly struck out and the name re-entered as John Fletcher under the same date.

I am inclined to believe, however, that Mary Wild died shortly before 18 January 1747 after the birth of her son Samuel, who may also have perished. For in 1746 we find Samuel Fletcher marrying Mary Richardson of Spondon. That these two marriages are the marriages of the same Samuel Fletcher has not yet been established beyond doubt, though it is significant that in the pedigree of Fletcher, in the possession of Messrs. Robert Barber and Sons, the specific allegation is made that the wife of Samuel Fletcher and mother of the eventual heirs of Goodere on the death of the eldest son, Samuel, Goodere's nephew, was Mary Richardson of Spondon.

This marriage at Spondon on 2 May, 1746, seems on the face of it, a highly probable marriage for Samuel Fletcher, the younger brother of Goodere, to have made. For Mary Richardson was his second cousin, being the daughter of William Richardson of Spondon. Since in the days prior to the invention of the Joint Stock Company almost the only means of preserving a family fortune was through the marriage of cousins, it seems likely that the preservation, and perhaps extention, of the valuable coal lands worked by Robert and John Fletcher and Partners would be an important consideration in determining the affections of a bereaved member of the family.

Unhappily, Goodere Fletcher's Will gives no indication as to whether this surmise is correct or not. For in leaving his estate in remainder to his nephew, Samuel, he calls his nephew the son of his brother Samuel "by his now wife Mary". Does that imply a previous marriage and perhaps children? All that can be said is that she might have been Mary Wild or Mary Richardson: and the only suggestion I can make for settlement of the question is through a careful examination of the Charlton Papers and of Wills and Administrations not only of Fletchers but of Wilds and Richardsons.

Mr. Samuel B. Fletcher has always averred, and undoubtedly believes, that his own ancestress was Mary Wild. I do not think, however, that this belief, sincerely as it is held, is irreconcilable with the possibility of his ancestress having been Mary Richardson. Samuel Fletcher, the younger brother of Goodere, lived until 1788 and was thus 66 when he died. Since his family did not continue in the coal trade after the sale of the estate to Robert Sutton, I think it not improbable that local tradition, handed on from father to son in somewhat loose conversation, may well have confused the two Marys by overlooking the early bereavement of Samuel Fletcher.

If this is not the case it would seem to imply the existence of two Samuel Fletchers in the parish of Heanor contemporaneously, and there is no evidence as to the birth of a second Samuel. To be sure there might have been one bred outside, who came to Heanor, perhaps as a protégé of the Fletchers of Heanor Hall. But if so, it is very difficult to account for his origin and for Goodere Fletcher's phrase "by his now wife".

It is clear, however, that a great deal of further research lies awaiting the interested. In particular, the Charlton Papers need careful examination.

It is to be hoped this examination will not be confined to the name of Fletcher alone, but will include such names as Zouche and its variants Souche, Sowche and South, Wild and its variants, Wyld, Wylde, Wilde, Draycot, Wright, Roper, Goodere and Hunter. For the key of this genealogical puzzle is to be found in the breaking up of the estate of Grey de Codnor by marriages of heiresses and by such events as the sale of Codnor by Sir John Zouche; and in the struggle for control of the richest and most easily worked coal lands of the East Derbyshire coal field and their development.

When that work has been done thoroughly there will, I believe, emerge one of the most valuable contributions to the study of early capitalist enterprise and industrial development in these islands.

It will be found that the contribution arising from the enterprise of Robert and John Fletcher and Partners had a significance in the development of England, which has not yet found its way to recognition by historians.

One of our globe-trotting kinsmen who would like to remain anonymous has kindly allowed us to publish this abridged description of his travels and experiences.

LONDON, W.C.1.

20th November, 1956.

Dear Mr Fletcher,

I am looking forward to reading *The Fletcher House of Lace and its Wider Family Associations* very much, and wish the venture complete success.

As a commercially-minded individual, I cannot help thinking that a considerable number of copies could be sold in the United States.

On one occasion, when I was in New York, a Sherlock Holmes type of guy established the fact that a Fletcher was staying in the hotel and cordially invited me to enjoy the hospitality of the 'Fletcher Society' which, by 'phone, he claimed to represent.

Unfortunately, I could not accept the invitation, but have often wondered what would have happened to me, no doubt a deemed-to-be 'country cousin', had I been able to do so.

Anyway, on a later visit to New York, I tried to find the 'Fletcher Society' in the telephone directory but it was not listed, so at random, just for the fun of it, I rang a couple of Fletchers bearing the same initials as myself and chatted with them but, funnily enough, they were as suspicious of me as I was of the fellow who rang me, so we didn't get any further.

When I was in Johannesburg in 1947, I contacted the Fletchers who live both there and at Boksburg a few miles away. They made me very welcome, so I spent some happy months in that area which otherwise might have been very lonely.

There is a story of a Fletcher who lives in Victoria, Vancouver Island, British Columbia, who insists upon riding a horse down the one-way streets against the traffic and, as the existing laws of the Constitution of British Columbia do not apply to horses, the police cannot do a thing about it—virtually, an act of parliament would be needed to rectify this.

His other trick was to tether his horse to the parking meter stands, thereby monopolising at least two spaces for which he cannot be made to pay a parking fee. We never met when I was in Victoria, so I thought it best to give him a wide berth as he seemed a cussed old so-and-so—in fact, a typical Fletcher.

Yours sincerely,

'ONE OF THE CLAN."

J. W. S. Fletcher, Esq.,
Hieron's Wood,
Little Eaton,
Derby.

PLATE 28

THE COMPILER, his wife DOROTHY,
daughter ELISABETH, and son PHILIP FREDERIC

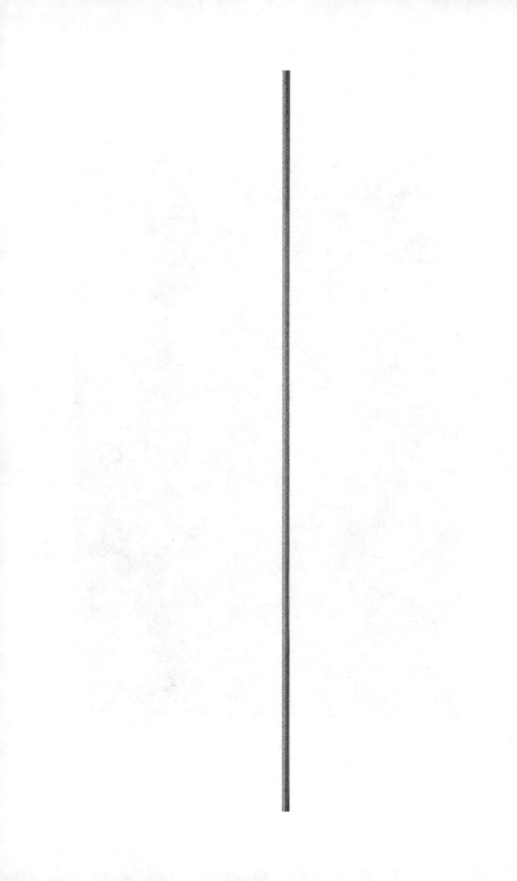

SUMMARY

The main object of this short Summary is to point out that besides interesting the reader, one of the chief purposes of the documentary part of this work is to provide a springboard to use for further research into the origins of The Fletcher Family, the pattern for which is outlined in "Note for a History of the Fletchers of Horsley and Heanor".

A first step to be taken could well be to discover the exact identity of both Samuel Fletcher and Mary Wild of Heanor Wood who, judged by the phrasing of the former's Will were, in my estimation, undoubtedly the grandparents of Edward of Heanor, founder of The Fletcher House of Lace.

So informed, we might go a stage further and try to learn whether we are related or not to John Fletcher, the son of William Fletcher and Mary (Hodgkinson) his wife, of Pentrich Common, who occupied a little homestead and farm in the Smalley Mill district, and similarly to the Allens, who owned a woodyard nearby, and to other Fletchers, whose histories are recorded by The Rev. Charles Kerry in his History of Smalley.

Indeed, if we delve into the wider field sufficiently, we might even discover that the penurious young Heanor man mentioned in The Gentleman's Magazine of 1812 was, in his generation, "very much one of us". And from p. 496, vol. 1 of that reference, I quote— "F. Bullivant Esq. of Stanton House, near Burton-on-Trent, has left the whole of his property to the son of a poor man of the name of Fletcher of Heanor, Derbyshire, which will amount, it is supposed, when the youth comes of age, to 200,000£".

The foregoing, rather loosely written reference, concerns the Will with two Codicils, proved in P.C.C. 25th February 1812, of Fletcher Bullivant, of Stanton p. Stapenhill, a wealthy landowner in East Derbyshire during the late 18th and early 19th centuries, died s.p. buried 22nd January 1812, who entailed his estate on the youngest son of Thos. Fletcher of Shipley Lodge, Heanor, Co. Derby, hosier. By codicil, the heir was to take the name Bullivant. Do these Fletchers, descendants of Thomas Fletcher of Shipley, believed to be the

305

eldest surviving son of Samuel Fletcher, mentioned by Kerry, or a son of the said Thomas, now pass as Bullivants? This is regarded as very important for future investigation, so information relating to members of the Bullivant family living in Leicestershire in this respect would be most welcome.

It would be very interesting if we could learn how this one-time man of humble means reacted to the claims and influence of great wealth. Did his good fortune persuade him to play the part of Fairy Godfather to the Fletcher Family at large? Such munificence might explain, what to me, has seemed to be the ease with which the sons of Edward Fletcher, a poor man by comparison, found the wherewithal to establish businesses of their own after serving their apprenticeship with father.

This is a fantastic thought, but may I remind you that persistent genealogical research has produced innumerable delightful surprises, and also shed the light of reality upon a host of equally fanciful surmises. "Seek and ye shall find" is the spur of the ardent genealogical searcher!

Samuel B. Fletcher

July 19th, 1956

306

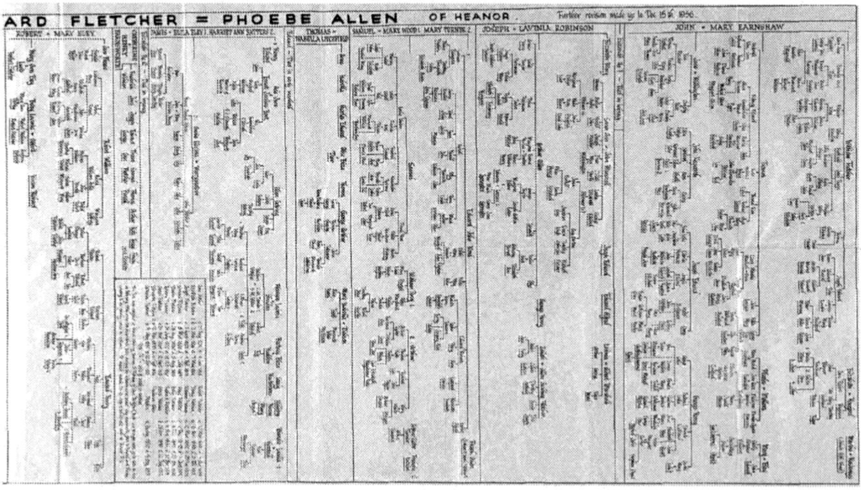
ARD FLETCHER = PHOEBE ALLEN
OF HEANOR.
Further revision made up to Dec 15th 1956.
ROBERT = MARY ELEY.
JAMES = ELIZA ELEY 1. HARRIET ANN SHIPTON 2.
THOMAS = ISABELLA LITCHFIELD
SAMUEL = MARY WOOD 1. MARY TURNER 2.
JOSEPH = LAVINIA ROBINSON
JOHN = MARY EARNSHAW

THE FAMILY TREE OF THE HEANOR LACE FLETCHERS